D1604004

# Spokane's Legendary Davenport Hotel

Tony Bamonte

Suzanne Bamonte

# Spokane's Legendary
# Davenport Hotel

Tony Bamonte
Suzanne Schaeffer Bamonte

Tornado Creek Publications
Spokane, Washington 2001

Published in 2001
Printed in the United States of America
by
Walsworth Publishing Company
Marceline, Missouri 64658

Library of Congress Control Number: 2001130462
ISBN: 0-9652219-7-0

**Front cover photo**: The Davenport Hotel and Restaurant, circa 1914.
(Eastern Washington State Historical Society photo.)

**Back cover**: Sheet music for *The Davenport Waltz,* published in 1909.
(Courtesy Jamie Baker.)

**Tornado Creek Publications**
**P.O. Box 8625**
**Spokane, Washington 99203-8625**
**(509) 838-7114, Fax (509) 455-6798**

## Other Books by Tony & Suzanne Bamonte:

*Miss Spokane: Elegant Ambassadors and Their City*

*Spokane and the Inland Northwest: Historical Images*

*Manito Park: A Reflection of Spokane's Past*

*History of Newport, Washington*

*History of Pend Oreille County*

## Books by Tony Bamonte:

*Sheriffs 1911-1 989: A History of Murders in the Wilderness of Washington's Last County*

*History of Metaline Falls*

**The Authors:**

Tony and Suzanne Bamonte have turned their pastime and passion for writing and publishing Northwest history into a vocation. This is their sixth publication together. They are always looking for access to private photo collections for future publications. If you are interested, they can be contacted at the address or telephone number listed below.

Tony was born in Wallace, Idaho, in 1942 and raised in Metaline Falls, Washington. He was elected and served as Pend Oreille County sheriff for three consecutive terms from 1978 until 1991. He has a Master's Degree in Organizational Leadership from Gonzaga University and a Bachelor's Degree in Sociology from Whitworth College. Tony began his law-enforcement career in 1966 as a Spokane city police officer. He has also been a logger, miner, construction worker and an army helicopter door gunner during his tour of duty in Vietnam. In addition to coauthoring and publishing history books with wife Suzanne, he is a licensed Washington State Realtor.

Suzanne was born in lone, Washington, in 1948 and raised in Metaline Falls, Washington. She graduated from Central Washington University with a Bachelor's Degree in Accounting, subsequently becoming a Certified Public Accountant. Prior to their marriage in 1994, Suzanne lived in Seattle where she worked as the controller of an art glass studio from 1988-1993 and of a publishing company from 1982-1988. Previous to that, she worked in the field of public accounting.

# Acknowledgments

Piecing together the history of Louis Davenport and his accomplishments was a complicated process. Much conflicting information abounded. As a result, this project entailed a great deal of research and the assistance of many people. We thank the following for helping to bring this project to fruition.

Two people, in particular, to whom we feel a great depth of gratitude are **Laura Arksey**, retired librarian and archivist from the Eastern Washington State Historical Society, and **Nancy Gale Compau**, Spokane Public Library Northwest Room historian. We are honored by their remarkable dedication and efforts on behalf of our numerous writing projects. We also extend our appreciation to: **Gary Zagelow** for his extensive research on the Davenport buildings and sharing resource materials; **Evelyn Conant** for proofreading our entire manuscript – twice!; **Louie and Nita Davenport** for sharing the personal Davenport history and the family albums; **Walt and Karen Worthy** for the information about the hotel renovation, sharing historic photos, and for making the hotel so easily accessible to facilitate our book research and the video process.

We thank and acknowledge the following people (listed in alphabetical order) for their assistance, which came in a variety of ways, including interviews:

Maggie Aldridge
Jamie Baker
Sheri Barnard
Susan Beamer
Jim Bolser
Barbara Brazington
Robin Briley
Edna Mae and Thoburn
   Brown
Parker Compau
Mark Danner
Larry and Bernice
   Davenport
Ed Ellefsen
Kaye Hale
Melville Holmes

Butch Jacobson
Grayden Jones
Judy Knaack
Donald MacDonald
Ann McCoy
Lillian McGuinness
Gillian Melcher
Ron Miller
Bill Morlin
Glen Oberg
Jean Oton
Dorothy Powers
John Reed
Ellen Robey
Maxine Rolie
Al and Mae Schaeffer

Lura Sheahan
Rick Sherman
Roxanne Siegert
Jan Smith
South Hill Family History
   Center volunteers
Spokane County Title
   Company
Spokane Public Library
Norma and Dick Stejer
Angela Sterling
Nancy Venziano
Clint Weyrauch
Yvonne Wilhelm
Charlie Willis
George and Jean Wood

We also wish to thank the **contributors of photographs**, who have been acknowledged in the credit lines throughout the book. Due to limited space, the abbreviation **EWSHS** designates photos from the collections of the Eastern Washington State Historical Society/Northwest Museum of Arts & Culture.

# Table of Contents

Dedicated to
# Louis & Verus Davenport,
# Walt & Karen Worthy, and the
# Friends of the Davenport

"The history of the Davenport Hotel is the history of Spokane."

Nancy Gale Compau, historian.

# Introduction

The affectionate regard people far and wide have for the Davenport Hotel began with the inception of Davenport's Restaurant in 1890. Its owner, Llewellyn Marks "Louis" (or "Louie") Davenport, was able to infuse an indefinable charm into his hotel that was indelibly etched into people's memories. Davenport was a quiet, unassuming man who gave Spokane, Washington, its greatest landmark. His success grew out of service that was so exceptional it bordered on perfection, and it came with a fair price. However, after suffering an unfortunate decline, the great hotel closed in 1985. Its fate hung in the balance for a number of years, while talk of demolition sent an alarm throughout the community. Caring people rallied in its defense, leaving no stone unturned in their search for someone who cared enough and had the resources to bring the hotel back to its glory. After a succession of owners and a number of unsuccessful attempts to revive the hotel, Walt and Karen Worthy stepped forward. The restoration and renovation under the Worthys' direction makes one almost believe Louis Davenport had returned to lend his guidance. The quality of workmanship and materials used and the attention to detail would certainly please him. As the original public function rooms undergo their respective restorations, one wonders if they could ever have been more beautiful.

Louis Davenport enjoyed talking about his hotel, but not about himself or his accomplishments. While we may never know the answers to all the questions about this man who succeeded in developing a restaurant and hotel that attracted some of the most famous people in the world, this book contains more information about him and his family than has previously been compiled in any one document.

The Davenport legend is also the story of others whose vision, talents and hard work created and sustained the hotel: architects Kirtland K. Cutter, G.A. Pehrson and others who designed and constructed the landmark building, as well as longtime employees such as legendary chef Edward Mathieu, manager Jim McCluskey and countless others who carried out Louis Davenport's mandate for the highest quality of service.

What made the Davenport Hotel better known than the city of its location? What about it attracted hotel men from around the world who visited for the sole purpose of learning its secrets? Louis Davenport's secret cannot be summed up in a few words. He was truly a genius in his chosen field and remains a legend in Spokane – an example of success without greed. May this book, with an emphasis on the Davenport establishment's glory years, help to preserve the story of Louis Davenport and his legendary hotel and to welcome the reopened Davenport, a grand hotel for the 21st century.

# Chapter 1

## Long-held Myths and Misconceptions

Long before his death in 1951, Louis Davenport had established a legacy destined to keep his name alive. Davenport was a hospitality-marketing genius who possessed a genuine desire to serve his community and please those whose paths he crossed. His influence and efforts created more goodwill and attracted more events and festivities to Spokane than any other individual in the city's history. The reputation of Spokane's finest restaurant and hotel, which bore his name, stretched far beyond the shores of this continent.

Many stories have been told and much has been written about Davenport's rags-to-riches legacy following his arrival in Spokane in March 1889. But do these long-held stories hold up under scrutiny? Extensive research into his past and his family's history has revealed some inconsistencies, questionable elements or misleading facts. This chapter will address a few significant misconceptions about his life story. Nothing is intended to detract from the greatness of the man or his character, but rather to broaden the perspective on one who cut such a wide historical swath in the Northwest and acknowledge others who contributed to his success.

### Myth of Louis Davenport's Arrival

**Almost without exception, historical accountings explain Louis Davenport's arrival in Spokane as somewhat of a fluke or chance occurrence. According to the accounts, he boarded a train (his point of departure varies) and traveled as far as his money would take him, which just happened to be Spokane. He is portrayed as a 20-year-old man who arrived in Spokane alone with less than $2.00 in his pocket.**

While these colorful and somewhat romantic stories are in keeping with "how the West was won" and the emergence of self-made millionaires who exploited its great natural resources, they are not consistent with Louis Davenport's nature or the facts. His arrival in Spokane in March 1889 does not appear to have been a chance event or the whim of an irresponsible youth, but rather a predetermined and deliberate move. In a tribute to Louis Davenport over 30 years later, William C. Gray, who had built the California House, Spokane's first upscale hotel, wrote: "I well remember when you came here as a young chap. There was even then a certain something which many of us felt certain meant big things for you – a steady persistence, a willingness to work, **an inclination to consider well and then to act decisively** [emphasis added]." Perhaps he did arrive with just pocket change, but he was likely assured of some assistance and had a sense of direction in a town bursting with activity.

Most of Louie's youth was spent in Red Bluff, California, where his father, John S. Davenport and, for a period of time, John's younger brother, Elijah J. Davenport Jr., operated a mercantile store. The two brothers were from a large extended family, originally from Cold Spring, New York, who had since settled in Nebraska. They were the only members of the immediate family to migrate farther west. Louie was about seven years old when his family settled in California. Being a familiar figure in his nephew's youth, Elijah may have been influential in some of Louie's later decisions.

In the early 1880s, Spokane was becoming nationally recognized as a booming town with the potential to become a great city. The discovery of the Inland Northwest's abundant natural resources and potential for wealth was attracting people from all over the United States. News of Spokane's growth and exploding economy brought an enormous influx of people to the area – and a great need for services of all types. Specifically, there was a significant demand for hotels and restaurants, as evidenced by numerous articles appearing in Spokane newspapers during that time.

Among those attracted to Spokane were Louis Davenport's uncle, Elijah, with his wife Eva. Although one report states they arrived as early as 1883, this date could not be verified. The first city directory was not published until 1885 and many omissions of names occurred in the early directories. But according to his 1906 marriage certificate, Clifford Davenport (Elijah and Eva's first child) was born in Spokane in 1885. City directories and early Spokane newspaper accounts provided evidence of Elijah having established himself in the hotel business in Spokane by 1887. The following article appeared in the *Spokane Falls Review* on April 28, 1887:

> E.J. Davenport has fitted up the machine shop recently owned by Carter Bros. into a hotel. The gentleman has made such a complete change in the structure that one would not recognize the place. Mr. Davenport proposes to conduct a good home-like house, and knows how too.

By 1890 the Spokane city directories had listed Elijah Davenport as the proprietor of four hotels and a restaurant in Spokane as follows (the addresses reflect an old numbering system, which was revised in 1891):

> 1887 – Davenport E.J. propr. **U.S. Hotel** 109 Front. [This was the machine shop referenced in the above quote as the directory also listed this hotel as the residence of the two Carter brothers from whom Elijah had purchased the shop.]

> 1888 – Davenport E.J. propr. **Commercial Hotel** r. same. [A *Spokane Falls Review* article on March 15, 1889, stated, "Mr. E.J. Davenport, who has so successfully conducted the Commercial hotel of this city for the past year, has disposed of the same to Mr. W.H. Bell . . . Mr. Davenport has made a success as a hotel proprietor, both by his genial manners and excellence of his table."]

1889 – Davenport Elijah J. propr. **Pride of Spokane Restaurant**, 313 Howard, res. 302 1/2 W. Sprague. [Although Elijah was listed as the proprietor at the time the directory was published, just prior to the Spokane fire of 1889, which destroyed the restaurant, Louis Davenport became the proprietor. Also note that the residence address was that of the Chamberlin Lodging House listed in the next entry.]

1890 – Davenport Elijah J. propr. **Merchants' Hotel** Riverside Ave. W of Monroe and propr. **Chamberlin Lodging House**, Sprague N.W. corner of Lincoln [located next door to the Commercial Hotel].

No city directory was published in 1891, but the 1892 *Spokane Falls Directory* lists Elijah's residence as 1211 Sprague. There was, however, no mention of a business. That same year, Louie's mother, Minnie, is also listed in the directory. She had relocated to Spokane in 1891, bringing Louie's younger brother Arthur and sister Jessie.

***Drawing of the Commercial Hotel as it appeared in the 1890 Polk Directory.***

An interesting aside, which further corroborates Elijah's vocational status while in Spokane, was his bid to feed the prisoners. The following entry was made during a Spokane City Council meeting on June 27, 1888: "Two bids for feeding prisoners – E.J. Davenport offered to feed the prisoners for 25 cents per meal delivered at the jail or would furnish the meals at his house [the Commercial Hotel] for 20 cents." Following this entry was another bid, submitted by J.H. Seaman, for 20 cents delivered and 18 cents if the city picked them up. Seaman was awarded the contract.

The foregoing information paints a picture of the situation awaiting Louis Davenport upon his arrival in Spokane. **In summary, for a number of years prior to his arrival, Davenport had an uncle living in Spokane who was well established in both the hotel and restaurant businesses and in a position to help his young nephew starting out in his own business.** While it is not known to what extent Elijah may have helped Louie financially, both were known to have been proprietors of the Pride of Spokane Restaurant. Elijah gave Louie a job in the restaurant, where he acquired the experience necessary to become its proprietor. Some years later, when Louie's father (Elijah's brother) died in 1909, he bequeathed to his siblings and his children equal shares of his estate (with the exception of Louie's brother, Arthur, who also received the father's real estate holdings in Red Bluff, California). However, Elijah made legal arrangements for his share of the estate to go to Louie. This further establishes a connection between uncle and nephew, but by this time, Louie was quite well to do. Perhaps it was repayment of a loan?

*Dedication of the Masonic Temple on West Riverside Avenue in 1904. Between the Temple and the Monroe Street Bridge in the background is the Merchants' Hotel, Elijah Davenport's fourth hotel. An excerpt from a newspaper article on May 4, 1922, entitled "Landmark Is Demolished," read as follows: "One of the oldest landmarks in the city – the Merchants' hotel . . . – is being wrecked today to make room for the new [expansion of the] Masonic temple. The old building was erected immediately after the fire in '89 and served to house many of Spokane's homeless while their razed residences were being restored. For a time it was the largest building and the finest hotel at Spokane Falls. Up to about six years ago it was used for a lodging house. City officials condemned it as a fire trap, and the ground floor has since been used to house an auto paint shop." (Detail of EWSHS photo L93-66.271)*

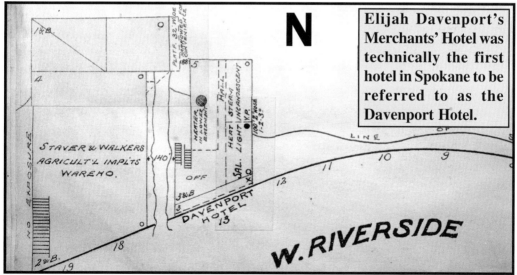

*A reproduction from an 1890 Dakin Spokane Fire Map showing the location of the Merchants' Hotel, listed on the map simply as "Davenport Hotel." The 1890 Spokane City Directory listed it as the Merchants' Hotel and the following year it appears on the Sanborn Map as the Merchants' Hotel. (EWSHS archives.)*

## Misconceptions About Davenport's First Restaurant

**Most accounts claim Louis Davenport's first restaurant was the Waffle Foundry, which was started in a tent after Spokane's Great Fire of 1889. The most popular story has Davenport scraping together enough money (the sum usually cited is $125) to start a bare-bones establishment directly across the street from what became the permanent location of his popular Davenport's Restaurant. He is said to have earned this sum by joining the manual-labor force with pick and shovel, cleaning up debris and wreckage left in the fire's wake.**

An advertisement Louis Davenport ran in the *Spokane Falls Review* for several days beginning on August 6, 1889, two days after the big fire, raises some curious questions. The advertisement (see facing page) contains four key points: (1) Prior to the fire, Louis Davenport had taken over as the proprietor of the Pride of Spokane (of which his uncle had also been the proprietor), making that his <u>first</u> restaurant in Spokane. (2) He opened another restaurant (his second) <u>immediately</u> after the fire. (3) The restaurant he opened after the fire was simply referred to as "Restaurant, L.M. Davenport." (4) The site of his new restaurant, the address of which is on the old numbering system, was located in an existing building on Sprague between Lincoln and Monroe, a block beyond the burned-out section.

To have opened a restaurant this quickly, it appears Louis Davenport had access to the necessary supplies or some financial means or assistance to open a restaurant. The Pride of Spokane Restaurant, located at 313 Howard Street, was destroyed in the fire. According to a newspaper account on August 7, 1889, the restaurant was insured, although it was Elijah Davenport who was named in connection with the restaurant. This is a good indication that both Davenports were involved with the restaurant at the time of the fire. Another interesting bit of information that may help explain how Louis was able to open the restaurant immediately comes from *Supplement II, Summer 1968* to a book entitled *Thomas Davenport, Philipstown Pioneer 1682-1759 and His Descendants* compiled by Dorothy Giles and Irma Franklin. It states: "At the time of the great Spokane fire, he [Louis] loaded furniture, dishes, cutlery, cooking utensils, etc., from his uncle Elijah's restaurant, bought 2 large tents, and after the fire, started serving meals . . . "

The story of setting up his restaurant in a tent is interesting because of the images it conjures up. After the fire, little time was wasted in resuming business in the growing metropolis and business owners sought any available shelter, many of which were truly tents. In the case of the Waffle Foundry, however, analysis of the temporary locations of Davenport's Waffle Foundry and study of the drawings provided by the Davenport establishment create questions about its being housed in an actual tent. It is unknown how long the restaurant referenced in the ad remained at the given location, but in an interview in 1895, Louis Davenport stated the opening date of his

Waffle Foundry was December 8, 1889. In a letter to Davenport in 1922, William S. Hayford wrote: "I recall going to work for you on the 8th of January, 1890, in your waffle foundry, located in a tent where Sherman-Clay Piano House now stands [the Miller Block – not the Whitten Block as listed in some sources – at 808-810 West Sprague Avenue], as a waiter." According to Robert B. Hyslop in his book *Spokane's Building Blocks,* both the Miller and Whitten buildings were constructed immediately after the fire. The drawings (see page 21 for one rendition) show a tent-like roof, but framed windows and doors with glass panes. Perhaps temporary canvas tarps were stretched over the rafters to provide some protection during the construction of the building. This does not, however, appear to have been merely a poor man's attempt to break into the restaurant business but more likely an expedient and only way to capitalize on the tremendous demand for food services until he was able to establish his business in a more permanent location and facility.

*This notice appeared in the Spokane Falls Review on August 6, 1889, two days after Spokane's fire burned most of the business district. There is a commonly held belief that Louie Davenport's first restaurant was Davenport's Famous Waffle Foundry. This advertisement is significant because it establishes that he had two restaurants – this one (which appears to have been short-lived) and the Pride of Spokane – prior to the Waffle Foundry.*

*Note the bottom ad for "Robinson & Davenport, Successors to Mead & Co." The meat market would have faced Sprague, with the restaurant located be-*

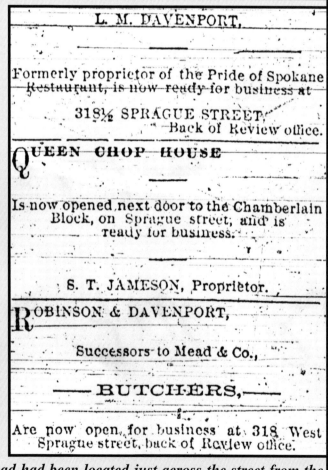

L. M. DAVENPORT,

Formerly proprietor of the Pride of Spokane Restaurant, is now ready for business at

318½ SPRAGUE STREET,
Back of Review office.

QUEEN CHOP HOUSE

Is now opened next door to the Chamberlain Block, on Sprague street, and is ready for business.

S. T. JAMESON, Proprietor.

ROBINSON & DAVENPORT,

Successors to Mead & Co.,

—— BUTCHERS,——

Are now open for business at 318 West Sprague street, back of Review office.

*hind it. Before the fire, Mead had been located just across the street from the Pride of Spokane, and Robinson was named with the company in the 1889 directory. Another source stated Elijah Davenport had owned meat markets, but this is the only reference found corroborating the claim.*

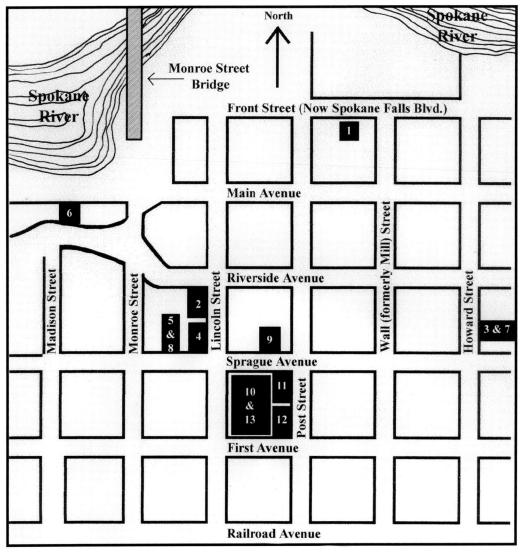

## Davenport-owned establishments and dates of their initial occupancy:

### Elijah Davenport

1. U.S. Hotel (1887)
2. Commercial Hotel (1888)
3. Pride of Spokane Restaurant (1889)
4. Chamberlin Lodging House (c. 1889)
5. Robinson & Davenport Meat Market (1889)
6. Merchants' Hotel (1889)

### Louis Davenport

7. Pride of Spokane Restaurant (1889)
8. L.M. Davenport Restaurant (1889)

9. Davenport's Famous Waffle Foundry, first location (1889)
10. Davenport's Famous Waffle Foundry, second location (1889)
11. Davenport's Restaurant/Wilson Block (rented in 1890, purchased in 1905*)
12. Pennington Hotel (purchased 1904*)
13. Davenport Hotel (1914)

*Offer to buy was in 1903. Date reflects when sale was finalized and deed filed.

**Note:** In 1891 Spokane's Street numbering system changed. Davenport's Restaurant was 207-209 West Sprague at the time it opened and, with this change, became 807-809.

With Davenport's ability to open a restaurant immediately after the fire, what about the story that he scraped together $125 mucking out fire debris to start his restaurant? A program distributed by the Davenport Institutions in 1922 to celebrate its 32nd anniversary stated: "With an actual capital of less than $125, which [Davenport] had accumulated following the fire by working with a drill and pick and shovel as a member of an excavating partnership into which he had entered for a short time following the fire, he managed to acquire a tent restaurant . . . "

From the news accounts following the fire, nearly every able-bodied man participated in some of this grimy activity to salvage what he could and reestablish businesses. Further, in a city council meeting called immediately after the fire, the council members adopted a motion that " . . . any person offered employment and refusing to work, be notified to leave the city." Of course, anyone who had an interest in the city and was physically able would naturally pitch in and do his part. Plus, it may well have been to Davenport's advantage to participate in this activity to secure a more desirable location for his restaurant in the heart of the business section. However, in another 1922 letter, W.C. Ufford, manager of the Spokane Lumber Company, refers to his work after the fire as follows, " . . . the gruff but kindly Insurance Adjuster seeing among many workers one apart, different, perhaps even less capable than the others in cleaning burnt mortar from bricks amidst the ruins of the great fire, but whose tapering and bleeding fingers attracted him, and who needing a Clerk asked, 'Can you write?'" This type of work, of which he had experience (he was listed as a clerk in both the Red Bluff, California directory in 1885 and in the San Francisco directories in 1887 and 1888), was much more akin to Davenport's business nature.

Other elements of the story about Louie Davenport's early days in Spokane, such as arriving with $1.25 in his pocket, are also included in the program mentioned above. One would assume that Davenport himself contributed to the story – or at least approved it – but he includes no mention of being the proprietor of the Pride of Spokane prior to the fire (it does, however, state he "worked as buyer and general utility man" in "one of the principal restaurants of the city of that day") or the restaurant he opened on August 6, 1889. Nor does it mention his Uncle Elijah, who according to living descendants, loaned Louie some money to help him start his restaurant. There are also no references in any available literature about the other family members who joined him in Spokane. By all accounts, Davenport was a humble and very private man who did not like to draw attention to himself. This was perfectly illustrated in a newspaper article following his marriage in August 1906, which stated: "The marriage comes as a complete surprise to all except the nearest friends. . . . The secrecy of the marriage is in keeping with Mr. Davenport's modesty, probably few men in Spokane having a stronger dislike for notoriety . . . " He may simply have been unwilling to share the personal details and was content with the abbreviated version of his early history, which made a good story.

*Looking southwest from the Spokane River at a section of downtown Spokane, circa 1885. The cross streets in the foreground are Front (now Spokane Falls Boulevard) and Mill (now Wall). The two-story building facing Front Street (see arrow) was Carter Brothers' machine shop. It became Elijah Davenport's U.S. Hotel in 1887, which was the first known Davenport-owned hotel in Spokane. (Detail of EWSHS photo L86-275.2)*

*Looking north on Post Street in 1888. Victor Dessert's Pacific Hotel, the tallest building on the right, was on the corner of Post and First. The Russ House adjoining it was a lodging house, also owned by Dessert. The fire in 1889 destroyed all the buildings seen here, but the block north of First on the left became the future home of Davenport's restaurant and hotel. (Photo courtesy Jerome Peltier.)*

Before moving into his permanent site in the Wilson Block on the south side of Sprague at Post Street, Louie had a second temporary location in the fire district. The Hayford letter, cited earlier, further stated: "On July 1st, 1890, I aided in your moving to the tent of the old Tycoon Saloon [later the site of the Davenport Hotel, which adjoined the Wilson Block on the west] . . . On July 4, 1890, the tent burned down . . . Thereafter you moved into a room at your present location . . . " Another letter, written in 1922 by Arthur D. Jones, a prominent Realtor, stated: "I proposed to rent you a couple of small storerooms on the ground floor in this building [Wilson Block] and [Henry L. Wilson, one of the owners] answered that he wanted no restaurants in the place, nor waffle signs on his building and I assured him that you had fight (energy) enough in you to keep the crumbs off and that the place would be such a credit to his building that he would ultimately be satisfied." After Jones's lobbying efforts on his behalf for this location, Davenport did move into the Wilson Block. The July 5, 1890 *Spokane Falls Review* reported Davenport would ". . . reopen his restaurant on Monday, July 7 [the opening was delayed until July 10th] . . . "

On July 13, 1890, the *Spokane Falls Review* printed a lengthy article, excerpts of which follow, praising his restaurant. This was only nine days after the tent burned, less than a year after the city's fire and 16 months after Davenport arrived in Spokane. The description of this restaurant further illustrates that Louis Davenport was not a near-penniless laborer, as historically portrayed, when he arrived in Spokane and obviously had more financial means available to him than the stories indicate. But more importantly, it highlights his quick advancement to the ranks of Spokane's top restaurateur and portrays the markings of a brilliant man with outstanding work ethics and ideas. This article was his first public accolade and an important preview of his future in the hospitality industry.

## SUITABLY SITUATED
### Davenport's Establishment Opened to the Public –The Place to Patronize – A Description of the Interior of This Popular and Prosperous Restaurant.

One of the requisites to life's contentment, and which affords the greatest happiness, is to enjoy our daily repasts amid pleasant surroundings, together with an inviting cleanliness and a good service. This tempts the ruling need of our existence, and which should be followed by wholesome edibles. An establishment possessing these features has been a long felt want in this city, the supplying of which many futile attempts have been made by various caterers, but only until Thursday last was it shown that the proper idea had finally been grasped, and that by L.M. Davenport, who opened to the public for the first time a restaurant managed in accordance to fill this popular demand.

This establishment, located at 207 West Sprague Street, is without doubt the most elaborate in finish, the best in general management and the most complete in equipment of any ever started in this city. The exterior is particularly inviting, there being two entrances on either side of a spacious bay-window, which is decorated with a novel miniature flour mill. The interior is perfect in management, and magnificent in appearance. It comprises two departments, one for ladies and the other for gentlemen, which are entirely distinct from each other, but both show that neither expense nor effort has been spared to perfect every detail necessary for the comfort of the patrons, and rapid supplying of their wants.

The ladies' department to which special care has been devoted, is 20x40 feet in dimension, and is particularly beautiful in appearance. The walls are artistically decorated with rich designs on paper and bordered by gold trimmings. The tables are well arranged, all covered with snow white linen and adorned with silver utensils, together with an electric call-bell within easy reach, showing that every possible comfort for the fair sex has been the main object in view.

The gentlemen's department, which occupies the principal part of the establishment, and to which the ladies' portion adjoins, situated to the right of the entrance, is 23x78 feet in dimension. This department also shows that the wants of the men have not been neglected in the lavish expenditure of money to give a uniformity in general comfort and an elegance in appearance throughout the establishment. The room artistically frescoed, and in arrangement comprises an enormous oval dining counter, encircling the center of the room, around the base of the outside of which is a foot rail, for the convenience of the patrons who sit at the counter on unique stools made for this purpose. From over this counter is where you are served by attentive employees, or if preferred you can select the gentlemen's retreat, which is an inviting small apartment, furnished with tables and chairs, taking up the back portion of the room, from which is separated by massive draperies suspended from the ceiling to the floor. The cash counter is located in front and encircles the inside of the display window . . . . The entire establishment is finished in dark and light wood of an impaneled design, and ornamented with solid cherry trimmings. Over the entrances to the ladies' department suspend heavy, rich portieres, while the floors are covered with fancy matting, and the establishment lighted throughout with numerous electric lights.

The kitchen . . . will undoubtedly be the finest in the city, both in management and equipment. It is located in the adjoining portion of the building, and is ventilated by an electric blower. The air here even seems particularly pure and sweet, and the arrangement has been so closely studied that the accumulation of dirt of any kind seems to be impossible. When completed it will be equipped with every conceivable culinary utensil, enormous ranges, the latest improved refrigerators, and every modern appliance for handling orders with dispatch and keeping all edibles fresh and wholesome. This department is provided over by a competent chef, . . .

Every detail of the establishment throughout shows that strenuous efforts have been made to practically make this a retreat where the most fastidious taste of the connoisseur can be satisfied, and for which the proprietor, L.M. Davenport, deserves much credit, having had many obstacles to overthrow in connection with this business.

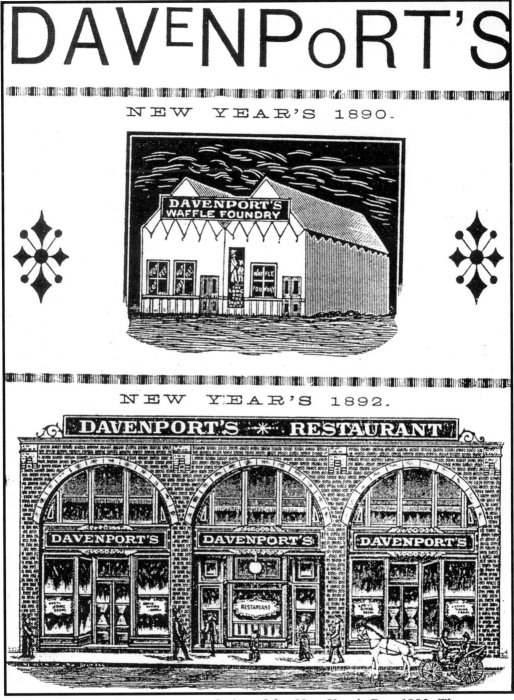

*A reproduction of a menu cover designed for New Year's Day 1892. The top portion is a drawing of Louis Davenport's "tent restaurant" from which he operated shortly after the Great Fire of 1889. The bottom drawing shows Louis Davenport's Restaurant in the Wilson Block at 805-809 West Sprague Avenue as it is appeared in 1892. A physical description of this restaurant, which appeared in a July 13, 1890 newspaper, is recorded on the preceding pages. (EWSHS L95-16.129)*

He has spared neither trouble nor expense to make this restaurant strictly first-class in every respect, and every detail shows that much study and labor have been expended to completely satisfy every want that his patrons could possibly desire.

# Louis Davenport Did Not Initiate the Hotel Project

**Historically, it is believed among those with interest in and knowledge of the Davenport Hotel, that Louis Davenport conceived the idea to build the hotel and that it had been his planned ambition and dream.**

By 1908 Louis Davenport was well established in the restaurant business. He owned and operated the most popular and elegant restaurant in the Inland Northwest and was comfortably reaping its profits. In fact, he was so well established and successful that he was in the process of building the most magnificent home in the Spokane area.

As early as 1906, a number of prominent businessmen began formulating plans to build an elegant, first-class hotel in Spokane. Their intent was for it to be the finest hotel in the Northwest, which they felt would attract a vast amount of business to Spokane and greatly enhance the city. Because of the city's excellent economy and projected growth, it was a sound business idea. This plan was developed to the point of reality, both conceptually and financially, by 1908. The major ingredient still lacking was a competent manager with the talent and intelligence to put the plan together and manage it.

Having already proven himself as a successful entrepreneur in the hospitality business, Louis Davenport was the natural choice and the perfect person for the project. His business acumen in the hospitality industry was unsurpassed and he had a reputation as a fair, honest and likeable individual. However, had Davenport been anticipating the assumption of such a major responsibility, it is unlikely he would have committed himself and his financial resources to the construction of such an elaborate new home (and, in fact, did sell it only about two and a half years after moving in to raise needed capital for the hotel). But once he agreed to the management position, he became the powerhouse and creative force behind the project.

A public announcement of the plan for the new hotel was made on October 8, 1908. The following article appeared in that day's *Evening Chronicle*:

## MILLIONS FOR A FINE NEW HOTEL
### Plans Are Afoot for Building a New 11-Story Hostelry Here.

The finest hotel in the entire northwest is to be built in Spokane. The costs of the building will be in the neighborhood of $2,000,000 and the money will be furnished by Spokane men.

The new hotel will be 11 [later changed to 12] stories high and will be the tallest building in the city, being 175 feet from the street to the top of the block. . . .

The building will be constructed of reinforced concrete, and will have brick and terra cotta on the outside. It is to be entirely fireproof, and one of the most sightly structures in the west.

In the center of the hotel will be a lobby 110 by 50 feet, and that space will be open to the top of the building. In this way there will not be a dark room in the entire hotel. There will be 450 rooms in the establishment, and there will be closets and a bath connected with each.

There will be bridal suites, small and large banquet halls, and in every way the equipment will be the best in the northwest.

### Several Sites In View

Three locations have been inspected for the hotel, but the site just west of Davenport's restaurant is believed to be the most probable choice. This would give three streets, from which entrances would be made to the lobby. The building would be bounded by Sprague and First avenues and Lincoln street. In addition to that location, the company has in contemplation a site on Riverside avenue, between Madison and Monroe and also the old Merriam site on First and Howard. There are several other good sites in view.

**The business men of Spokane have been working on the proposition for the last two years, but the difficulty was to secure a competent manager. The money was raised, and then the promoters went to Louis Davenport, owner and proprietor of Davenport's restaurant.**

**Finally Mr. Davenport concluded to undertake the proposition, and plans have already been drawn for the beautiful building** [emphasis added].

The plan of the builders is to construct for Spokane one of the finest hotels in the country. It is expected to provide a fire proof, comfortable, well cared for hotel at reasonable rates. Everything is to be first class, and as good as any hotel in the country. The hotel is planned to be as beautiful as Davenport's restaurant, and is expected to be as famous for a hotel as is Davenport's restaurant for a restaurant.

The restaurant attachment is to be conducted by Mr. Davenport, and the city is to be advertised through the hotel, in a way so as to bring fame to Spokane.

This article is significant to Spokane's history and especially to the history of the Davenport family. It highlights the degree of respect Spokane's community leaders had for Louis Davenport. Most importantly, it documents how Spokane's most famous building was conceived, not to discredit Davenport for its original concept, but to acknowledge the significant roles of the others involved.

*An architectural rendering of the proposed hotel, which appeared in the Spokes-man-Review on Sunday October 11, 1908, below the following headline: "Sprague Avenue Perspective of $1,750,000 Hotel on Lincoln Street, Sprague to First Avenue." A modified version of this hotel became the famous Davenport Hotel.*

The following article appeared below the drawing of the proposed hotel:

> The above illustration shows the Sprague avenue and Lincoln street frontage of the 11-story hotel to be erected by Spokane and eastern capitalists on the block bounded by Sprague and First avenues, Post and Lincoln streets. The big structure will occupy all of the block excepting L.M. Davenport's restaurant, which it adjoins on the west. It will be 155x200 feet, and the building alone will cost about $1,000,000. It is estimated that the furnishings will cost $250,000, and the site about $500,000, making a total investment of $1,750,000.

> In design the structure is old Spanish. It will be built of steel construction with brick and terra cotta exterior, highly ornate. At each corner of the building will be a tower with the dome rising 200 feet above the pavement. Besides the four towers there will be pinnacles on the building. The roof will be red tile, and the brick and terra cotta will be light grey.

> . . . The building will have a lobby 46x90 feet with fine mosaic floors and huge terra cotta pillars forming arches . . . These arches will support a balcony 30 feet wide extending all the way around the lobby, and over this will be a huge dome of art

glass 35 feet above the lobby floor. There will be a 14-foot corridor with marble walls running through the building from Sprague to First avenue, intersecting the lobby midway.

. . . It will require four large passenger elevators to accommodate the hotel, besides the service and freight elevators. The top story, the windows of which are not shown in the above picture, will be used principally for employees' quarters.

The hotel will have a large dining room at the southeast corner, facing on First avenue. It will also connect with Davenport's restaurant. There will also be a men's cafe on the Lincoln street frontage and a grill room in the basement.

Cutter and Malmgren are the architects of the building. While the floor plans and principal features have been worked out, these are subject to change. Mr. Cutter and L.M. Davenport, who is one of the Spokane men behind the project, will make an extended trip east in the near future to make a study of big hotels with the idea of embodying their most attractive features in the Spokane hostelry.

*The home built by Louis and Verus Davenport at 34 West Eighth Avenue. They began construction of this home prior to being approached by a group of Spokane businessmen to become involved with their hotel project. This was the grandest home in Spokane, but the Davenports lived there about two-and-a-half years before they arranged a trade and sale of this home to Richard B. Porter to free up capital for the hotel. Although the Davenport Hotel project deprived the family of their new home, it destined Louis Davenport to become one of the nation's foremost hotel entrepreneurs. (Photo EWSHS, L88-404.19.2.1)*

# Chapter 2

## Spokane Falls, 1883–1888, During Elijah Davenport's Early Years

In 1862 President Lincoln signed into law the largest land grant act in the country's history, the Pacific Railway Act. This law granted public lands for the purpose of connecting the East and West coasts by rail. Union Pacific and Central Pacific, both chartered that year, were the first recipients of the land grant. The Northern Pacific Railroad was chartered in 1864 to provide the link to the Pacific Northwest.

The Inland Northwest was known to possess enormous stands of old-growth timber, plus vast mineral deposits in the Colville, Metalines, and Coeur d'Alene mining districts. Because of these known timber reserves and the obvious mineral potential in the Northwest, the Northern Pacific Railway was eager to build the northern transcontinental line. However, various obstacles delayed construction until the late 1870s. The line finally reached Spokane from the west in 1881 and, with the completion of the cross-country connections in 1883, the Northern Pacific was well into a national advertising campaign to sell its vast land holdings. The facing page, which contains a partial clipping from a Northern Pacific Railroad advertisement, illustrates a typical promotional piece from that era. This advertising campaign was the most significant factor in attracting huge numbers of people to the Northwest, and the railroads profited both in their transportation and real estate dealings.

Passage of the land grant and subsequent construction of the railroad created an attractive new frontier. Although the driving factors for building the railroad into the Pacific Northwest were the timber reserves, homestead land and the agricultural potential, it was the discovery of gold that triggered the first major rush and population explosion. With the railroad line running through Spokane, the city quickly became a hub of activity and the economic center of the Inland Northwest.

## Spokane Falls in 1883

In addition to the railroad's advertising campaign, a constant barrage of promotion was carried on in both local and national news media regarding the opportunities in Spokane Falls, as the city was then called. One article described 17 new buildings under construction in downtown Spokane, 12 of which were brick. An ongoing theme in the majority of promotions was the need for hotel accommodations. The following excerpt is from a lengthy article in the June 8, 1883, *Spokane Falls Review*:

# PUBLIC ATTENTION

Is now largely directed to the

 ## VAST NEW REGIONS

Opened for Settlement by the completion of the

# NORTHERN PACIFIC RAILROAD

Through MINNESOTA, NORTH DAKOTA, MONTANA,
NORTHERN IDAHO, WASHINGTON and OREGON,

The widely known and prosperous

# Northern Pacific Country

☞The important Geographical Divisions traversed by this New **TRANS-CONTINENTAL LINE,** possess unusually large and varied Natural Resources.

**THERE ARE** New Towns growing into important trade centers, and there is a steady advance in the values of all property.

**THERE ARE** Large unoccupied areas of FERTILE LANDS especially adapted to Wheat Growing and General Farming.

**THERE ARE** EXTENSIVE GRAZING RANGES, the best in the United States for Stock Raising.

**THERE ARE** RICH MINERAL DISTRICTS to be developed and HEAVY BODIES OF TIMBER for lumbering purposes.

**THERE ARE** Navigable Rivers, Lakes and larger waters and innumerable water powers ready to be utilized.

**THERE ARE** Profitable Fisheries on the Rivers, Lakes and Puget Sound. The fish are of great commercial value.

**THERE ARE** Exceptionally good opportunities for Merchants, Manufacturers, Professional Men, Mechanics and Traders to engage in business.

## The Diversified Resources of this Grand Region

ready to be developed into innumerable paying industries, will put in use much capital AND REQUIRE A LARGE NUMBER OF OPERATORS AND WORKING MEN.

# THERE IS AMPLE ROOM

*In this Great Belt of Productive and Prosperous Country*

# For Millions of Settlers

To secure COMFORTABLE HOMES and become INDEPENDENT. ☞ Each State and Territory traversed by the NORTHERN PACIFIC possesses abundant resources to support a compact population. The countries are well watered, the soil is rich and productive, while the climate is superior in the qualities which assure healthful and pleasant living, is favorable for the production of crops, and usually more propitious than elsewhere found for the growth of wheat, oats, rye, barley, fruits and the vegetables.

. . . Brickmakers are hard at work burning new kilns and delivering that already burnt, while as far as we can ascertain there is not a carpenter out of employment in the city. And the new growth is of a lasting kind. It is not temporary shelters thrown hastily together regardless of appearance, but houses that will endure for years, substantial, well finished and handsome in appearance . . .

Following this paragraph, the writer described the new brick and frame structures and included a general discourse that presented Spokane as an enticing place to live and start a business. By that time, Spokane had eight major business blocks, five significant hotels, nine manufacturing plants, two banks, two colleges, a high school and four churches. The Echo Roller Mills had just been completed on Havermale Island and was billed as one of the largest flour mills in the Northwest. The first bridge in downtown Spokane, which actually consisted of three spans, connected the south bank at Howard Street to Havermale Island, Havermale Island to Big Island, and Big Island to the north bank of the river. On August 11, 1883, plans were announced for a second bridge to cross the Spokane River at the foot of Post Street. This bridge was proposed to be 526 feet long, 22 feet wide ("wide enough for a double drive way and foot walks on each side") and 56 feet above the river.

## Spokane's Hotel Accommodations are Inadequate

Another excerpt from the July 28, 1883, *Spokane Falls Review* article stated:

> The advancement of Spokane Falls is founded upon a foundation of lasting stability. It is here for all times, and every year will see it progress . . . There are more buildings than ever in course of construction. Brick blocks and frame residences on every hand. There is not a street, alley or byway in the city that is not the scene of some improvement. . . . **The hotels are crowded to capacity and "the cry is still they come."** . . . The prospects of Spokane Falls were never more encouraging than at the present writing, and there is no reason to doubt but that it will continue on indefinitely.

On July 14, 1883, shortly before the announcement of the gold discovery and ensuing rush to the Coeur d'Alenes, the *Spokane Falls Review* reprinted an article from the *Northern Pacific Railway Journal*. This article highlighted reasons to move to Spokane Falls, again asserting the need for hotels, which likely was the kind of publicity that attracted Elijah Davenport to Spokane. Following is a portion of that article:

### SPOKANE
#### "A Land Flowing with Milk and Honey"

SPOKANE COUNTY is the most easterly of the Territory. . . . Its area is 10,000 square miles. Its soil, climate, timber, stock ranges and mineral resources is perhaps unsurpassed by any other like area on the continent. Tributary to it are the Great Bend agricultural and grazing lands, the pine forests of the Coeur d'Alene and Pend d'Oreille lakes. The rich mineral lands of the Okanagon [*sic*], Colville and Kootenai ranges, tributary streams, and many lakes, all of which are supplied with fish in endless variety . . . a great source of revenue . . . . Its chief attractions are pleasant, healthful climate, freedom from malaria, absence of strong winds and severe thunders and lightnings (tornadoes being entirely unknown), and the great productiveness of its soil . . .

The article continued to describe Spokane with the following headings: real estate, railroads, high schools, churches, the press and hotels. Regarding hotels, it stated the following:

The hotel accommodations are entirely inadequate to the rapidly increasing development of the town and to receive the many who are daily finding their way from the east in search of homes in Eastern Washington. The Sprague, a first-class hotel in every particular, is situated but a few yards from the depot. Here pure spring water is conveyed thro' pipes to every part of the house, which is provided with bathrooms, wash rooms, etc., and all modern improvements. The dining room is provided with an experienced corps of waiters, and the table is supplied with all the delicacies of the season. The California House, on Howard street, is also a first-class hotel, free busses conveying travelers to and from all trains. The N.P. House, now being enlarged, is very centrally situated. Here, as in all others, the too frequent reply to somniferous inquiries: "Rooms and cots all engaged, will try and make you a 'shake-down'"! There are also some five or six hotels of minor importance.

## Mineral Discoveries in the Coeur d'Alenes

The subsequent discovery of gold initiated the first major boom to the Inland Northwest, creating an even greater demand for lodging and services. Elijah Davenport came to the area, not as a prospector seeking a fortune in mining, but as an entrepreneur aware of the services needed in the booming area.

Andrew Prichard is given credit for making the first discovery of placer (loose surface) gold in the Coeur d'Alenes. Although he only told a few close friends, his discovery soon leaked out and, by 1883, was being reported nationally. The first newspaper ad in Spokane announcing this discovery was on September 1, 1883. During early stages of the gold-rush era, placer gold was worth between $25 to $30 an ounce and relatively inexpensive to obtain as the only equipment needed by the first prospectors were a shovel, pick, gold pan and living supplies. Even the poorest and least educated of men stood a chance of fulfilling dreams of becoming wealthy.

The discovery of silver and lead came on the heels of the gold rush. The first major discovery occurred in 1885. Noah S. Kellogg, along with his partners Phil O'Rourke and Con Sullivan, discovered the mineral deposit that grew into the now world-famous Bunker Hill Mine. As the story goes, they stumbled upon the outcropping while searching for Kellogg's jackass after he wandered away. Between the years

*Spokane newspaper headlines announcing the discovery of gold in the Coeur d'Alene Mountains. The announcement on the left appeared on September 1, 1883 in the weekly edition of the Spokane Falls Review. It was the first of many. The headline shown on the right appeared in this same newspaper on September 22, 1883.*

1886 to 1946, over $60 million in dividends were paid. In the combined production of lead and zinc, it was the largest single-lode-mine producer in the United States.

With its brisk development prior to the gold and silver discoveries, Spokane had become the economic center for the Inland Northwest. It became more established in that position as further mineral discoveries were made and mining enterprises developed. Initially serving as an outfitting supply point, Spokane later became home to many of the region's successful mine owners and investors. Wealth from the mines poured into the city, and it soon became the Inland Northwest showplace for the wealthy, who built elaborate mansions and handsome business buildings.

*A typical example of hard rock mining in the late 1800s using a pneumatic drill called a "buzzy." (Photo courtesy Butch Jacobson.)*

Obviously, with all the excitement brewing in and around Spokane Falls, there were plenty of reasons for Elijah and Eva Davenport to move to the area in 1883, but Eva's health topped the list. While living in California, Eva had contracted malaria and was in search of a healthier climate. Spokane was being nationally advertised as an exceptionally healthy place to live, even specifying that it was free of malaria. And, the economy was booming. Elijah was a businessman, and Spokane offered abundant opportunities, especially in the hotel business. The following quote, which first appeared in the *Walla Walla Union* and was reprinted in the *Spokane Falls Review* on March 8, 1884, illustrates the type of publicity Spokane Falls received:

> . . . We have studied the Spokane Falls problem [its exceptionally rapid growth] since 1881, and each time we have visited the place have found other reasons for faith in its future. The local reasons are its beautiful site, admirably adapted for the residence of man, sloping towards a rapid river, making a perfect system of drainage possible, an atmosphere rarified by an elevation of 1821 feet above the sea, purified by frequent Chinooks, medicated by their passage through pine forests, combine to make it a health resort; a river tumbling over falls . . . furnishes water power for turning thousands of wheels, while extensive forest of cedar and other timber, easy of access, furnish material to be worked up. Spokane Falls is the chief starting point for the Colville and Big Bend countries, the place where the immigrant designing to settle in those regions obtains his supplies. It is also a prominent starting and outfitting point for the new mines. It is claimed to be the trading point for the rich and extensive agricultural region south of Hangman's Creek, and it is the supply depot for the lumbermen in the Pend Oreille country. . . .

A partial quote from *Thomas Davenport: Philipstown Pioneer, 1682-1759, and His Descendants (Supplement III)* offers some information about Elijah up to and including his time in Spokane:

> Elijah John Davenport, Jr., born in Philipstown (Cold Spring), N.Y., Mar. 8, 1850. In 1867, he joined the 6th Kansas Volunteer Cavalry and was a scout in western Kansas against Indians. In 1870, he went to San Francisco and Mr. Spreckles (his father's friend) gave him a job driving a horse-car on Market Street and assisted him in buying a half-interest in a little ranch at Gridley Station north of Marysville, California. He hired as many as 40 Chinese laborers to cut wood for the boilers on the steamboats on the Sacramento River. In 1881, he went to Pawnee City for his grandmother's last illness [probably was his mother's, as she died in 1881 following a prolonged illness] and married there Mar. 11, 1882, Eva (Phenia Roseha) Beaver, born Mar. 8, 1863, Crawfordsville, Ind., died Feb. 7, 1937 . . . After their marriage, Elijah and Eva went to Marysville and while in the Sacramento Valley, Eva contracted malaria so in the fall of 1882, they drove a covered wagon north to Walla Walla, Wash. Terr., where they wintered. **In the Spring of 1883, they moved to Spokane Falls. At the time of the big Spokane fire, Aug. 4, 1889, Elijah Davenport owned a restaurant on south Howard Street, the two largest meat markets, the slaughterhouse [Editor's note: only one tiny reference could be found to owning a meat market and nothing to confirm the slaughterhouse], and the Chamberlin Block at Lincoln and Sprague . . . By 1890 he had built 4 hotels and was considered a wealthy man but lost everything in the Panic of 1893**. [It should be noted here that Louis Davenport's father, John, and his uncle Elijah's mercantile partnership in California is not mentioned in this particular writing.]

## The Developing Timber Industry

After the initial mining boom, the magnificent forests of the Inland Northwest can be cited as the primary catalyst that drew Eastern capital to this area. As the forests in the eastern United States were becoming depleted, lumbermen began to look to the West. Unlike the mining wealth hidden underground, the endless stands of huge evergreen trees were clearly visible. The vast timber reserves were, in fact, the main incentive for the Northern Pacific Railway to build its line into the Pacific Northwest, in spite of the unrelenting challenges presented by its rugged terrain. As soon as the transcontinental railroad was completed, industry representatives were sent west to begin the acquisition of timber and timberlands.

Just as the gold rush and subsequent silver and lead discoveries had contributed to a growing population and an increasing demand for goods and services, so, too, did the developing timber industry in northern Idaho and Eastern Washington. Like mining, such enterprises could be boom or bust, but some were enduring and significant. In the early stages of the region's development, local demands were supplied by countless small sawmill operations. However, by the early 1900s, large multi-regional companies had expanded their activites to the Pacific Northwest and many independent lumbermen had built substantial enterprises. Many fortunes were made.

One timber venture to have considerable, but short-lived, impact on the regional economy was the B.R. Lewis Lumber Company, which established the first major sawmill in the Inland Northwest. When Byron Lewis arrived in 1900, he was already an experienced Minnesota lumberman with financial backing, who had been acquiring timberlands in northern Idaho. In 1904 he purchased a small sawmill being built by the Kennedy Brothers at Coeur d'Alene, Idaho, near the mouth of the Spokane River and expanded it into what was advertised in 1907 as the second largest saw-mill west of the Rocky Mountains. At its peak, the mill employed 450 workers and turned out from 40 to 70 railroad cars of lumber a day. His extensive horse logging operation included 200 large draft horses. Although his entrepreneurial pursuits were headquartered in Coeur d'Alene, Lewis made his home in Spokane, building a large home at 2319 West Pacific Avenue in the fashionable Browne's Addition. However, expenses outpaced income and his venture failed in 1908.

**B.R. Lewis**

*B.R. Lewis skidding operation, circa 1907. (Photo courtesy Spokane Public Library)*

The failure of B.R. Lewis presented an opportunity for another lumberman who had arrived the same year, Frederick A. Blackwell. As president and general manager of the William Howard Land and Lumber Company, one of the largest Eastern lumber companies, Blackwell came to the Northwest in 1900 to begin securing timberlands for the company. He settled in Coeur d'Alene, where he proceeded to build an empire of lumber mills, railroads, and other diverse investments, as well as beautiful homes. He founded the Panhandle Lumber Company, around which he developed the town of Spirit Lake, Idaho. He was also instrumental in the development of Usk and Ione, Washington, the latter being the location of his second Panhandle Lumber sawmill, the largest mill in Pend Oreille County at the time.

**Frederick Blackwell**

In 1908 Blackwell purchased the B.R. Lewis Company. Under his ownership, the lumber manufacturing operation become one of the largest in the region. Blackwell's successes were due in large part to his role in developing railroad transportation in the Inland Northwest. He built the Idaho & Washington Northern Railroad from McGuires (near Post Falls), Idaho, to its terminus at Metaline Falls, Washington, the location of the Inland Portland Cement Company, which he was instrumental in founding in 1909. The line, with its connections to Spokane, was built to service his sawmills in Spirit Lake and Ione, as well as the cement plant. Although a major consideration was moving logs to his mills and lumber and cement to markets, Blackwell spent a great deal of money providing comfortable first-class passenger service on both this line and his electric railroad between Coeur d'Alene and Spokane.

Just as with the mining activity, Spokane prospered from the development of the timber industry in the Inland Northwest. The tycoons of both industries needed an appropriate venue for their formal and informal gatherings, a place to raise capital, build networks and conduct other business. Most specifically, they needed a hotel where they could proudly host their conventions and trade shows. It is hard to overestimate the importance of such a place to business and industry and, ultimately, to the overall prosperity of a region. Early entrepreneurs on the Spokane hospitality scene, such as Elijah Davenport, had provided the modest first restaurants and hostelries that served the influx of people initially attracted by mining and timber developments. After the fire of 1889, which destroyed most of these businesses, some distinguished, mid-sized hotels, such as the Spokane Hotel, were built. However, none of them could accommodate large conventions. Thus began the quest toward the sophistication of Spokane's hotel industry, which ultimately resulted in the construction of the Davenport Hotel.

## Spokane's First Hostelries

In 1877, Spokane Falls consisted of two business houses, a small grist mill, a few small residences, a log military barracks and a some scattered settlers in the outlying area. One business was James Glover's small store and post office. It was situated on the southwest corner of Howard and Front streets, across from his home on the southeast corner. The other business was a boarding house, called the Western House, which belonged to James Masterson, a "horse doctor" with an entrepreneurial spirit. It was located one block east of Glover's establishment on Stevens and Front. Spokane's business center grew up around the intersection of Howard and Front, along the south bank of the Spokane River. (Front was later named Trent Avenue and, in the mid-1970s during the gentrification of Spokane's downtown area for Expo '74, the downtown portion of Trent was renamed Spokane Falls Boulevard.)

In addition to sleeping accommodations and a dining hall on the main floor, the Western House had a second floor, accessed by a ladder and furnished with bearskins and buffalo hides for sleeping. These rustic quarters, nicknamed the "corral," were used mainly by miners and other laborers. Although the Western House was unsophisticated in appearance, it filled the needs of those checking out the area or passing through. Just before it was destroyed in the fire of 1889, the boarding house was listed in the Polk Directory under the Western Hotel.

*The Western House (below arrow), built in 1877 by James Masterson, was the first hotel in Spokane Falls. Room rates were 50 cents a night. On the right is a rear view of the California House, built in 1878. (Detail of EWSHS photo L86-275.2)*

William Gray

*The California House, Spokane's second hotel, was built in 1878 on the northeast corner of Howard and Front streets. It was operated by William Gray (see inset), his wife Clara and W.H. Smiley, Clara's brother. After being partially destroyed by fire in 1887, it was rebuilt as the Windsor Hotel. Less than two years later, it was completely destroyed in Spokane's big fire. (Photo courtesy Jerome Peltier.)*

In 1878, William Chandler "Bill" Gray began construction of the California House, the second hotel in Spokane Falls, with more sophisticated accommodations and amenities than the Western House. At a time when most lots were selling for around $50, Gray paid $200 for the most choice business corner in the fledgling town. His 60 x 142-foot lot was at the northeast corner of Front and Howard, near the present site of the Looff Carousel at Riverfront Park. During its heyday as Spokane's first significant hotel, the California House was the setting for many of Spokane's momentous social and business gatherings. The three-story frame building housed a large dining room on the main floor, which also included a kitchen and banquet room, private guest rooms on the second floor and a large open dormitory on the third floor for male guests. By 1883 a billiard table was added to the main floor.

Although Gray's roots originated in Maine, he spent much of his early productive life in California, making his mark in both the railroad and hotel businesses. He was married to Clara F. Smiley, the daughter of one of California's pioneers, Foster F. Smiley. The promise of the railroads and the potential for business opportunities drew the Grays and Clara's brother, William H. Smiley, to Spokane Falls in 1878. During construction of the California House, they lived in the deserted log barracks that had previously housed a company of soldiers. Smiley, who was also involved in the California House and later practiced law in Spokane Falls, pastured his cow on land where the Davenport Hotel now stands.

Shortly after his arrival, Gray became quite involved in civic affairs. He was one of the organizers in the formation of both the city and county of Spokane and served as a member of the first city council. During his time in the Inland Northwest, he was active in building railroads, farming (they owned a large farm in Stevens County), mining and politics.

On May 18, 1887, a fire broke out on the top story of the California House. It was determined to have been caused by a defect in a chimney. Fortunately, the local volunteer fire department was able to extinguish the flames before the entire building was destroyed. Within three months, it was remodeled and reopened as the Windsor Hotel, greatly expanded to 100 guest rooms.

*The Windsor Hotel was only in existence for two years. After the California House was damaged by fire in 1887, it was remodeled, as shown above, and renamed the Windsor House. In 1889 it was completely destroyed in the big city fire. (Photo courtesy Spokane Public Library Northwest Room.)*

From the time the first hotel was built in Spokane Falls, the demand for living accommodations continued to escalate. Temporary or short-term accommodations fell into three categories: (1) Hotels, both small and medium sized, most of which provided some type of dining facilities. (2) Lodging houses, which were typically small or temporary dwelling houses and often crude, provided only sleeping quarters. (3) Boarding houses offered both sleeping and eating accommodations. At the time, there was no such designation as "apartments."

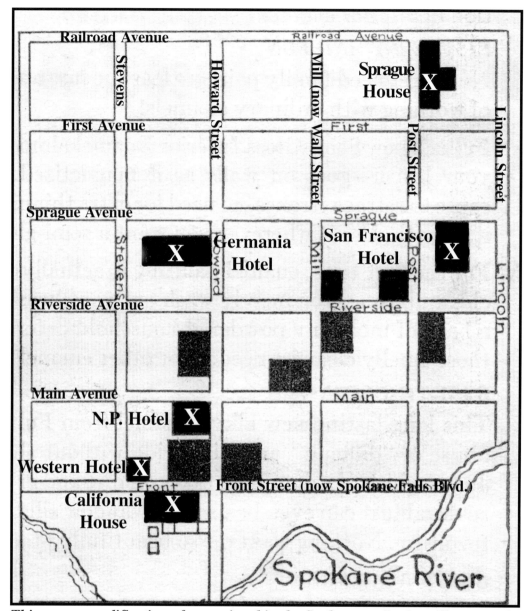

*This map, a modification of one printed in the Spokesman-Review, illustrates the Spokane downtown business district in 1884. The solid black squares mark the business blocks, while those with the X's were the noted hotels at that time. This map does not reflect the existing residences or the many smaller businesses.*

When the Western Hotel was built in 1877, there were about 50 people living in or near Spokane Falls. During the mining rush to the Coeur d'Alenes in 1883-1884, the population quickly rose to about 3000. The need for lodging was so great that many families took in boarders and often private homes and even stables or barns would be outfitted to serve as lodging houses. They were frequently identified by the attachment of a crudely-fashioned "Rooms" sign.

## A Sampling of Early Spokane Falls Hotels

*The N.P. Hotel, a two-and-a-half-story frame building on the northeast corner of Main and Howard, was built in 1879. Although the Northern Pacific Railroad didn't reach Spokane until 1881, the hotel was named in anticipation of its arrival. The Arlington Hotel was later built on this site. (Photo courtesy Spokane Public Library.)*

*The Sprague House was built in 1882 at the northwest corner of Railroad Avenue and Post Street by William Kaiser. During construction it blew down, was rebuilt and then, in 1884, burned down. (EWSHS photo L89-267)*

*The Falls View Hotel was located on the site of Spokane's current city hall, origi-
nally the Montgomery Ward building. In 1876 Frederick Post, who had the first
flour mill in Spokane, built a two-story home (the structure jutting out on the
right) on this site north of Front near Post Street (named for Frederick Post). The
three-story addition to Post's former home was built about 1887 to become the
Falls View. (Photo courtesy Spokane Public Library.)*

*The Pacific Hotel at the southeast corner of First and Post, was built in 1888 by
Frank Johnson for Victor Dessert. This building was destroyed in 1889 fire, but
rebuilt and later named the Desert Hotel. (Photo courtesy Spokane Public Library.)*

The 1889 Spokane Falls Polk Directory, published before fire destroyed downtown, included 18 hotels, 31 lodging houses and 13 listings for furnished rooms. As Spokane grew, the demand for a first-class hotel continuously held promise. With that potential in mind, the Arlington Hotel had been built in 1887. It was destroyed in the fire two years later, but during its short life-span, it was Spokane Falls's most elegant hotel.

An outstanding description of the new Arlington Hotel, which also reflected the mood of the times, appeared in the *Spokane Falls Review* on February 26, 1887. The obvious interest in luxury and refinement expressed in this lengthy article shows that Spokane's aspirations for first-class accommodation long predated the Davenport. Excerpts of that article follow:

## THE ARLINGTON HOTEL
### Ready for the Grand Opening Tuesday March 1st.
### One of the most Complete Hotels in the Territory.
### A Hasty Description of the New and Promising Enterprise.

Next Tuesday the new Arlington hotel will throw open its doors to the public. The event is one of more significance than the casual observer would imagine. It means the supplying of more hotel facilities of a better class, something that the city has been sadly deficient in for years. If there is any one thing . . . that reflects credit or discredit upon a place it is the character and extent of its hotel accommodations. A town can show evidence of the most phenomenal growth and enterprise, and yet if the stranger, accustomed to a superior class of hotels, finds that he is compelled to put up with poor and crude accommodations he goes away with a bad impression of the place . . . . Spokane Falls has always been troubled by limited hotel facilities. One hotel has been called upon to fill most of the requirements of the city. Large though it is it has always been inadequate to meet the demand. . . . The excessive poverty in rooms has been so great as to at times work a hardship upon the traveling public. During the past four years, there have been innumerable schemes set on foot for the building of a modern hotel in this city. Hardly a month passed but what the papers made note of some strangers in the city looking around with an idea of going into the hotel business, but the news would never materialize into any tangible shape. So the city grew, demands for accommodations increased each day, fine blocks and handsome homes were under way, a spirit of progress manifested itself on every hand and yet the new hotel so necessary to fill a long felt want failed to appear. . . . the wonder has continually been expressed that some one conversant with the business had not seized the opportunity, . . . . It began to look as though the city would be compelled to make shift with the hotels in sight when a couple of enterprising gentlemen stepped into the breach and announced their intentions to supply the deficiency. The announcement was made public last spring and the parties who proposed to invest their means in an enterprise of this description were Del S. Lashier and Samuel T. Arthur. . . . the result of their labors is seen in one of the most complete and elegant hotels on the Pacific coast, and we do not except any city, large or small.

*An artist's sketch of the Arlington Hotel, at the northeast corner of Howard and Main, as it appeared in 1887. When it opened, it was the finest hotel in Spokane Falls. The only death resulting from the great fire of 1889, which destroyed the hotel and most of the business section, occurred at the Arlington. As the hotel became engulfed in flames, a civil engineer by the name of George Davis leaped from the burning building. He later died at Sacred Heart Hospital. (Sketch from Spokane Falls Illustrated (1890) by Harry H. Hook and Francis J. McGuire.)*

The building is three stories high with a mansard roof, containing nicely furnished and comfortable rooms, with a basement the full size of the ground floor of the structure. The edifice is of brick, substantially constructed of modern plans . . . There is another main entrance on Howard street opening into a large hall . . . . The dining room is a model of neatness and comfort. It contains seating room for a large number of guests. The furniture and appointments . . . are of the very best quality.

The kitchen is off the dining room separated by two sets of double doors. The kitchen is finished supurbly [*sic*] . . . Off from the bar room are the stationary marble wash stands, supplied with hot and cold water, and the water-closets, set up with a special care for sanitary protection. On the second floor are the parlor, sleeping apartments single and en suite, ladies' toilets and bath rooms. The third and fourth floors are also finished in the same style. . . . The proprietors have a hobby that runs to first-class, and every thing pertaining to the furnishing of the building is of the very best. Few private residences are better furnished than the Arlington Hotel.

Not only is the building equipped in the very best style, but it is supplied with every modern convenience. There are sixty rooms in the hotel, and every one of them are connected with the office by an electric enunciator. There are also speaking tubes from every hall to the main office, so that every part of the building is in direct communication with headquarters. The building is heated throughout with hot water, . . . illuminated with incandescent electric lights . . . From the basement to the roof everything about  and pertaining to the Arlington hotel is of the most modern patern [*sic*] and is of the very best finish and quality. Most of the rooms are large, while every one is well lighted and arranged with the single aim of comfort to the patrons of the house. . . .

*Many of Spokane's early fires were fought with bucket brigades. The first fire department in Spokane Falls was organized in August of 1884 by a small group of volunteers. On October 1, 1884, an ordinance officially established the city's fire department. Soon thereafter, Rescue No. 1 and Spokane Hose No. 2 were added to the new department. Following the fire of 1889, the fire department was reorganized and its fire fighters became paid city employees. (Photo courtesy Jerome Peltier.)*

# The Constant Threat of Fire

As has been noted, most of Spokane's early hotels were destroyed by fire. Long before the one that destroyed the business section, fire was a constant threat. During the gold rush years of 1883-84, as Spokane Falls began rapidly expanding, fire was a constant concern. Up until 1880, all the buildings in Spokane Falls were of wood construction, heated by wood and illuminated by kerosene – all potential fire risks. On January 19, 1883, the first serious fire in Spokane Falls broke out in F.R. Moore and Company's store at the southeast corner of Howard and Front. Five businesses were completely destroyed and a number of other structures damaged. Among the burned-out businesses was Charles Carson's restaurant, one of Spokane's first restaurants. Carson later built the Pride of Spokane Restaurant, of which both Elijah and Louis Davenport subsequently served as proprietor.

The fire in 1883 had been the worst to date in the history of Spokane Falls and prompted the installation of a new water system and a fire department in 1884. Prior to the Great Fire of 1889, a number of serious fires occurred, the worst of which was on September 14, 1888. This fire, which centered around the area of Howard and Main, was termed "the most destructive conflagration in the history of Spokane Falls." Over 22 downtown businesses were damaged or destroyed, with a total loss of over $50,000.

# Spokane Falls in 1888:
# The Ultimate Business Climate

In July 1888 the Spokane Falls *Morning Review* conducted a census of Spokane. According to the *Review's* statistics, Spokane's population had grown by 60 percent over the prior year and was stated to be 11,888. Elijah Davenport had become well established in Spokane Falls, and promotion of the city had reached an all time high.

The following quotes, taken from articles appearing in the *Morning Review* on various dates (as noted) throughout 1888, provide a descriptive glimpse of the conditions and excitement building in Spokane Falls. Undoubtedly well aware of the state of affairs in the growing town bursting with opportunity, Louis Davenport arrived the following year to make his home in the city whose future he would greatly affect:

July 17, 1888, under "News of Spokane":
**Over Two Million Being Expended in Buildings**
Next to the increase in population the building developments are most important to the people of Spokane. They watch with unabated interest to the rapid growth of the city in this connection. The sound of the carpenter's hammer and the echo of the saw is everywhere heard as the bustle of building life continues from morning until

night. And one grand point of the building this year is the fact that all the leading blocks are brick and stone. Travelers from Tacoma, Seattle and other towns along the coast – and east as well – remark on visiting the city that Spokane is outstripping all competitors in point of substantial brick buildings and the number of them. The building in Spokane this year beats all previous records. . . .

September 21, 1888

## AS OTHERS SEE US

**Spokane Graphically Pictured By a Visitor –**
**Our Advantages Over Many Other Communities –**
**Mining, Lumber, Agricultural and Manufacturing Industries**
**Described by a Chicago Writer**

**[The writer's name was only given as Leubrie and the article, from which this excerpt was taken, had first appeared in the *Chicago Inter-Ocean*.]**
As a mining center Spokane will stand without a peer in the country which in itself will warrant the building up of a large city here. Second in importance would appear the lumber interests. The adjoining mountains are thickly covered with a heavy growth of timber, which can be easily floated down the Spokane river to Spokane, where the necessary mill, run by the fine water power, prepare it for market. While no aggressive steps have as yet been taken in this direction, it is very evident that a great lumber market will be established at this point in a few years.

It is seldom that a mining and agricultural region are close allies, yet such happens to be the good luck of Spokane Falls, which boasts of a large and fertile an agricultural region tributary to it as can be found anywhere. Directly south of the city lies the great wheat belt of Palouse, conceded the richest agricultural land on the Pacific coast.

October 6, 1888

## OUR GREAT FUTURE

**Capacity of Spokane as a Manufacturing Center –**
**A Glowing Picture That Other Cities Might Envy**

. . . Here we are in a city that is geographically situated for large growth, in the presence of preponderate means for manufacturing which is always equal in importance to raw production from the soil. The two go together because of the requirements of civilization in the application of raw materials to the wants of mankind.

. . . Four years ago there were but three manufacturing establishments here. There was one saw mill that turned out 5000 feet of lumber per day; one shingle mill that made 6000 shingles, and the Post flour mill, with a capacity of sixty barrels a day. Now 25,000 shingles are daily manufactured, with a constant demand for more; three flour mills grind out 500 barrels each day; one sawmill that has a capacity of 80,000 feet daily; three planing and wood manufacturing mills, six shingle mills, an iron foundry and a cracker factory. All these give employment to hundreds of men direct, and an unknown number in various tributary directions.

But all this is as nothing to what might, and surely will, be done here in the manufac-turing line; and we can safely say this without in the least arousing any jealousy on the part of the proprietors of the extensive works now here. They are all making money and prospering, and know that the demand is greater than their capacity to supply. . . .

October 18, 1888

## A MODEL CITY

### Spokane Falls the Metropolis of Eastern Washington
### What a Delegate to the Press Convention Saw in the City of Falling Waters
### [A reprint in the *Morning Review* from the *Seattle Post-Intelligencer*.]

If Seattle merits the title of the Queen City of Puget Sound, Spokane Falls may justly lay claim to the title of Queen City of Eastern Washington. In all that gives promise of future wealth and greatness, it is incomparably ahead of the towns and cities east of the Cascade mountains in our territory. . . .

Already has it out-run in the race for population and wealth, towns and cities many years older, and today bids fair to rival even the Queen City of Puget Sound. The population is not far from 15,000, while on all sides are seen evidences of wealth and refinement far exceeding other communities of that number. Its growth is phenomenal; indeed, it is questionable if its parallel can be found in America. In few cities of 50,000 can be seen more palatial residences; more substantial, costly or commodious business structures; larger or better hotels; while the schools, hos-pitals churches, etc., will compare favorably with those of cities much older and more populous than Spokane Falls.

. . . To adequately describe the surroundings of this beautiful city – to speak fittingly of the lovely natural parks, the boiling, foaming, rushing waters that furnish the motive power for the industries mentioned, with other matters worthy of note, would require more space than can now be spared. It goes without saying that Spokane Falls is the cleanest, the brightest, the handsomest, the liveliest and most attractive, the most enterprising, the most hospitable city of Washington territory – save alone the Queen city of Puget Sound.

Although the devastating fire that destroyed most of the business district the following year created a setback and an enormous loss of property, Spokane Falls continued to experience intense growth and development. The city rebounded in an astonish-ingly short period of time; the destruction left by the fire was quickly transformed into a metropolitan city of greater strength and beauty than before the fire. As the barrage of newspaper articles following the fire attest, though saddened by the great loss, the community spirit and drive remained positive and strong. Everyone pitched in to rebuild. Opportunities for those wanting to establish a new business or rebuild an old one abounded. Louis Davenport was among those who excelled at seizing the opportunity and established a business whose reputation was heralded far and wide in much the same way as was the city's reputation.

# Chapter 3

## Louis Davenport's Early Years in Spokane and the Evolution of His Restaurant.

Louis Davenport arrived in Spokane Falls in March 1889. That year President Grover Cleveland signed an omnibus bill admitting Washington State to the Union, Benjamin Harrison was inaugurated as the twenty-third president of the United States, more than 10,000 men were engaged in the Coeur d'Alene mining operations in northern Idaho, and Spokane Falls reached a pinnacle of development that secured its position as the largest city in Eastern Washington – and still it continued to boom. Railroad and street car transportation was at full throttle. Spokane Falls was well established as a main stop on the Northern Pacific's transcontinental line; the Seattle, Lake Shore & Eastern Company completed their line to the town of Davenport, while the Northern Pacific extended its Central Washington branch 40 miles west from Davenport into the Big Bend Country; the Oregon Railway & Navigation Company reached Spokane Falls from the south, with trains running regularly to and from Pendelton, Oregon; and D.C. Corbin and his associates were constructing the Spokane Falls and Northern Railroad to the north through Stevens County. Streetcar service was affording residents the opportunity to build homes away from the heart of the city while still being able to take advantage of the services it provided. By the end of 1889, sixteen-and-a-half miles of street railway were in operation and the first Monroe Street Bridge was completed that year. Ground

*Howard Street looking south from Riverside Avenue as it appeared at the time of Louis Davenport's arrival in Spokane. (Photo courtesy Spokane Public Library.)*

*A construction crew on Riverside Avenue prior to the fire of 1889. (Photo courtesy Spokane Public Library.)*

was broken at the northwest corner of Main Avenue and Post Street for the new $300,000 five-story Auditorium Building. On March 31, 1889, a *Review* article stated, "The entire force of the Review establishment will go to church today. The office will be removed to its new quarters, formerly the Presbyterian church, at the corner of Riverside avenue and Monroe street [a move that saved them from being burned out by Spokane's big fire the following August]." Spokane acquired its first zoo, located opposite the post office, which contained two wild buffalos, a huge grizzly bear, "a monster devil fish and many other rare novelties." In 1889, Spokane Falls even had a drug problem; around the time of Davenport's arrival, Police Chief Joel Warren conducted a large raid on Chinese opium dens and arrested nine people from five establishments.

When Louis Davenport came to Spokane Falls, it was a wide-open, rapidly growing town. People worked hard, but enjoyed many good times as well. An article that appeared in the *Spokane Falls Review* on March 30, 1889, provides one example, quoted as follows:

### Two Foot Races
Jake Berkenstock, a saloon keeper at the corner of Main and Stevens streets, and H.B. Rogers bus man at the Windsor hotel, both fat men, will run a foot race at the fair grounds, Sunday April 1, for $25 a side; distance one quarter mile, turn and back. Berkenstock has also made a race with a colored man one quarter of a mile, with a 15-foot, 2x4 scantling on his shoulder; the race to take place at the same time and place.

Following his arrival in Spokane Falls in March 1889, Louis Davenport went to work for his Uncle Elijah, who was the proprietor of the Pride of Spokane Restaurant, located at 313 Howard (the old numbering system) between Riverside and Sprague. Elijah was also in the hotel business and, that same month, he gave up his Commercial Hotel. Soon thereafter, he became the proprietor of the Chamberlin Lodging House and started construction on his Merchants' Hotel.

Louis's prior work history had been primarily as a clerk, but in the employ of his uncle, he also gained restaurant experience. Coupled with his instinctive business sense, he soon became the proprietor of the Pride of Spokane. He assumed responsibility for this, his first restaurant, possibly just days before the August 4, 1889 fire destroyed most of the city's business section, including his restaurant.

Naturally, the fire garnered more news coverage for a longer period of time than any other event in the city's history. The front page of the *Spokane Falls Review* on August 6, 1889, cried "MILLIONS LOST," followed by ten subheadings:

**An Appalling Calamity Visits the Proud City of Spokane Falls.**

**Thirty Blocks of Its Most Magnificent Buildings Devoured by Flames.**

**The Entire Business Portion of the City Wiped Out of Existence.**

**A Night of Terror, Devastation, Suffering and Awful Woe.**

**Hundreds of Dwellers Down Town Turned into the Streets Destitute.**

**One Man Killed and Several Others Severely and Painfully Injured.**

**An Official to Be Investigated for an Apparently Inexcusable Blunder.**

**The People Not Discouraged and the City Will Be Rebuilt Better Than Ever.**

**Notes and Incidents of the Disaster and a History of Many Heroic Deeds.**

**A List of the Sufferers, with Amounts of Losses So Far as Received.**

Although the Pride of Spokane was destroyed, one account states that Louis Davenport salvaged some of his restaurant equipment and supplies during the fire. Two days later he advertised in the newspaper that he was again open for business (see page 15). In addition to this restaurant, which was outside the burned-out area, he also became involved in the cleanup effort, as did every other able-bodied man living in Spokane Falls at the time. This was a major event as many of the destroyed buildings had been constructed of rock and brick. There were piles of solid rubble and numerous brick walls left standing. On August 14, 1889, the city superintendent of streets was authorized to hire workers to blast down some of the remaining hazardous freestanding walls, as shown in the following photo, at a cost of $98.

*Looking northeast at Riverside Avenue after the 1889 fire. This photo was taken from the Commercial Hotel on Lincoln. (Photo courtesy Spokane Public Library.)*

Available literature offers scant details about Louis Davenport's life, especially before his restaurant's growing popularity caught the attention of the media. What little information there is, unfortunately, is contradictory in nature and, in some cases, simply inaccurate. But the sketchy newspaper references do confirm that Louie had two previous restaurant establishments in Spokane Falls, however short-lived, before his famed Davenport's Waffle Foundry.

According to an interview with Davenport, which appeared in the December 8, 1895, edition of the *Spokesman-Review*, that very day was the sixth anniversary of the opening of his restaurant in its temporary "tent" location. This, no doubt, was referring to his Waffle Foundry. Because of the emphasis given to that date as his well-known restaurant's point of inception, it appears the restaurant he opened immediately after the fire did not continue for a long period of time.

Davenport's Famous Waffle Foundry, as the sign read, was located on the north side of Sprague Avenue near Post Street, across the street from what became his permanent site in July of 1890. (For a more detailed account of what is known about Louis Davenport's first year in Spokane Falls and the locations of his restaurants, refer to Chapter 1, beginning with page 14). One fact is undisputed: Once Louis Davenport got his foothold in the restaurant business, his soaring success was unstoppable; he immediately began expanding, improving and beautifying – a process that continued until his retirement in 1945.

FEB. 14-1889
Chief of Police
Joel F. Warren
appeared at the
opening of Davenports
in full dress uniform

On February 14, 1922, a celebration was held at the Davenport Hotel to commemorate Louie's 32nd year in business and officially reopen his newly remodeled restaurant, now called the Italian Gardens. An album (now at the Northwest Museum of Arts & Culture) of letters, photographs and artwork was compiled by close friends and business associates.

**Joel Warren, c. 1889**

**Joel Warren, 1922**

One of the contributors was Joel Warren, who served from 1884 to 1890 as both a police officer and the chief of police. Warren was Spokane's most popular law-enforcement official and his term covered one of the roughest periods in its history, namely during the gold rush and early mining years in the Coeur d'Alenes. In Warren's letter to Davenport, he stated: "If my memory serves me right I ate one doz of your waffles on the occasion of the opening of the door that led to the many years of successful catering to the wishes of hundreds of thousands of people. At that time I was Spokane Chief of Police, and appeared for the first time in full uniform. Am inclosing a sketch [see above] of the occasion as I remember it."

*Looking north on Post Street in the 1890s, showing the east side of Davenport's Restaurant prior to the addition of the Mission-style facade designed by architect Kirtland Cutter. (See page 21 for a sketch of the front.) The three-story brick building on the left is the Bellevue Block, where the Hazelwood Dairy had a creamery on the main floor. The horse-drawn wagons in front were used for the dairy's deliveries. Directly north (right) of Davenport's is the Whitten Block. The Auditorium Building is visible at the end of the street. (Photo courtesy Spokane Public Library.)*

## Louis Davenport's First-Class Restaurant

On July 10, 1890, Louis Davenport opened his restaurant at a permanent site, 207-209 West Sprague Avenue, located in the newly constructed Wilson Block on the southwest corner of Sprague and Post. The Wilson Block, built at a cost of $11,000, was owned by Henry L. Wilson and F. Lewis Clark and adjoined the Bellevue Block (later known as the Wellington Block and finally the Pennington Hotel) to the south. Spokane's first public schoolhouse had been moved to this site in 1881 because it had been built on a railroad right-of-way. The Spokane Falls Review took over the building in 1883, but moved it to another location long before the big fire.

Davenport initially occupied less than half the ground floor of the Wilson Block, but sometime before 1892, he expanded east to include the next address number. (In 1891 the city revised its street numbering system. The first directory published following this revision listed Davenport's Restaurant at 805-809 Sprague. It also gave Louie's residence as rooms in the Whitten Block, across the street from his restaurant.) In 1893 fire gutted the restaurant, resulting in the first of Louie's many major remodeling projects. It also temporarily put the restaurant's 43 employees out of work.

*The first Post Street Bridge and lower Spokane Falls, circa 1889, just a few blocks north of Davenport's Restaurant. (Photo courtesy Spokane Public Library.)*

**Ladies and Gentlemen**

will be most courteously served at Davenport's new restaurant, 207 West Sprague street. The apartment is especially attractive. Opening to-day about noon.

*The first newspaper announcement at the opening of Louis Davenport's restaurant in the Wilson Block. (Clipping from the July 10, 1890, Spokane Falls Review.)*

**DAVENPORT'S**

**Spokane's Leading and Popular Restaurant.**

207 AND 209 WEST SPRAGUE ST.,

SPOKANE FALLS, - - WASHINGTON.

*The first Davenport's Restaurant advertisement to appear in Polk's Spokane Falls City Directory, as shown above, was in the 1890 directory. Some accounts claim Davenport initially occupied only the space at 207 Sprague and expanded into the 209 space the following year. However, this directory would have been published shortly after his move, confirming that he immediately occupied 207 and 209, which was the entire west end of the Wilson Block. (See pages 19 and 20 for a detailed newspaper account of the restaurant three days after it opened.)*

SOUP.

Clam Chowder.                                          Maccaroni.

FISH.

Fried Herring, 25                    Tom Cod, 25                    Fried Smelts, 25

Boiled Sea Bass with Anchovey Sauce, 25

TO ORDER.

Broiled Fresh Spanish Mackerel, 50        Broiled Fresh Shad, 35

BOILED.

Capon with Oyster Sauce, 35  ·     Turkey with Egg Sauce, 40

Ox Tongue with Cream Sauce, 20        Leg of Mutton with Caper Sauce, 20

Brisket of Beef with Horse Radish, 20        Sugar Cured Ham, 20

Pickled Pigs Head with Sauerkraut, 20        Corned Beef and Cabbage, 20

ROAST.

Stuffed Turkey with Cranberry Sauce, 40            Saddle of Mutton, 20

Domestic Goose and Apple Sauce, 40        Loin of Pork, 20

Prime Roast of Beef, Brown Gravy, 25            Stuffed Chicken, 35

Duck with Currant Jelly, 40        Lamb with Mint Sauce, 20

Suckling Pig and Apple Sauce, 35            Saddle of Venison, 25

Shoulder of Veal with Dressing, 20

ENTREES.

Pillau of Chicken a la Creole, 35        Lobster Cutlets a la Hollandaise, 30

Maccaroni a la Cream, 20        Frogs Legs any Style, 35

Pork Chops Breaded with Sauce Robert, 25            Beef a la Mode, 20

Tenderloin of Beef Larded with Mushrooms, 25

Pate de Foie Gras aux Truffes, 50        Venison Steak with Currant Jelly, 25

Croquette of Chicken aux Petits Pois, 35        Half Grouse, 35

Fried Calves Brains with Cream Sauce, 25            Half Pheasant, 30

Paupiette of Veal with Puree of Asparagus, 25

Broiled Quail on Toast with Bacon, 40        Pineapple Fritters au Rhum, 20

Half Spring Chicken on Toast, 40        Antelope Chops with Jelly Sauce, 25

Eastern and Olympia Oysters every Style.

*This two-page menu for Davenport's Restaurant was prepared for New Year's Day 1892, only a year and a half after establishing the restaurant in its permanent*

## COLD.

Fresh Crabs, 25          Veal, 20          Turkey, 40          Mutton, 20

Corned Beef, 20          Beef, 20          Pork, 20

Sugar Cured Ham, 20          Fresh Lobsters, 50          Goose, 35

Boned Turkey with Aspect Jelly, 40

## RELISHES.

Los Angeles Comb Honey, 10          California Grapes, 10

New Celery, 10          French Olives, 10          Lettuce, 5

Sweet Pickles, 5          C. & B. Chow Chow, 5          Pitted Olives, 10

Imported Anchovies in Oil, 25          Spiced Chicken, 5

Hamburger Aale, 20          Caviara Russe, 25          Pickled Eels in Jelly, 25

Imported Pate de Poissons, 25          Scotch Kippered Herrings, 25

## SALADS.

Chicken, 10          Potato, 5          Shrimp, 10

## VEGETABLES.

Asparagus on Toast, 15          Schnittbohnen String Beans, 10

Boiled, Mashed and Baked Potatoes.          Potatoes in Cream, 5          Beets, 5

Sugar Corn, 5          Stewed Parsnips, 5          Boiled Rice, 5

Green Peas, 5          Stewed Tomatoes, 5          Mashed Turnips, 5

Bowl of Rice and Milk, 10          Baked Sweet Potatoes, 10

Lima Beans, 5          Succotash, 5          String Beans, 5

## PASTRY.

Pies of all kinds, 5     Jelly Tarts, 5     Home Made Fruit Cake, 10

Chocolate, Cocoanut, Pound and Sponge Cake, 5          Cream Tarts, 5

Lady Fingers, 5

## DESSERT.

English Plum Pudding, Hard Sauce, 10          Vanilla Ice Cream, 15

Strawberry Preserves, 15          Raspberry Preserves, 15          Lemon Ice, 15

Preserved Pine Apples, 15          Brandy Peaches, 15          Brandy Cherries, 15

Peaches and Cream, 10          Sliced Pine Apples and Cream, 15

*location in the Wilson Block. This menu provides a glimpse of the elaborate and exotic fare offered in the restaurant at that time.*

Davenport made every effort to keep his prices affordable while offering an ever-expanding menu and excellent service in beautiful surroundings. His reputation grew, and the citizenry of Spokane patronized his establishment. On December 8, 1895, an article appeared in the *Spokesman-Review* with the headline, "ONLY ONE IN 410" and a subheading, "**Only One First Class Restaurant in Spokane Has Lived to Tell the Story**." The article claimed statistics showed "only one first-class restaurant out of 410 succeeds" and that Davenport's was the single exception of first-class restaurants to have survived in Spokane. The writer queried Louie Davenport about his continued success when so many others had failed. Davenport's response was:

> I don't know as I am [an] authority. . . . I am learning something every day, and expect to as long as I am in the business. The restaurant business is like any other mercantile pursuit [his father was in the mercantile business when Louie was young]–for that's what it is–we buy and sell merchandise. . . . If a restaurant man's ideas for conducting, furnishing and managing his business strike the class of people he is catering to, and he can hold up to that point and keep adding to and improving, he will naturally succeed. I attribute the failure of so many first-class restaurants to the fact that they start at a gait that they can't keep up. They give more than they can afford to for the money and get a big trade at first. Then they find they are losing money and begin to decrease the service to cut down expenses. Naturally, the patronage begins to fall off . . .

The interviewer then asked, "Has the restaurant business always been profitable in Spokane?" Louie's response is noteworthy in light of the questionable story that he opened his restaurant on $125 earned cleaning up debris after the fire (see Chapter 1):

> There has been a time during the last four years [which covered the period of the 1893 economic panic and the difficult times that followed] when all the first-class restaurants were giving more than they could afford to for the money, and many had to close. For a period of 15 months this house lost an average of $1000 a month. **I happened to have the money to lose,** and the others didn't. [Emphasis added.]

"There has been a time during the last four years when all the first-class restaurants were giving more than they could afford to for the money, and many had to close. For a period of 15 months this house lost an average of $1000 a month. I happened to have the money to lose, and the others didn't. I grinned and bore it, and kept up the service just the same, knowing it was only a question of time when the others would have to fall out. It was inevitable that the weaker ones would have to go."

*A copy of the newspaper article quoted above in which Louis Davenport refers to his financial status as it related to the success of his hotel.*

Following the interview with Davenport, the writer offered further accolades regarding the restaurant, some of which are quoted below:

> . . . It is as grand today as it was the first day it opened in the present quarters. The yearly outlay in improvements and repairs is enough to keep half a dozen ordinary restaurants looking new. Changes and improvements are being made nearly all the time. . . . its grandeur is never allowed to fade. . . . Mr. Davenport has kept on improving, until Davenport's is known from Chicago to San Francisco. Spokanites feel as much pride in the place as though they owned a personal interest in it. [This sentiment is expressed even today by supporters of the Davenport Hotel.] . . . one may travel a thousand miles in any direction without encountering a restaurant that can approach Spokane's palatial establishment. . . .

*This is one of the earliest photos available of Louis Davenport (right), circa 1890, shown here with Daniel F. Wetzel, a jeweler who, at the time of the big fire, was in partnership with the founder of Dodson's Jewelers. (EWSHS photo L88-404.19)*

The following month, on January 27, 1896, the *Spokane Daily Chronicle* published an article reviewing some of Spokane's leading businesses. Among those reviewed was Davenport's Restaurant, which stated as follows:

**Davenport's**

That Spokane is emphatically a "restaurant town" is evinced by the large number of excellent cafes we possess. But one that is especially popular is Davenport's, at 805, 807, 809 Sprague avenue. It contains 10,000 square feet of floor space and is furnished in white and gold. Besides the public dining rooms there are seventeen private ones and a delightful little banqueting hall, recently has been added. The service is unexcelled, and the menu includes every delicacy. There are thirty-nine assistants employed. The charges are surprisingly moderate considering the excellence of the service. This is the finest restaurant in Washington. Mr. L.M. Davenport is a young man and a native of San Francisco, where he had wide experience in this line. [This statement is inaccurate. See the text following this quote.] He is very popular in the city and the institution he has built up is not only an honor to Spokane but reflects the highest credit upon himself.

This article may have been the original source of a mistaken notion perpetuated in various accounts about Louie Davenport's life. He was *not* a native of San Francisco and it appears he did not have restaurant experience prior to moving to Spokane. Louie was born in Pawnee City, Nebraska, on July 14, 1868. At about age seven, the family moved to California and settled in Red Bluff. Louie was listed as a clerk in a stationary and variety store in Red Bluff in the 1884-1885 Tehama County Directory. In 1887 and 1888, he appears in Langley's San Francisco city directories as a clerk for the Del Monte Milling Co., a flour mill. In summary, between the ages of 16 and 20, references to his work history are that of a clerk, and not with the restaurant business. Being a mere 20 years of age when he arrived in Spokane Falls in 1889, he would hardly have had time to gain "wide experience," if any at all, in the restaurant business prior to working for his uncle in the Pride of Spokane. What makes this conclusion so remarkable is that Louie Davenport possessed a natural propensity and brilliant mind for his chosen line of work in which he had few equals.

## Always Expanding and Updating

Davenport's expansion continued and, by about 1900, he had taken over the entire Wilson Block and most of the ground floor of the Bellevue Block, where the kitchen was located. Although he was only leasing his space, Davenport commissioned the services of architect Kirtland Cutter to significantly remodel both the interior and exterior of the restaurant. The exterior Mission style design was unique and somewhat of a novelty amidst the business section's more conservative architecture; the white stucco provided an eye-catching contrast to the surrounding brick and granite structures. It attracted attention and exuded a welcoming gaiety.

*Looking south at a section of Davenport's main dining room, with windows facing Post Street, circa 1910. The fireplace at the far end was directly below the one in Davenport's second-floor apartment and was removed during the restaurant's remodel in 1922 as the Italian Gardens. (Photo courtesy Walt and Karen Worthy.)*

*Hallway to private dining rooms in 1908. (EWSHS Libby Studio photo L93-68.9-4)*

*Davenport's Restaurant after architect Kirtland Cutter created the Mission-style facade, transforming the plain two-story brick building into a work of art. The design, influenced by the Spanish missions of California, drew upon the use of arched windows, parapets, bell towers and red-tiled roofs (also see page 68). The first phase of the exterior remodel, completed around 1900, involved only the building shown above (the Wilson Block). After Davenport purchased the adjoining Bellevue Block in 1904, Cutter redesigned its exterior to tie in with the restaurant, creating the appearance of just one building. (Photo courtesy Spokane Public Library.)*

In 1903 Louis Davenport negotiated the purchase of the property his restaurant was occupying and the adjoining Bellevue Building (by now, technically the Wellington Block, but still commonly known as the Bellevue). This transaction, finalized in 1904, allowed him to take the restaurant to a greater level of sophistication, securing his place in history as Spokane's greatest restaurateur and hotel entrepreneur. The following article, announcing the pending sale, appeared in the *Spokesman-Review* on November 9, 1903:

## BIG REALTY DEAL BY DAVENPORT

### He Gets Possession of Two Buildings for $120,000

### To Remodel Them

### Will Transform the Bellevue Building Into Modern Apartment House,

### Will Look Like One

## Intends Building Hothouse on Top of Restaurant,
## and Wine Cellars Under it.

L.M. Davenport has completed negotiations for the purchase of the building in which his restaurant is situated, and for the Bellevue building immediately adjoining it on the south. He contemplates extensive improvements. The deal is the largest real estate transaction consummated in Spokane in many months. While none of the parties to the deal will disclose the exact purchase price, it is understood that the two properties represent to Mr. Davenport an investment of about $120,000.

The Bellevue building is three stories high. It has a frontage of 70 [75] feet on Post street and of 100 feet on First avenue. It was purchased from Frank P. Hogan. The restaurant building, which was purchased by Mr. Davenport from the F. Lewis Clark interests, is two stories high, and has a frontage of 80 feet on Post street and 100 feet on Sprague avenue. In length, therefore, it is the same as the Bellevue building.

### To Build Apartment House.

Commencing April 1 next Mr. Davenport will remodel the Bellevue's two upper stories into a fine modern apartment house at a cost of $25,000. The entire interior of the two floors will be torn out, and rearranged. All the modern improvements will be installed. The apartments will be leased unfurnished for stated intervals, Mr. Davenport says, and not rented from month to month.

The exterior of the Bellevue building will be remodeled, and stuccoed, after the fashion of the restaurant building. While there will be no connection between the two buildings, they will look, from the outside, exactly like one building. The ground floor of the Bellevue building will be rented for store buildings. The second story of the restaurant building, which is now used for lodgings, will probably be undisturbed. [The following year, a major renovation project, which included construction of the exquisite Hall of the Doges, was undertaken.]

### Greenhouse and Wine Cellars.

In addition to transforming the Bellevue into an apartment house, Mr. Davenport announces that he will build a greenhouse on top of the restaurant building, where he will raise all the flowers and hot house plants which have been such a feature of his restaurant. He also intends constructing under the restaurant, he says, the most modern wine cellars in the northwest.

The construction of the wine cellars may be commenced this winter. The other improvements, as stated, will not be commenced until April, and Mr. Davenport hopes to have them completed next summer. Mr. Davenport has had the improvements in mind for some time, and has been negotiating for the purchase of the two pieces of property for about three months.

A follow-up article appeared in the *Spokesman-Review* almost a week later, on November 15, 1903, announcing:

# PRICE OF $550 PER FOOT FRONT

**SPRAGUE AVENUE BUSINESS PROPERTY SHOWS INCREASED VALUATION**

. . . Sprague avenue business lots are worth about $550 per foot front, on the basis of the purchase just made by Louis M. Davenport, while the same deal establishes a valuation for First avenue property of about $325 per foot front. . . . Mr. Davenport's purchase of the building wherein the main portion of his restaurant is located is from the Consolidated Improvement company on a basis of $67,000. . . . Mr. Davenport has been located in the building for 14 years and for three years has had an exclusive lease of the premises. Under this lease, which was for ten years, Mr. Davenport agreed to return the old building practically in the shape in which he received it. In consequence of all the many improvements made to the structure have been at his own expense. He has about reconstructed the building, even to the floors, and in consequence he estimates that the equity in the improvements of the Consolidated company is only about $12,000, which leaves $55,000 as the value of the naked ground.

**Was Built After Big Fire.**
The building was erected originally by Henry L. Wilson and F. Lewis Clark, in 1889. Building and land were valued at about $32,000. . . .

The adjoining property, covered by the deal, is the Bellevue building. It was owned by Frank Hogan and is covered by a three story building of common red brick. . . . For ten years past all of the main floor of the Bellevue except store rooms at the southeast corner, has been occupied by Mr. Davenport, as part of his restaurant. This is bought for $52,500 from Mr. Hogan. The building was built in 1890. . . .

In 1902 and 1903, prior to Davenport's purchase of the two buildings, a listing for Mrs. M.C. (Maud) Pennington at South 6 Post (in the Wilson Block, above Davenport's Restaurant) appeared in the city directory under "furnished rooms." By this time, Louie Davenport also lived in the Wilson Block, likely even renting a room from Maud. The year of Louie's purchase, Maud's rooms in the Wilson Block were listed in the city directory as "The Pennington," but by the following year (1905), the Pennington Hotel was listed at the address of the former Bellevue Building, and Maud was named as the proprietor. In 1907 Maud married Harry W. Hollis, who also became her business partner in the management of the Pennington Hotel. Davenport's association with Maud was not strictly business. In 1906 he married her sister, Verus E. Smith.

## Wastes No Time Making Improvements

The first improvement to be made on Davenport's new buildings was announced on December 13, 1903, even before the sale became final (early 1904 for the Pennington and the Wilson in 1905). As was typical with most anything associated with the Davenport establishments, it was unique and innovative:

# DAVENPORT'S UNIQUE ROAD

## COMBINATION RAILROAD, CABLE LINE AND ELECTRIC POWER PLAN.

### USED IN EXCAVATING CELLAR

**Modern Methods Used – Cellar Will Be 80 x 100 Feet Under His Building.**

A miniature railroad, with cable cars moved by electric energy, is a unique feature of Spokane building improvements this week. This decidedly modern application of up to date methods is in connection with excavating a basement under Davenport's restaurant, on the west side of Post street, between Sprague and First avenues.

The work is being done by Contractor J. Little, who this week will begin moving the first of 96,000 cubic feet of earth called for in his agreement. . . .

From a platform, wagon bed high, on First avenue, at the rear of the building, an inclined roadbed has been constructed running beneath the south wall of the restaurant. On the slanting roadbed ties have been placed and heavy T rails have been laid.

### Is a Narrow Gauge Line.

The gauge of the "Davenport" road is narrow, being but 33 inches. Upon these rails steel cars will be operated. The cars are of the side dump pattern and transport 18 cubic feet of earth each trip.

An electric motor furnishes power which operates a system of cable and pulley by which the cars are hauled to the top of the incline. From the platform the earth from the cars is dumped into waiting wagons and the earth is hauled to the Main avenue fill, west of the Monroe street bridge.

### Some Pick and Shovel.

The excavating under the building will be carried on in the old fashioned pick and shovel way, except that it will be shoveled directly into the cars. . . .

It is probable that as the work progresses under the building electric lights will be used, so the workmen can see to labor. The plan described is said to be entirely new in the northwest and to be cheaper than old ways.

The excavation is part of Mr. Davenport's plans for improving the property he purchased  recently. He intends constructing a cellar 12 feet deep and 60x100 feet in size. Heavy granite walls will be built to support the existing building . . . .

The article further described their plans for the new basement, including wine cellars, cold storage and refrigerating rooms, but it is not known if they materialized as planned. Eventually a bowling alley and an archery court occupied part of that space. The railroad was only a temporary feature used to carry out the excavation.

## Davenport's Famous Hall of the Doges

On June 8, 1904, the *Spokesman-Review* printed an article detailing Davenport's plans to build a ballroom above his restaurant, the famous Hall of the Doges. It became Spokane's most popular place for weddings and other social functions. Its name was suggestive of the palaces of the Italian doges of medieval times. A doge was a leader, specifically the chief magistrate, in old Venice and Genoa. In Venice the doge was originally chosen by the vote of the people and held office for life. He was regarded as the civil, military and ecclesiastical chief, and had almost unlimited power. The description in the following article, announcing the ballroom plans, is fairly close to what actually happened, but some changes did occur during the construction and remodel process:

## DAVENPORT PLANS UNIQUE BALLROOM

### RESTAURATEUR WILL SPEND $30,000 IN CREATING PLACE FOR ENTERTAINMENTS

### ITS EQUAL NOT IN THE WEST

### Big Promenade Around the Dancing Floor Will Be a Feature of the Place.

Louis M. Davenport will spend about $30,000 in an elaborate ball and reception room to be built over his restaurant at the southwest corner of Sprague avenue and Post street, which will eclipse in luxury and splendor anything of its kind west of the Mississippi river and will make his establishment unique in the west as a place of public entertainment. The ballroom, with a magnificent promenade surrounding it on all sides, and the banquet and reception rooms will occupy the whole of the upper floor of his main building, 85x100 feet [actually 80x100].

The ball floor proper will be 40x60 feet in size. It will be supported by nine steel pillars reaching from the rock foundations in the basement of the building to the second floor. Along the tip of the pillars will be immense steel girders to support the steel joists upon which the dancing floor will be laid. The joists will be hung to the girders by stirrups, which will give spring to the floor and remove vibrations from the building. The floor will rest entirely upon the steel pillars, so that people in the restaurant below will never know dancing is going on . . .

Over the ballroom will be a beautiful dome. It will rest upon 36 steel pillars around the four sides of the room. The columns will be of Byzantine style. Along the top of them will be a hand carved frieze and relief work. The base of the dome, in hand painted and relief work, will rest upon the frieze. Above it will be the skylight in harmonious colors of art glass, making the room suitable for day or night occasions.

*The 990 sq. ft. Hall of the Doges prepared for a dance. (EWSHS photo L93-68.9 14)*

*Hall of the Doges decorated for the 34th wedding anniversary, September 11, 1911, of railroad capitalist Robert E. Strahorn and his wife. The occasion also was to celebrate a book Mrs. Strahorn had just published called "Fifteen Thousand Miles by Stage." The tepees in the back were part of the decorations depicting the Strahorns' early travels in the West, the book's topic. (Photo courtesy Walt and Karen Worthy.)*

## Promenade All Around It.

A promenade 20 feet wide will completely surround the ballroom and will be one of the most attractive features of the building. Arches between the 36 pillars will connect it with the main hall on all sides. In the promenade will be every device known to give an air of ease and comfort. It will be laid in expensive imported rugs. Cozy corners and lounging nooks, furnished with all kinds of divans and easy furniture will be in it in profusion. A whole carload of ferns and palms will be brought from Rutherford, N.J., for its decoration.

The main entrance to the hall will be at the northwest corner of Davenport's restaurant. [This is somewhat misleading in regards to what actually happened. On the main floor, the stairway was located at the southwest corner of the restaurant, reaching the second floor at the south entrance to the ballroom.] The ascent to the second floor will be by a luxurious stairway . . . A large reception room will be at the left of the landing above. The women's dressing rooms will open off the reception room, while the men's smoking and dressing rooms will be at the southeast corner of the building.

At the west end of the building will be two banquet halls, one for 25 guests and one for 50 guests. Large banquets will be served in the ballroom or in the promenade, with the ballroom left for dancing. A complete kitchen, with steam tables, serving rooms and elevators from the kitchen on the first floor will occupy the southwest corner of the building. Separate services of imported china and silver will be on hand for feasting parties from 10 to 250. The best orchestra that can be secured will be maintained to play in the restaurant and in the ballroom.

## Fit for Any Entertainment.

The whole plan of Mr. Davenport is to have a large assembly room fit for any kind of entertainment, such as parties, banquets or weddings . . . and will shed upon the guests the atmosphere of private ball or reception. Artistic curtains, hangings and palms will throng the archways. The rooms and corners will be lighted with subdued and diffused lights from ornamental chandeliers. The woodwork and carvings will all be light in coloring.

The plans were prepared by Cutter & Malmgren. Mr. Cutter said: "Mr. Davenport has instructed us to **spare no expense in making it the finest ballroom and reception hall in the west** [emphasis added]. Everything will be of the finest construction for ease, comfort, safety and entertainment of the guests. . . ."

Historically, the Hall of the Doges is important to Spokane's early interior architecture because Kirtland Cutter followed Davenport's instructions to "spare no expense." Knowing that Davenport's Restaurant was the top social establishment in Spokane, Cutter was given an opportunity to display and publicize his talents and abilities on a grand scale. Over the course of its life, the Hall of the Doges was the queen of Spokane's ballrooms.

In addition to the new ballroom and banquet rooms, the layout of which varied somewhat from the newspaper description, another major development took place on the second floor around the same time. Cutter designed an attractive apartment in Art Nouveau style for Louie Davenport at the northeast corner of the building, adjacent to the Hall of the Doges. It had large, arched leaded-glass windows facing on Sprague and Post, oak paneling and a hammered copper fireplace as the center focus of the living room (see photo on page 84). With Davenport's approval, Cutter also designed a men's bar and a small dining room within the main restaurant, called the Peacock Room, in the Art Nouveau style. The men's bar, originally called the Orange Bower, was located on the main floor of the Pennington in a space earlier occupied by the Hazelwood Dairy's creamery and was accessible from either the restaurant or Post Street. The use of the Art Nouveau style is noteworthy because it was rarely used in Spokane.

In conjunction with the extensive interior remodeling, Cutter also extended the Mission style facade, created a few years earlier on the Wilson Block, to the Bellevue/Pennington building, giving the two buildings the appearance of one.

*The Orange Bower, a men's bar, opened about 1904 on the Post Street side of the Pennington Hotel. During prohibition, it was converted into a soda fountain. Following various remodels, it was also the Aladdin Fountain, the Apple Bower, the Copper Strike Tap Room and the Audubon Room. (EWSHS photo L84-207.4.78)*

*A view of Davenport's Restaurant, the Pennington Hotel and the Pfister Block from the northeast corner of Sprague Avenue and Post Street. The Pfister was demolished in 1912 to make way for the construction of the new Davenport Hotel, which was opened in September 1914. When the Davenports were first married, they lived in an apartment above the restaurant, located at the corner with the smaller tower at the center of the photo. (Photo courtesy Dorothy and Bob Capeloto.)*

## Louis Davenport Reaches a Pinnacle by 1906

By 1906 Louis Davenport had reached a significant pinnacle in his life. He had positioned himself in the right place at the right time and had established a history of making excellent business moves. His restaurant was nationally known and even had acclaim in some international circles.

On March 2, 1906, the *Spokesman-Review* ran an article summing up the impression of an editor from a national magazine. This article addressed both Spokane and Davenport's Restaurant:

### SPOKANE, MODEL OF AMERICA

**"FRA ELBERTUS" HUBBARD GIVES HIGHEST PRAISES TO THIS CITY**

**TELLS IT IN THE "PHILISTINE"**

**Declares Davenport's Restaurant is the Finest Thing
of the Kind in the Country.**

"Spokane is the model city of America," declares Elbert Hubbard ("Fra Elbertus") in the March *Philistine*, of which he is editor. He visited Spokane this winter, and his impressions are embodied in this article:

At this writing it seems to me as if the city of Spokane, Wash., quite surpasses any city of America in it attention to the excellent and fit in architecture. Here is a city of 75,000 people, built up in about 15 years, not by struggling pioneers, squatters and speculators, but by people who came intending to stay. Spokane skipped the shanty stage.

Spokane is being built by young, ambitious, hopeful people from the east, who came with money expecting to make more. . . .

### Not a Mining Camp.

Mining towns always have a camp like quality of instability . . . But while Spokane has a very large mining interests, you at once see that they are not supreme. There are lumber, agricultural, stock raising – a vast territory on every side that looks to Spokane for supplies.

. . . The best example of Spokane spirit, crystallized, is Davenport's restaurant. Fifteen years ago the owner of this concern ran a waffle wagon. Then he rented a hole in the wall, and was himself a cashier, cook, waiter, scullion. The business soon outgrew its quarters. Davenport grew with the business.

---

It was fitting that Louis Davenport received his first national review from someone of Hubbard's renown and social standing. Hubbard, a native of East Aurora, New York, was truly a national phenomenon in his day and one of the nation's most prolific and popular writers.

Following a walking tour of England in 1893, Hubbard returned to America and tried to find a publisher for a series of biographical sketches he had written, called "Little Journeys." Being unsuccessful, he decided to print them himself, thus founding the Roycroft Press. His business expanded into the manufacture of furniture and other crafts, and soon developed into an artists' colony of over 500 people. He became a leading figure in the American Arts and Crafts movement.

**Elbert Hubbard**
**1856 - 1915**

It has been estimated that during his lifetime Hubbard published more than seven million words, most of his writings were contained in his periodicals, one of which was called the *Philistine*.

Hubbard and his wife were lost at sea when the British ship *Lusitania* was sunk by a German submarine on May 7, 1915. A total of 1198 died in that attack.

## Nearest Perfect in America.

This is not a biography, so just let me say that Davenport's restaurant is the best, the most unique and nearest perfect restaurant in the world. . . .[it] represents an investment of a little over a quarter of million dollars.

Davenport often feeds 5000 people a day. The yearly receipts are $400,000 and the net profits are $65,000.

The prices are moderate, but we must remember that Spokane is in Washington, where fruit, vegetables, dairy products and meat are produced at a cost so slight that it would make a Massachusetts gardener faint away.

Where a single acre produces 400 bushels of potatoes, or three tons of melons, where there are two crops of strawberries a year, there is a fortune for the gastronomic artist who can serve the people.

Davenport's is as snug, clean and complete as an ocean liner ready to sail. It contains no rat holes, chuck holes or unsightly corners. The retiring rooms are dreams in marble and tile. Between the serving room and the kitchen there are immense plate glass windows, so the customers can get a look at the kitchen, a place resplendent in copper, nickel and glass, dotted with quick moving men in spotless white.

The style of architecture is Early Mission, . . . Then there is a lunch counter and a buffet, commonly called a bar, where carved woods rival hammered brass and wrought iron.

## Didn't Meet Davenport.

. . . I know Davenport, but he does not know me. At his restaurant I pay cash. I purposely avoid meeting the man – I see the creation of his head, hands and heart. It is enough! A man is known for his work. Davenport's restaurant proclaims him.

I am told Davenport is a gentleman; low voiced, quiet, tireless, systematic, imaginative, with a patience and persistency like that of Pericles.

The art side of Davenport's restaurant is debtor to Kirk Cutler [*sic*], a designer and architect, who has keyed Spokane in an artistic way, . . . Residences, stores, clubs, banks, proclaim Kirk Cutler's quiet good taste, and his safe unbizarre lines and color schemes.

Davenport has collaborated with Cutler and the result is Davenport's restaurant, the finest thing of the kind in America, a proposition no visitor to Spokane will dispute.

When a man does a thing well beyond compare, though it be but the making of mouse traps, the world will make a pathway to his door, says Emerson. All trails lead to Davenport's.

*Looking east from the entrance to Davenport's Restaurant in 1914. The windows at the left face Sprague Avenue. (Photo courtesy Dorothy and Bob Capeloto.)*

*Davenport's Restaurant decorated for Easter in 1912. Many who had occasions to visit the hotel in earlier years often comment on the lasting impression left by the banks of flowers used in the decorations for special occasions, especially at Easter. (Photo courtesy Dorothy and Bob Capeloto.)*

***Throngs lined the street for President William H. Taft's arrival at Davenport's in September 1909. (EWSHS photo L93-68.9-40)***

For nearly two decades prior to Louis Davenport's involvement with the proposed Davenport Hotel project in 1908, his restaurant was the most popular establishment of its kind in the Inland Northwest. It was typically the gathering spot of choice for most major functions in Spokane. For example, when President William H. Taft visited Spokane in 1909, he had both breakfast and lunch there. The occasion was reported in the September 27, 1909 edition of the *Chronicle* as follows:

> The ride from the depot to Davenport's assumed the nature of a triumphal procession, with the president bowing his appreciation of his reception right and left. Every available space along First avenue between the buildings and curbing, every window and doorway and the roofs of adjacent houses were jammed with a mass of humanity eager to get a glimpse of the nation's chief. After entering Davenport's where breakfast was served, fresh arrivals among the crowd of sightseers thronged the streets until the initial meal of the president in this city was concluded. . . . Arriving at Davenport's, the cavalry executed a right wheel, bringing them in line on the north side of the street, saluting the president as he passed. The infantry, which brought up the rear of the possession, took its position on the street immediately in front of the building . . .

Davenport's Restaurant, although already widely known and popular, would assume a greater place of prominence as the new Davenport Hotel's main restaurant after the hotel opened in 1914. The restaurant was completely remodeled in 1922 to become the beautiful Italian Gardens. Although the restaurant would undergo additional revisions and name changes in later years, this would be the form it retained until after Louie Davenport sold the hotel and restaurant in 1945.

# A Photo Tour of Davenport's Restaurant

*Looking west along the Sprague Avenue side of Davenport's Restaurant in 1908. Imagine the excitement of seeing such a rarity as palm trees on the sidewalks of downtown Spokane! (EWSHS Libby Studio photo L87-12.47.08)*

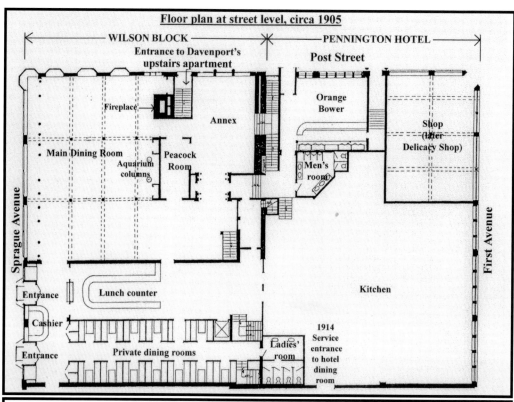

**Floor plan at street level, circa 1905**

WILSON BLOCK — ⊀ — PENNINGTON HOTEL

Entrance to Davenport's upstairs apartment

Post Street

Fireplace

Annex

Orange Bower

Shop (later Delicacy Shop)

Main Dining Room

Aquarium columns

Peacock Room

Men's room

Sprague Avenue

First Avenue

Entrance

Lunch counter

Kitchen

Cashier

Entrance

Private dining rooms

Ladies' room

1914 Service entrance to hotel dining room

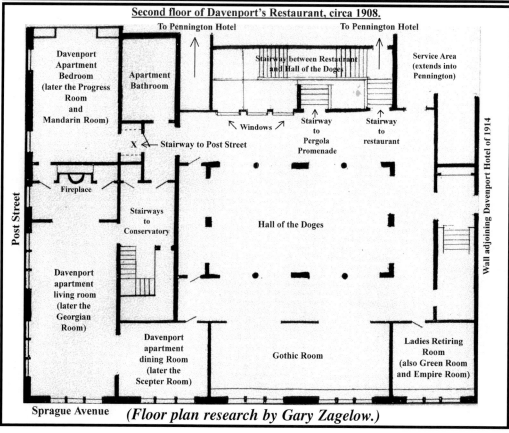

**Second floor of Davenport's Restaurant, circa 1908.**

To Pennington Hotel

To Pennington Hotel

Davenport Apartment Bedroom (later the Progress Room and Mandarin Room)

Apartment Bathroom

Stairway between Restaurant and Hall of the Doges

Service Area (extends into Pennington)

Windows

Stairway to Pergola Promenade

Stairway to restaurant

X ← Stairway to Post Street

Post Street

Fireplace

Stairways to Conservatory

Hall of the Doges

Wall adjoining Davenport Hotel of 1914

Davenport apartment living room (later the Georgian Room)

Davenport apartment dining Room (later the Scepter Room)

Gothic Room

Ladies Retiring Room (also Green Room and Empire Room)

Sprague Avenue

*(Floor plan research by Gary Zagelow.)*

*Left: The entryway to Davenport's Restaurant decorated for a group of visiting Japanese Commercial Commissioners in September 1909. It was typical of Davenport to create a theme or decorations befitting the occasion for major functions held at his establishment. (EWSHS Libby photo L93-68.9-48)*

*Below: The cashier's counter and entrance to the main dining room in 1908. (EWSHS Libby Studio photo L83-68.9-3.)*

*Looking south in the dining room toward the music balcony in 1908. The archway at the left is one of the entrances to the Annex. (EWSHS Libby photo L93-68.9-10)*

*The Peacock Room in 1909. This was a small dining room within the main dining room, designed in Art Nouveau style by architect Kirtland Cutter. (EWSHS Libby Studio photo L93-68.9-20)*

*The Annex, a smaller dining room on the south end of the main dining room, in 1908. The windows face Post Street. (EWSHS Libby Studio photo L93-68.9-9)*

*Main dining room area in 1908 showing glass columns containing live fish. (EWSHS Libby Studio photo L93-68.9-8)*

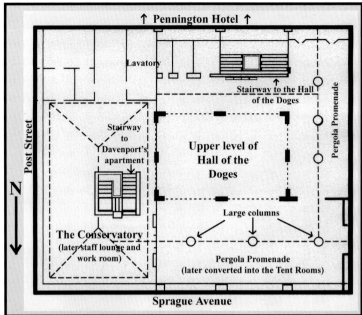

General layout (not an exact representation) of the third floor of Davenport's Restaurant, circa 1908. The north section of the Pergola Promenade, which surrounded the Hall of the Doges on three sides, was converted into separate party rooms, called the Tent Rooms about 1922. The Conservatory became a staff lounge. (Plan research by Gary Zagelow.)

The roof garden on the third floor, called the Conservatory, in 1908. The stairway landing to the left of the railing led to the Davenports' apartment below. This view is looking toward Post Street. A door at the far left corner of this room led to the Pergola Promenade (see facing photo). (EWSHS Libby Studio photo L93-68.9-22)

*Left: Looking east into the north end of the Conservatory in 1909. This was converted into a staff lounge and work room in 1922. (EWSHS Libby photo L93-68.9-20)*

*Bottom: Looking east along a section of the Pergola Promenade that bordered Sprague in 1908. The door at the far end opened into the room shown above. (EWSHS Libby Studio photo L93-68.9-24)*

*Ladies' retiring room. This 255-square-foot room was later also known as the Green Room and the Empire Room. (EWSHS photo L93-68.9-18)*

**The Gothic Room was another banquet or meeting hall on the second floor. The dining room of the Davenports' former apartment was opposite the back wall. The wall to the left bordered Sprague Avenue. (EWSHS photo L93-68.9-17)**

*General business office in 1908. (EWSHS Libby Studio photo L93-68.9-48)*

*Refrigeration room in 1908. Louie Davenport was invested in various ways in the production of some of the restaurant's food supplies, which helped keep the prices low and the quality high. He was a major investor and vice-president of the Ryan & Newton Co., a wholesale produce business in Butte, Montana. For a period of time, he had a chicken ranch in Deer Park. (EWSHS Libby Studio photo L93-68.9-29)*

## Davenport Marries and Starts a Family

On August 30, 1906, Llewellyn M. "Louis" Davenport, age 38, and Verus E. Smith were married at St. Thomas Episcopal Church in New York City. The following day an article appeared in the *Spokesman-Review* describing this event:

# WAS SURPRISE TO FRIENDS

### L.M. Davenport Will Bring Home a Bride – Married in New York

Louis M. Davenport and Miss Verus E. Smith were married yesterday afternoon at 3 o'clock at St. Thomas Episcopal church, probably the most fashionable church in New York City. The ceremony was performed by Rev. Ernest M. Stiles, the rector.

Mrs. M.C. Pennington, the bride's sister, with whom she has made her home, has received a dispatch announcing the marriage and stating that they will return to Spokane in two or three weeks.

Mr. Davenport left Spokane last Friday to meet his bride, who just arrived last Saturday from a trip abroad. Miss Smith came to Spokane five years ago with her sister, Mrs. Pennington, with whom she has made her home, coming from Portland where she received her education. She has made many friends in Spokane during the time she has been here and has hosts of friends in Portland.

The marriage comes as a complete surprise to all except the nearest friends. Few men are more typical of the west and of Spokane than Mr. Davenport. Coming to Spokane about 15 years ago, practically without means, he has in that time built up a fortune said to approach half a million, and has done it by strict business methods and prompt attention to even the details of business.

**Louis Davenport**                                    **Verus Davenport**

Few restaurants are better or more favorably known than Davenport's, built up entirely by Mr. Davenport within a few years, till it now has a reputation for elegance extending even beyond the confines of America. The secrecy of the marriage is in keeping with Mr. Davenport's modesty, probably few men in Spokane having a stronger dislike for notoriety than has this eminently successful man of business.

He has quietly fitted up a home for his bride on the upper floor of the restaurant building, where they will make their home on their arrival in the course of a few weeks.

On June 4, 1907, Verus Davenport gave birth to Llewellyn Marks "Lewis" Davenport II in their home on the second floor of Davenport's Restaurant. The Spokane County auditor's Register of Births gave the location of his birth as the "corner of Sprague and Post." To avoid confusion, a different spelling of the name was used for father and son, but neither ever used "Llewellyn." Both preferred to be called "Louie," as does the grandson, whose name is also Llewellyn Marks Davenport.

## HAPPY LOUIS DAVENPORT

An heir has been born to L. M. Davenport, proprietor of the famous Davenport restaurant. The baby is a 10 pound boy, hale and strong, and there is a great deal of rejoicing as a consequence today in the Davenport family.

The young heir to the palatial restaurant was born yesterday afternoon and in time is expected to take his place at the head of one of Spokane's big institutions which has helped to make this city famous.

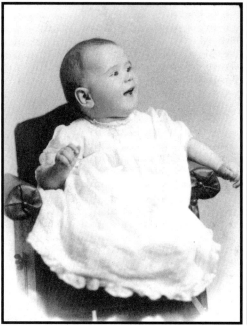

*Clockwise from upper left: Verus Davenport with her infant son, Lewis; an article announcing his birth from the Wednesday evening edition of the Spokane Daily Chronicle on June 5, 1907; Lewis at about age three with his father, Louis Davenport, and as a baby. (Photo courtesy Louie and Nita Davenport III.)*

*The living room of the Davenports' apartment above the restaurant before moving to their new home on Eighth Avenue in early 1910. The photo was taken after the suite was decorated for former president Theodore Roosevelt's stay during his visit to Spokane in April 1911. Davenport provided Roosevelt with a French chef and private valet. Everything was done to insure his privacy and comfort. This room later became the Georgian Room. (Photo EWSHS L94-36.314)*

*Private stairway to the roof garden (the Conservatory) on the third floor in 1911. The door at the right opened into the living room of the Davenports' suite. (EWSHS Libby Studio photo L93-68.9-36)*

*The dining room, just off the living room of the Davenports' former apartment, furnished and decorated for Teddy Roosevelt's visit in 1911. The window on the right faced Sprague Avenue. (EWSHS Libby Studio photo L87-1.5915X-11)*

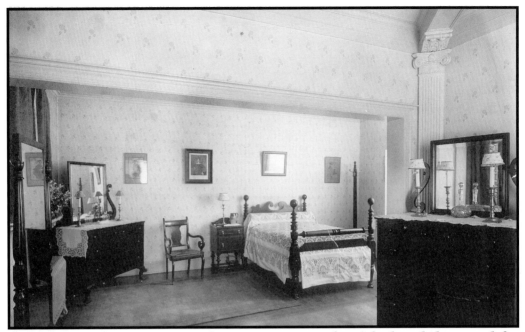

*The bedroom in Davenports' former apartment furnished and decorated for Roosevelt's visit in 1911. An alcove in this room provided the sleeping accommodations for Roosevelt's personal secretary. (EWSHS Libby Studio photo L87-1.5913X-11)*

## Louis and Verus Davenport Become Millionaires

On January 20, 1909, the *Spokane Daily Chronicle* announced that Spokane had 26 millionaires. By today's standards, this might seem insignificant and the reporting of it likely would be seen as an indiscretion, but in 1909 it was noteworthy.

The purpose of this announcement was to further promote Spokane and the potential for success. Following is a list of these millionaires and their vocations:

1. Blackwell, F.A. – Railroad builder and operator and timberman.
2. Breen, James – Mining.
3. Browne J.J. – Real estate and banking.
4. Brownlee, Malcolm B. – Capitalist.
5. Campbell, Amasa B.– Mine owner and operator.
6. Clark, F. Lewis – Real estate and capitalist.
7. Clark, Patrick – Mine owner and operator.
8. Corbin, D.C. – Railroad builder and operator.
9. Corbin, Austin – Mining man and capitalist.
10. Cowles, William H. – Newspaper publisher.
11. Day, Harry L. – Mine owner.
12. Davenport, Louis M. – Restaurant and real estate.
13. Finch, John A. – Mine owner and operator.
14. Graves, Jay P. – Railroad builder and operator, and mine owner.
15. Heath, Sylvester – Real estate.
16. Hogan. Frank P. – Real estate.
17. Hay, M.E. – Capitalist.
18. Hutton, L.W. – Mine owner and real estate.
19. Humbird, T.J. – Lumberman.
20. Jenkins, Colonel D.D. – Capitalist.
21. Kuhn, Aaron – Banker.
22. Monaghan, James – Mines and real estate.
23. Paulsen, August – Mine owner.
24. Peyton, Colonel I.N. – Capitalist.
25. Welch, Patrick – Railroad contractor.
26. Winters, William – Railroad contractor.

*The home built by Louis and Verus Davenport at 34 West Eighth Avenue as it appeared in 1927. Construction on this Kirtland Cutter-designed home began in 1908 and took nearly three years to complete. The landscape design was the work of the Olmsted Brothers, a well known landscape-design firm from Brookline, Massachusetts. The Davenports only lived in their new home about two-and-a half years before selling it to the Richard B. Porter family, who lived there for many years. In 1967 the house was demolished to make way for an expansion of the Sacred Heart Medical Center. (EWSHS Libby Studio photo, L94-10.30)*

## Davenports Build Their First House

When it came to elegance, Louis Davenport's masterful touch reached a level that earned him national prominence. The success of his restaurant was partially due to the combined beauty of structure and decor. His concept in a home reflected this same taste. From the main structure to the grounds, Louis Davenport orchestrated the creation of Spokane's most elegant estate. Davenport's good friend Kirtland Cutter and Cutter's partner, Karl Malmgren, were commissioned to draw up the plans for the buildings. The beautiful building site overlooking the town, with a creek running through it, had been a natural gathering spot for the local Native Americans in earlier times. Frederick Law Olmsted, famed landscape architect from Brookline, Massachusetts, was hired to design and supervise the landscaping, which took over two years to complete. The plans for his new estate were announced in the Sunday morning *Spokesman-Review* on November 22, 1908. The entire front page of the second section described Davenport's house project in great detail, as follows:

# L.M. Davenport Residence Grounds Finest in Northwest
## Landscape architecture equal to finest improved park. Attractive residence for picturesque setting. Gate lodge, thirteen waterfalls, summer houses and fishes.

Cutter & Malmgren have completed the plans for an attractive residence which is to have a fit setting in the elaborate grounds L.M. Davenport has been beautifying for several months on Seventh and Eighth avenues and Division street. The house, while resembling the old German type of residence in most of its features, does not adhere closely to any style of architecture, but embodies many new and original designs which conform to the picturesque site.

When completed the house and grounds will be one of the show places of Spokane, adding to the distinctive architecture which has made this city the admiration of visitors and furnishing the most pretentious piece of landscape gardening that has been attempted by an individual in the northwest. . . .

### Three and One-Half Acres in Site.
The grounds are irregular in shape, having a frontage of 250 feet on Seventh avenue, 475 feet on division street, and 500 feet of Eighth avenue. The tract contains about three and a half acres. It is extremely rough and broken, there being a difference of 72 feet in the elevation of the ground on Eighth avenue, which is the residence site, and the lowest point at the Seventh avenue and Division street. There is a general slope to the ground to the northeast and the high ground commands an unbroken view of the city and the valley to the east and west.

Through the grounds from north to south runs a sharp ravine in which flows a crystal clear stream, fed by a big spring that rises from the earth near the city reservoir. The stream enters Mr. Davenport's grounds 50 feet west of the southeast corner . . . leaving the grounds near the northeast corner. From the rustic bridge under which the stream flows on Eighth avenue just before crossing Mr. Davenport's property line to the point where it flows under Seventh avenue there is a fall of 42 feet.

Naturally the stream, though small, is turbulent, and this characteristic has been taken advantage of to create a succession of 13 miniature falls and pools placed in alternate order. The dams which form the pools are made of rustic rock laid in cement, and across the stream at different places are stepping stones, or rustic bridges, according to the width of the channel. These bridges and stepping stones are approached by meandering paths which are laid out through the grounds, following the contour of the land. Standing at the lowest falls and looking up the ravine, the 13 falls are all to be seen in one view, and they are so close together as to produce the effect of a series of cataracts with no intervening still water.

At one place the boulders form a grotto down the sides of which the water spreads and runs in silver threads into a deep pool at the bottom. A drinking fountain has been built there, and a resting place with seats in the cool of the niche beneath the rock.

*Foot bridge crossing the stream on Davenports' estate. (EWSHS photo L84-207.4.72)*

*Grotto and pool on the Davenports' estate. (EWSHS photo L88-404.19.2.21)*

*A crew working on the landscaping on the lower terrace of Davenport's new home on Eighth Avenue. The entire grounds were surrounded by a rustic wall of basaltic rock, the height of which was a minimum of six feet and reaching a maximum height in places of 25 feet, the height of the wall shown in this photograph. (EWSHS photo L88-404.19.2.7)*

*Verus and Lewis standing on a path along Cowley Creek at the Davenports' estate on Eighth Avenue. (EWSHS photo L88-404.19.2.19)*

*Fishing in the lower pool of the Davenports' estate. (L88-404.19.2.32)*

In the larger pools fishes, rainbow trout, carp and gold fish will be placed and water fowls will add a touch of animated nature to the ideal setting of still life.

The ravine is already richly wooded with native trees, . . . The birches, cottonwoods, spruce and other trees in the ravine are being left undisturbed as much as possible, it being desired to preserve the natural wildness of the place, . . . The slopes, which are mostly bare, will be set with native syringas, rhododendron, laurel, azalea and other shrubs, while native ferns will be planted along the water's edge. The rocks and ledges are to be covered with moss wherever they are now devoid of that garnishment.

### Vines and Laurels Along Walks.

The paths that lead up the steeper slopes are to be cribbed with logs, over which laurel and clinging vines will hang, and where steps are necessary, these will be of thin slabs of rustic stone. One of the paths will be carpeted with pine needles. The paths will lead to the various bridges and stepping stones across the stream and to the summer houses which have been built at the best viewpoints.

Enclosing the entire grounds is a heavy rustic wall of basaltic rock, laid dry. This wall is not less than six feet high at any place and at some points it attains the height of 25 feet, giving the place a baronial appearance. In the higher places the wall is heavily battered and filled with earth in which ferns and vines are planted.

*A wagon load of trees to be planted during the Davenports' landscaping project at 34 West Eighth Avenue. This photo was taken in front of the main gateway entrance. (EWSHS photo L88-404.19.2.2)*

## Gate Lodge at Entrance.

The entrance to the grounds is near the southwest corner, where there is a covered gateway supported with massive stone piers, which are roofed over, forming a pinnacle effect. The swinging gates are of heavy timbers, with huge iron bars. The gateway connects with the lodge, or gardeners' cottage, which is built of rustic rock, . . . In front of the lodge stands the water tower, which throws out heavy buttresses, forming an approach to the rustic bridge crossing the ravine on Eighth Avenue.

Inside the lodge is a large room fitted up with fireplace, and in the water tower is a bathroom, under the lodge is a room for gardening tools and other implements.

Leading from the gate to the house is a gravel drive, which forms a true circle 65 feet in diameter, in the center of which is a fountain. A paved path leads from the circle across a low terrace, with lawn and garden on each side, to the front entrance, and continues east from the terrace down to the ravine. The terrace is 25x74 feet.

## House Modified German Type.

Back 200 feet from the gate, the house is set at an angle with the east end nearest the street. In style the house is an American adaptation of the old German type, being long, low and narrow, with duplicate fronts facing two ways. Two main gables or wings are connected by a narrower center part, which extends beyond the wings, forming east and west gables. There are seven gables in all . . . The roof is broken with dormers, giving a very irregular skyline. It is covered with wide hand-made shingles. The color is terra cotta, while the outside walls are weathered brown and the window sashes and trimmings are white.

## First Story Rustic Rock.

The low kitchen wing on the west and the second story of the house are covered with hand made shingles, laid wide to the weather. The first story is basaltic rock with deep-set joints and part of the gables are half timber and plaster. The second story has a heavy overhang, supported by 12x12 adzed timbers, the ends exposed.

The greatest length of the house is 143 feet, including the east terrace and high terrace wall, which are 18 feet wide. The greatest width is 88 feet, . . .

The north terrace is only two inches below the level of the main floor. It is a grass terrace 14x82 feet, with a two-and-a-half-foot wall. On the east it connects with a semicircular terrace at the end of the house, having floor of Welsh quarries and a fountain. Off this terrace in a niche at the end of the house is a huge outside fireplace, protected from the southwest breeze by the projecting sun room off the living room, and made further comfortable by the fireplace, . . . The wall which supports it drops 20 feet to the ravine slope.

## Formal Garden Level.

From the west end of the north terrace stone stairs descend to a formal garden north of the west wing of the house. From the kitchen wing two high stone walls extend to the west, enclosing the kitchen yard, and leading to the garage, which is on the west property line.

Entrance to the house is beneath a covered porch, having massive stone piers, supporting a balcony, set between the two main wings. The balcony has a heavy railing hung with flower boxes, while huge terra cotta urns are directly over the porch piers. The floor of the porch is tile.

Without a vestibule, entrance is directly into a large hall, from which stairs with two landings in view ascend along the north wall. Over the stairs is a large window lighting the hall and extending to the second story.

### Tropical Hardwood Finish.

All of the principal rooms are to be finished in tropical hardwoods: Philippine mahogany, Central American mahogany, Jenesero, Circassian walnut and the floors will be quarter sawed oak. The hall will be wainscoted in wood paneling seven feet high.

To the east of the hall is the living room, entered through a wide porch. This room is 22x35 feet, and opposite the arched entrance is a great inglenook 7x15 feet, entirely covered, including the ceiling, with Moravian tiles of quaint designs in relief. At each side of the fireplace are settees in old-fashioned design.

Large mullioned windows with heavy wood muntins open on the north and the south upon the open terraces, while other windows of the same type open upon the north and south porches and upon the semi-circular terrace, and into the sun room . . .

This sun room is 14x21 feet, and has a flat roof with extending beams in the pergola effect. Three sides of the room are glass and the flat roof is covered with flower boxes, ferns and vines. The room is to be filled with palms.

West of the entrance hall is the dining room, 16x22 feet. The room has a recessed fireplace with beveled sides built of rookwood tiles, and the north end is taken up with two built-in buffets, between which are folding glass doors leading to the smoking room. Wide French windows open from the dining room upon the south terrace. At one end of the room is a semi-circular alcove set off from the main room by a low beam, and intended for a breakfast room.

The smoking room is 15x16 feet and its wide windows overlook the north terrace and garden. It also has a French window opening upon the north porch.

To the west of the dining room is the service compartment, including the kitchen, 15x17 feet, butler's pantry, 8x13 feet; servants' dining room 8x10 feet; servants' hall, in which are a large ice chest and pastry room, filled up with shelves, bins and other equipment. Off the kitchen is a covered workroom porch for the servants.

In the east wing on the second floor is the owner's chamber, 16x23 feet. This connects with a sitting room, 14x17 feet, through an open arch, just opposite which is a large fireplace in the sitting room. The beds are so placed in the chamber as to give a view of the sitting room fireplace. A tile bath with shower attachment, pedestal basin and Roman tub connect with the owner's chamber.

### Chambers All in Ivory.

French doors open from the sitting room upon a sleeping balcony. The finish of these rooms and of all the chambers will be ivory.

Adjoining the owner's chamber on the south is the nursery, which also connects with the sitting room and has bath and connection with the south balcony.

In the west wing are two guest chambers with bath and fireplaces. Both of these chambers open upon balconies. The servants' rooms are west of the guest chambers and have private bath. There is a sewing room adjoining the servants' chamber. All of the chambers have large closets with outside light.

On the third floor is the attic, in which one large room is to be finished for a play-room. The basement equipment is complete, including a hot water heating plant, laundry, driers, storeroom, wine cellar, fuel room and fruit room. Underneath the north terrace will be a frost proof room for storing plants in the winter. . . .

*The front gate entrance to the Davenports' new home at 34 West Eighth Avenue following its completion in 1911. (Photo courtesy Louie and Nita Davenport III.)*

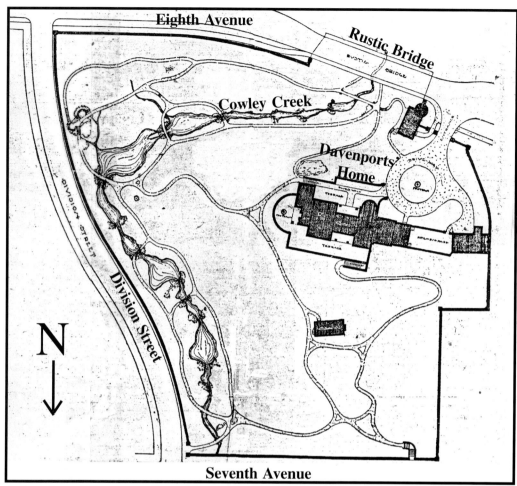

*A drawing of Davenport's residence site and grounds between Seventh and Eighth Avenues. This drawing shows the locations of the house, paths and Cowley Creek.*

When the world famous inventor Thomas Edison visited Spokane in 1908, he toured Davenport's new home site. Following the tour, he stated, as quoted in the *Chronicle*:

> I have seen no place in America with greater opportunities for making a beautiful home near the heart of a city . . . It struck Mr. Davenport, who through his persistence and natural artistic temperament, has built in Spokane a restaurant which is unsurpassed in many respects in America, if not in the world, to realize the natural beauty and the opportunities to be found in this little plot of ground on the northern slope of the rugged bluffs which bound the city on the south.

The Davenports only lived in their new $225,000 home about two-and-a-half years. They sold it to the Richard B. Porter family, who lived there for many years. The gorge and wooded areas were later filled and made level with the streets. The house was eventually turned into a nursing home and later torn down to make way for the expansion of Sacred Heart Hospital.

*Lewis Davenport II and an unidentified woman outside the Davenport home at 34 West Eighth Avenue, circa 1911. (Photo courtesy Louie and Nita Davenport III.)*

Another leading citizen in the early 1900s, and a close friend of Louis Davenport, was Aubrey L. White. The two men moved in the same business circles, shared a love of nature and were members of the Cathedral of St. John the Evangelist. According to an article in the *Chronicle* on October 7, 1907, they had even intended to build mansions on adjoining property bordered by Sixth and Ninth on the north and south, Hilliard (now known as Cowley) on the west and McClelland on the east. The article stated that Davenports had recently purchased four acres adjoining a three-acre lot White had owned for several years. They planned to create a most beautiful parklike setting in which to build their homes and had already engaged the services of Frederick Law Olmsted Jr.

White was a nature lover dedicated to preserving natural open spaces and parks for the public's enjoyment. He formed the "City Beautiful" movement and was instrumental in the creation of Spokane's first park board. Not only a charter member, he was also the park board's first president. In 1908 he recruited Davenport as a board member, a position he held until his death in 1951. In addition to his tireless city beautification campaign, White was also an entrepreneur who was active in numerous business ventures. His business connections and regard for Spokane were the impetus behind the development of Spokane's parks. His memory has been honored by the naming of the Aubrey L. White Parkway in Riverside State Park, and the preservation of an area he loved along the Little Spokane River as a park.

*Aubrey L. White at his desk in the Spokesman-Review office, where he was the garden editor and head of the Civic Development Department for more than 25 years. (Photo courtesy Charlie Willis, Aubrey White's grandson.)*

# The Aubrey L. White Family Photo Montage

*Ethelyn (Binkley) and Aubrey White on board a cruise ship, circa 1920.*

*Aubrey White (center) and his daughters, from left: Betty, Harriet, Mary and Louise, in the 1920s.*

*Whites' daughters in their adult years, from left: Mary, Betty, Harriet and Louise. (All photos courtesy Charlie Willis.)*

*Aubrey and Ethelyn White's daughters, from left: Louise, Harriet, Betty and Mary in the 1920s.*

*Aubrey and Ethelyn White's grandson (Louise's son) Charles Willis, and his family, from left: Herald, Melissa, Charlie and Winfield, in the 1980s.*

# A Collection of Photographs from the Davenport Family Album Showing Some of Lewis Jr.'s Early Toys and Costumes
### *(All photos courtesy of Louis and Nita Davenport III)*

*Lewis Davenport in toy wagon. The Davenports lived in the apartment above the restaurant until Lewis Jr. was nearly four, at which time they moved to their new home on Eighth Avenue, where this photo was probably taken.*

*Christmas at the Davenport home at 34 West Eighth Avenue, circa 1909.*

*Lewis, at about age two, with a stuffed toy lamb (left) and standing near a rocking horse ridden by an unidentified child at his home on Eighth.*

*Lewis Davenport about 5 years old in front of the entry way to the family's new home at 34 West Eighth Avenue. This photo was taken at the outset of the automobile's popularity. The opposite page contains a John W. Graham advertisement for this type of toy car, which appeared in the Spokesman-Review.*

*Lewis and his dog in his toy car at their home on Eighth and mounting a donkey.*

*Lewis with some unidentified children (left) and with his mother, Verus Davenport, in front of their home at 221 West Sumner, circa 1915.*

*Lewis and his mother, Verus Davenport.*

*Lewis in a donkey cart with an unidentified woman (left), possibly Louie Davenport's mother, Minnie, who lived in Spokane from 1891 until her death in 1924. The woman on the right is also unidentified, but because of the resemblance to Verus, it possibly could be her sister, Maud Pennington Hollis. Maud, who was Lewis's favorite aunt, managed the Pennington Hotel for many years. She is buried in the family plot along with Lewis and his parents.*

*During his younger years, life had its trying moments for Lewis Davenport II. The upper photos picture him dressed like a girl and George Washington for some type of costumed functions. In the lower photo he is being forced to dance, obviously to his disdain.*

*The former home of the Richard Porter family at 221 West Sumner and, at the time of this photograph, Davenports' home, which they owned from October 1912 to October 1916, before moving to an apartment in the new Davenport Hotel. The home is presently (2001) owned by Michael and Sarah Michalko, proprietors of The Kempis Hotel. (Photo courtesy Louie and Nita Davenport.)*

Prior to the completion of Davenports' new mansion at 34 West Eighth Avenue, they realized the new hotel project was going to require a significant financial outlay. Consequently, in October 1912, they sold their new home to Richard B. Porter of the Porter Brothers, one of the largest railroad contracting firms in the United States. The Porters' payment for the house included land in the Rockwood area, their home at 221 West Sumner and a cash payment of $95,000. The Davenports had lived in their new home only about a year and a half.

# Chapter 4

# A World-Class Restaurant and Hotel in Spokane

*The Davenport establishments in 1917, with a good view of the Post Street side of Davenport's Restaurant in the Wilson Block (on the right) and the Pennington Hotel at the corner of Post Street and First Avenue. The new (1914) Davenport Hotel towers behind them. The vertical sign on the corner of the Pennington, below the clock tower, read "Davenport Delicacy Shop." To the right, a "Bowling" sign marked the dividing line of the two buildings. When the new hotel was built in 1914, all three buildings were interconnected and Davenport's establishments occupied the entire city block. (EWSHS Libby Studio photo L87-1.13554X-17a)*

Contrary to popular belief and numerous historical accounts, Louis Davenport did not initiate the movement that resulted in the construction of the Davenport Hotel. The initial idea for the now-famous hotel was originally conceived in 1906 by a group of Spokane businessmen, which may have included Davenport. During that time, Spokane had its share of enthusiastic supporters who recognized the potential of the Inland Northwest, with Spokane as its axis, and were actively engaged in its development. The success and fortunes of these supporters were dependent on Spokane's growth.

To attract conventions or other outside business, a city needs first-class accommodations that can comfortably and conveniently handle large crowds, while offering the kinds of amenities and entertainment the business class has come to expect from competing entities. In the early 1900s, Spokane was in need of a such a facility. Numerous newspaper articles proclaimed the necessity for a convention center.

Although a number of upscale hotels, such as the Hotel Spokane, had been built after the fire of 1889, none were of the size or caliber to handle large conventions.

By fall of 1908, the vision of such a facility began to materialize when a group of investors organized specifically for that purpose. Funds were committed and plans for Spokane's largest hotel, which would also become the city's tallest building, were drawn up.

*Hotel Spokane in the early 1900s. (EWSHS Libby Studio photo L87-1.82435-55)*

The one major element lacking in this plan was a key person, someone who could manage an operation of the magnitude and complexity envisioned. Louis Davenport was the logical choice. Within a short time span, he had made a name for himself and was gaining national notoriety. On October 9, 1908, a *Spokesman-Review* article contained the following statement:

> . . . No definite announcement is yet obtainable from the men behind the project, but it is said that L.M. Davenport, owner of Davenport's restaurant, which has been such a big feature in advertising Spokane, is interested in the enterprise and will probably become active manager of the hotel.

Apparently, negotiations with Davenport had been ongoing, perhaps to the point of his acceptance, before the above information was released to the press. Two days later, a sketch designed by Kirtland Cutter of the proposed hotel was displayed in the *Spokesman-Review*. This design, as shown on the following page, was drawn to match, and included the west end of, Davenport's existing restaurant.

The exact agreement Davenport made with his backers is unknown, but as history indicates, he quickly became the controlling partner, with an apparent complete buy-out option. Upon his immediate assumption of the role as key man, he personally directed all aspects of the hotel's construction, development and management.

Davenport's first order of business was to finalize the architectural plans for the hotel. As previously mentioned, the firm of Cutter and Malmgren had already proposed a design using artistic elements compatible with the restaurant's exterior, drawing freely on the use of the Mission-style parapets, arches and towers, but more

*Copy of an ink drawing by F.C. Hutchinson of Kirtland Cutter and Karl Malmgren's*
*original design for the proposed Davenport Hotel. (Courtesy Spokane Public Library.)*

lavish in its ornamental trimmings. Historically, the original proposal is of importance to the Davenport legacy because Kirtland Cutter specifically designed the hotel to tie in with his earlier creation, the Mission-style facade on Davenport's Restaurant.

Because of the anticipated cost to build such an elaborate and complicated design, Cutter was requested to modify his original plans. As the result of a trip Davenport and Cutter took to study the latest trends in hostelry design, they concluded this type of ornate style had become somewhat passe. The current trend restricted the ornate features to the bottom and the top of the building, with simpler lines in between. With that in mind, Cutter redesigned the Davenport Hotel's exterior to its present Florentine Eclectic design. Arguably, though more consistent with the design of the restaurant, the complexity of the earlier proposal may have been overpowering.

In November 1908, even before the new drawings were underway, a modification was made affecting the roof line, a change that reflected Davenport's influence. In order to create a roof garden, to be designed by the Olmsted Brothers, the roof would be flat. However, the four big towers – and the hotel's position as the tallest building in the city – would remain intact.

During the preliminary planning stages, a number of sites on which to build the new hotel had been considered. With Louis Davenport's acceptance of the key position, the chosen site, of course, was adjacent to his restaurant. Prior to releasing the announcement about building the grand new hotel, Davenport and his associates had already secured purchase agreements for some of the property on the block west of Davenport's Restaurant. Unfortunately, after the announcement, some of the remaining owners greatly inflated the asking price for their property. Eventually, the group purchased all the remaining property on the block. The total estimated costs for the property alone was almost $600,000.

*A drawing illustrating the property owners and transaction amounts or terms they received for their property located within Block 6 of Railroad Addition, Lots 1 through 6, in 1908. Davenport's Restaurant and his Pennington Hotel occupied lots 5 and 6. In 1914 the new hotel was constructed on lots 1 through 4.*

The following year, on June 24, 1909, revised hotel plans were unveiled in the *Spokesman-Review*, highlighting several major changes. The headlines announced the hotel would be 12 stories high instead of 11. The top two floors were to be used primarily as sample rooms for sales representatives to display their wares. A decision had also been reached to build the hotel in a U-shape, providing every guest room with an outside window. The hotel was to be built to the full 12 floors on the Sprague Avenue half of the block, but only to a height of three floors along First Avenue (the open end of the U), allowing for future expansion (a major addition in 1929 raised the short section adjacent to the restaurant to the full existing height).

The article disclosed the anticipated cost of the project to be about $2.2 million. Although the exterior design had been simplified, larger guest rooms and added conveniences accounted for the increase in the expected costs. The modifications, according to Davenport, would place this new hotel among the best in the county.

## The Davenport Hotel Company is Formed

Although the article in 1909 that discussed the revised plans also quoted Davenport as saying, "There is a good prospect of work being started on the building this year," those plans did not materialize as anticipated. In fact, little else appeared in the newspapers until 1912. It was even some time before the names of those involved in the Davenport Hotel partnership were publicly announced. On October 8, 1908, the *Spokane Press* had stated: "Mr. Davenport says that the Spokane & Eastern stockholders are heavily interested," but the first public announcement concerning the major backers of the new hotel was not made until July 25, 1912. It appeared in the *Spokane Press,* with a headline stating:

### COWLES, HILLS, DAVENPORT, HEAVILY INTERESTED IN NEW $2,000,000 HOTEL.

#### FINE STRUCTURE TO BE ERECTED ON SITE OF DAVENPORT RESTAURANT – SPOKANE MILLIONAIRE ADDS TO INVESTMENTS.

W.H. Cowles, multi-millionaire newspaper man and real estate holder of Spokane; James J. Hill and Louis Hill, railroad magnates, and L.M. Davenport, restaurant man, are reputed to be the heaviest stockholders in the company which announced yesterday afternoon that a $2,000,000 hotel would be immediately erected in Spokane on the block bounded by Post and Lincoln streets and First and Sprague avenues.

On August 7, 1912, the Davenport Hotel Company's articles of incorporation were filed. There were six articles involved, which stated the usual information: Name of the corporation, its purpose, the principal place of business, term of existence, the number and names of the trustees, and the value of the capital stock.

There were seven trustees chosen to manage the affairs of the corporation. Their names, in the order they appeared in the articles of incorporation, were as follows: (1) L.M. Davenport, (2) R.B. Porter, (3) John A. Finch, (4) W.H. Cowles, (5) W.J.C. Wakefield, (6) T.J. Humbird and (7) R.B. Paterson. All were residents of Spokane.

This board of trustees represented a good mix of experience and success listed as follows: **Davenport,** as has been thoroughly discussed, was the owner of the most successful restaurant in Spokane and, since 1908, the manager of the Davenport Hotel project; **Porter** – Railroad builder with timber interests; **Finch** – An attorney with heavy mining interest; **Cowles** – Newspaper owner and, reportedly, Spokane's wealthiest businessman; **Wakefield** – One of Spokane's most prominent attorneys; **Humbird** – One of the Inland Northwest's most prominent timber industrialists; and **Paterson** – A leading Spokane businessmen and president of the Spokane Dry Goods Company and The Crescent Department store.

## Paying for the Project:
## Corporate Funding and Real Estate Serial Notes.

At the time of its official incorporation, the capital stock of Davenport Hotel Company, organized under the laws of the State of Washington, was valued at $1,300,000 (13,000 shares at $100 per share).

To complete the project successfully, an additional $750,000 was needed. To that end, the Davenport Hotel Company made a public offering of Real Estate Serial Notes, which paid 6% per annum. The investment capital, the land on which the hotel was to be built and the existing Davenport buildings provided the collateral. The combined value of the collateral was over two and a half times that of the total notes offered.

The second article of incorporation was significant in its broad intent. In addition to the construction and operation of the hotel business, it also allowed the corporation to construct, lease or otherwise acquire, manage and occupy buildings for stores, apartments, office buildings, restaurants, lunch and tea rooms, barber shops, billiard halls, cafes and bars.

From its inception, the Davenport Hotel was legally structured to become almost a miniature city within itself, which, as the hotel shops became established and the services expanded, it virtually did.

These articles of incorporation solidified six years of planning. Finally, with the financing in place, ground breaking could begin and Spokane would be forever changed by the construction of its most distinguished and recognizable historic landmark.

No. 32634

## ARTICLES OF INCORPORATION
### OF THE

*Davenport Hotel Company*

Place of business Spokane, Wash

Time of existence 50 years.

Capital stock, $ 1,300.000

State of Washington, ss.

Filed for record in the office of the Secretary of State, AUG 7 - 1912,

at 4:14 o'clock P. M., at request of

*Wakefield & Witherspoon*

Address Crypton Bldg

Spokane, Wash

Secretary of State.

Recorded in Book 98, Page 505,
DOMESTIC CORPORATIONS

Fee for Filing and recording, $ 25.00

Fee for 1913 license - - $ 15.00

Certificate No. 22494

Mailed AUG 31 1912

Indexed.

Checked. Compared.

**Source: State of Washington,
Secretary of State**

# The Davenport Hotel Stockholders

The list of Davenport Hotel stockholders, which was printed in the August 30, 1914 *Spokesman-Review*, included the majority of men who controlled Spokane's largest business interests and were the strongest body of stockholders ever joined together behind any enterprise in the Inland Northwest in the early 1900s. At the time of this venture, the aggregate wealth of these men was conservatively estimated by W.D. Vincent, vice president of the Old National Bank, at $100,000,000.

The stockholders' names, as follows, read like a "Who's Who" of Inland Northwest businessmen and industrial and commercial enterprises, and was a testimony to the faith in Louis Davenport and the success of his hotel.

## The Stockholders

F.A. Blackwell, president Blackwell Lumber; Thomas H. Brewer, president Fidelity National Bank; James C. Broad, contractor; George S. Brooke, treasurer Trustee Co.; W.H. Cowles; Centennial Mill Company; Chamberlin Bros.; Comstock & Paterson; Spokane Dry Goods Co.; James C. Cunningham, vice president Union Trust and Savings; L.M. Davenport, proprietor Davenport's Restaurant; Day & Hansen, Security Co.; George R. Dodson, jeweler; Eilers Piano Co.; John A. Finch, capitalist; H.A. Flood, president Trustee Co.; D.A. Foley, railroad contractor; D.B. Fotheringham, capitalist; B.L. Gordon, president B.L. Gordon & Co.; Fred B. Grinnell, president Fred B. Grinnell Co.; John W. Graham & Co.; Jay P. Graves, capitalist; Greenough Investment Co.; Holley Mason Hardware company; T.J. Humbird, president Humbird Lumber Co.; L.W. Huntley, capitalist; Arthur D. Jones, president Arthur D. Jones Co.; Jones & Dillingham, manufacturers; James Kennedy, contractor; Thaddius S. Lane, president Home Telephone Co.; F.T. McCollough, secretary-treasurer Crystal Laundry; McCrea & Merryweather Loan Co.; Agnes J. McDonald, property owner; McGoldrick Lumber Co.; R., Martin, businessman; A.P. Mitchell, contractor; W.H. Murgittroyd, druggist; August Paulsen, capitalist; M.A. Phelps, manager Phelps Lumber Co.; Phoenix Lumber Co.; Porter Bros., railroad contractors; Powell-Sanders Co., wholesalers; R.L. Rutter, vice president Spokane and Eastern Trust Co.; Ryan & Newton, wholesalers; J.D. Sherwood, capitalist; W.H. Shields, manager Mutual Life Insurance Co.; H.J. Shinn, president H.J. Shinn Wholesalers; J.K Smith, grain dealer; James Smyth, president Smyth Plumbing Co.; T.F. Spencer, treasurer Kelly-Clarke Co.; W.H. Stanley, realty owner; R.A. Strahorn, president Portland, Eugene & Eastern Railroad; Twohy Bros., railroad contractors, W.J.C. Wakefield, attorney; Washington Trust Co., Washington Water Power; A.L. White, capitalists; Elizabeth Winters, realty owner; W.H. Ziegler, capitalist; Winters Investment Co.; Thomas F. Wren, railroad contractor; Inland Portland Cement Co.; and Valentine Peyton, president Spokane Drug Co.

Charles Jasper

*The Davenport Hotel site prior to demolition of the preexisting buildings, circa 1910. The inset is of Charles Jasper, the man in charge of the demolition. The west end of Davenport's Restaurant is barely visible at the far left. Next to Davenport's is the three-story brick Pfister Building, built around 1904, which extended the full depth of the block and had matching facades at both the Sprague and First Avenue entrances. The Pfister had one of the city's best equipped billiard rooms on the main floor and a bowling alley in the basement. Part of the upper level was rented to Maud (Smith) Pennington Hollis and comprised a portion of her Hotel Pennington, most of which was located in the former Bellevue Block, owned by Louis Davenport, her brother-in-law. Davenport purchased the Pfister from George Lang for $175,000. The other buildings contained various shops and businesses, some of which rented furnished rooms on the second floor. A sign on the corner building advertised rooms for 50 cents. (EWSHS photo L95-97.52)*

On October 9, 1912, demolition of the existing buildings on the Davenport Hotel site began. Earlier thoughts had been given to relocating the Pfister Building. However, as that proved to be too expensive, a decision was made to raze all the buildings on the site. To accomplish that, the Davenport Hotel Company sold the buildings to Charles Jasper, a native of Denmark who had moved to Spokane in 1888 and starting a general contracting business. The terms of Jasper's contract allowed 60 days, which was easily accomplished with the help of a crew of about 50 men. The majority of the materials removed were used in other buildings Jasper was constructing.

Jasper was related to Lewis Larsen, the founder of Metaline Falls, who was a friend and business associate of Louis Davenport.

*The glass and china washing area in the Davenport Hotel kitchen in 1914 is at the right, with the silver washing department located at the far end of this photo. (Photo courtesy Walt and Karen Worthy.)*

## Davenport Prepares Kitchen for New Hotel

As the construction progressed on the hotel, Davenport made his first substantial improvements to his restaurant in preparation for the additional guests he would be serving in the new banquet and dining rooms. This project, budgeted at $55,000, called for the renovation of the existing kitchen, with the installation of the finest kitchen equipment money could buy, and an extensive remodeling of the restaurant. The new alterations equipped the kitchen to serve 2200 people, the combined seating capacity of the hotel's Isabella dining room, the existing restaurant and the banquet rooms. After the hotel opened, it reportedly served more than 3000 people a day.

On August 2, 1913, Davenport discussed some of the pending changes in an announcement to the local press. The primary change involved enlarging the existing kitchen, extending it to First Avenue on the south and removing some of the private dining areas, namely the German and French rooms, at the rear of the restaurant, for expansion to the north. Davenport discussed other plans for the restaurant that were intended to happen simultaneously with the kitchen remodel, but most of those did not actually take place until a much later date.

The kitchen was located in the Pennington Hotel portion of Davenport's establishment. The new kitchen was designed to ensure cleanliness and efficiency. The fresh, new look included red-tiled floors and walls of white tile and marble. An entrance led directly into the Isabella Room, the elegant spacious dining room at the southeast corner of the new hotel. Along with the kitchen remodel, the service room for the Hall of the Doges and second floor service kitchen for the hotel banquet room were enlarged.

The *Spokesman-Review*'s article on August 2, 1913 discussing Davenport's announcement about the kitchen remodel, contained the following information under the subheading "novel kitchen equipment:"

> The kitchen equipment will include new apparatus for the sterilization of silver and chinaware, power-driven silver polishers, electric buffers for silver, steam cookers and vegetable peeling machines. The new dishwashing equipment, which consists of wire baskets, lined with wood, operates on a traveling belt. The dishes are placed in the basket and automatically carried through and washed in soapy water, then taken to the rinse water. The machine is only 8 feet 6 inches by 8 feet 8 inches, but it has a capacity of throwing 37 barrels of soapy water per minute on the dishes, as well as 28 barrels of rinse water, besides being sterilized by high pressure steam. The capacity is 10,000 dishes an hour.

*The silver washing department, showing the silver burnisher at the far left in 1914. The hotel's reputation for also washing the silver coins, giving them a shiny new appearance, was known far and wide. The hotel's silver service ware was also cleaned in this department, which was part of the kitchen facility in the Pennington Hotel building. (EWSHS Libby Studio photo L87-1.10814X-14)*

On January 19, 1914, the following article from the *Spokesman-Review* provided another interesting glimpse of the new kitchen features:

## CONTRACT ICING PLANT FOR HOTEL

### Buffalo Firm Will Put in Refrigerating System for Davenport.

#### WILL BE OPEN TO VIEW

### Big Glass Doors Will Permit Patrons of Dining Room to See How Foods Are Kept in Cold Storage.

Contracts for the refrigeration of the Davenport hotel and restaurant have been let by L.M. Davenport . . . . The equipment will be designed by the John Van Range company of Cincinnati, and will be made by the Jewett Refrigerating company of Buffalo, N.Y., which has made the installations in many of the best hotels in New York, Cleveland, Detroit and other cities. The cost will be approximately $15,000.

The scheme in general provides a refrigerating system, with white enamel tiled walls, red imported tile floors and sanitary tile baseboards, with natural white maple wood-work and solid polished brass trimmings. This scheme of wood, brass and white enamel will be visible to diners in the lunchroom through spacious plate glass doors, and so spotlessly clean and sanitary will be the whole interior of the kitchen and the refrigerators that the guests will be invited to inspect them. [Though perhaps modi-fied, this feature of being able to view the kitchen through a glass partition from the lunch room/coffee shop had actually been in place for many years.]

#### Will Have Display Feature.

Triple plate glass doors, providing two air chambers, will open into almost every unit of the system, so that the foods of various kinds in their containers can be seen from any position in the kitchen . . . . The interior of the large storage refrigerator for meats will be similarly lined, and all of the large compartments which can be en-tered will have the bevel sanitary tile baseboards, and locks that can be operated from within and without. Double automatic fasteners will secure every door.

One of the newest features of the system will be the extensive use of refrigeration drawers rather than compartments opening by hinged doors. This will permit of access to any class of article wanted without letting warm kitchen air into the entire unit. A sanitary precaution that will eliminate any possibility of sewer gas getting back into the cold chamber is double drainage. . . .

#### Keep All Food Chilled.

The meat, fish and vegetable boxes will be conveniently arranged near the ranges, and all food will be chilled until taken out to go onto broilers or into kettles. The fry cook will have his own set of refrigerators and the second cook another set.

A specially constructed service bar refrigerator, equipped with metal racks for holding bottles of all sizes and shapes, will adjoin the dining rooms. The present contract provides new refrigeration for the banquet service kitchen adjoining the Hall of the Doges and also for the present restaurant.

The system provides caves, drawers and compartments designed for all manner of containers, small individual milk bottles, butter, both in prints and small squares, cheese, salads, oysters, cold meats and 10 different kinds of ice cream, including special arrangements for fancy molds.

The working board and the serving counter in the kitchen will be equipped with steel tops, covered with 20-gage German silver, beneath which will be cold plate refrigerators, supplying cold plates on one side to the waiter, and on the other to the servers. All interior hooks, shelves and racks will be of metal and removable.

When the state-of-the-art kitchen was completed, it was a model of efficiency. However, Louis Davenport was never quite satisfied with it, feeling it was not centrally located to all the rooms it served. For months he sought the advice of some of the most noted hotel and kitchen experts in the country. As a result, and also because of his decision to create the Delicacy Shop along the First Avenue side of the Pennington Building, in 1916 the kitchen was remodeled again and expanded 30 feet north. In his reach for perfection, Davenport was constantly upgrading and improving his facilities.

*Cooks at work in the Davenport Hotel kitchen in 1914. The cooks are standing between the polished steel cooks' table and the range and boilers. (EWSHS Libby Studio photo L87-1.10741X-14)*

*The Davenport Hotel building site in April 1913, during the early stages of exca-vation for the hotel's foundation and two basements. The first basement would later contain, among other facilities, the Early Birds Club, the Arena Dance Hall, the billiards room and barber shop. The electrical and mechanical systems were located in the subbasement. The Pennington Hotel, along with a small portion of Davenport's Restaurant, is visible to the left. Also note the two sets of streetcar rails on both Lincoln Street and Sprague Avenue. One of the more interesting buildings in this photo is the O.K. Stables (see arrow), located on the south side of First Avenue, across from the excavation. The site is now the intended location for the Davenport Hotel's new parking garage. (EWSHS photo L87-1.2.11)*

## An Early Description of the New Davenport Hotel

In July 1913, *The Western Architect,* a national journal published monthly by the American Institute of Architects, printed the following article, entitled "**The New Davenport Hotel, Spokane. Cutter and Malmgren, Architects.**" Although the hotel was still in the early phases of construction, the article called attention to the artistry in its design and the utilization of some of the latest technology in America.

> Far out across the country in the thriving city of Spokane, where the fame of its wondrous water power, years ago, found a rival in the fame of its Davenport's Restaurant, a beautiful new monument to western progress is now building.

> There . . . the most modern hotel in the United States is climbing aloft. It is to be the Davenport Hotel.

**Louis Davenport**

*A view of the Davenport Hotel construction in 1913 from the southwest corner of Lincoln Street and First Avenue. By this time, the steel frame had reached the full 12-story height. This is one of the more illustrative photos of the construction, which shows a number of the early building trades in progress. In spite of the size and complexity of the project, from ground breaking to completion, not one person was killed or even seriously injured. Construction of the frame, which used over 42 million pounds of steel, was contracted out to Gerrick & Gerrick of Seattle. At the time, it was considered a "tradition" among structural steel workers that at least one worker was killed on every big building project. Fortunately, in this case, the tradition failed. (EWSHS Libby Studio photo L87-1.2729X-13)*

The world, all time, and the most advanced steps in science have been drawn upon to make this $2,000,000 hostelry the most complete, the most artistic and accommodating home-and-club-in-one . . . Louis M. Davenport and the other prominent citizens of the Northwest are not aping New York. They are not copying Chicago. They do not desire to make this wonderful hotel the replica of any hotel in the world.

They are building their ideal and where money and art are capable of surpassing similar existing institutions they are assuredly being surpassed.

From Florence, Italy, where Michael Angelo [sic] gave his influence to Florentine Art, comes the exterior design; . . . France contributes to the ornamentation and arrangement of the ballrooms; the lobby will look the role of silent, powerful romance, while heavily carved Spanish chests of oak . . . will serve as desks . . .; Elizabethan style in the treatment of the banquet rooms lends the English touch.

But . . . art has not been worshipped to the loss of service, for the builders know hotel patrons are not forgetful of attentions poorly given even in artistic surroundings.

The most up-to-date elevators that are installed in any building of the world is one step that has been taken with science. The use of every known safety device is promised and the movement of the big speedy cars will be without noise . . . .

Trunks will not be at the mercy of smashers, either in going to or from the Davenport Hotel. The sidewalk elevators can be raised to the level of any wagon that may back to the curb and baggage will not be dropped an inch.

The best barbershop that architects could design, with marble floors, marble pilasters separating elliptical panels in bas-relief and a vaulted ceiling; 405 large "homey" rooms; billiard rooms; a 500 foot driven well to supply the water; refrigerating plants to cool the air in summer; a heating system that washes and purifies the warm air for winter, also cleaning the air in the summer; fire escapes that are within the building and are enclosed in fireproof shafts with curtained glass doors; 50 sample rooms with baths; a regular staff of manicurists, hair dressers and chiropodists; these are some of the details that have been considered in giving service.

. . . In quiet spectacular features, there will be none from the sub-basement to the roof garden on the twelfth floor that will excel the effect of the moonlight scene in the marvelous patio, which is the lobby. The walls and huge square columns of the lobby will be in Caen stone, and the beams above will be of fireproof material representing carved oak.

Upon this the glass of the skylight will cast a mackerel shade. The arbor effect will be present and at night whether the moon be out to the rest of the world or not, the Davenport Hotel will have moonlight. By means of a large automatic silver arc the patio will be flooded with these moonbeams and the "moon" will travel its course from east to west each night, taking several hours to at last disappear in the west.

*The spacious 4200-square-foot Davenport Hotel lobby in 1916, looking west toward Lincoln Street. (EWSHS Libby Studio photo L87-1.12758X-16)*

From without, the great building covering a block of ground will present a dazzling appearance, especially so at night. The first two stories will be of beautiful white stone and the remaining stories will be of brick with terra cotta trimmings and polychrome effect. Thirty-eight Florentine lamps, each set on twelve foot piers, will surround the building and at each entrance will be clusters of bracket lamps. Each marquise [marquee] will have special lighting and the cresting of the cornices will also have special indirect lighting from concave ornaments decorated with gold leaf at three foot intervals.

. . . Little touches such as fountains scattered here and there, a great massive stone fire-place in the lobby, alabaster urns, bronze lanterns, bronze sconces placed in attractive corners, the great Isabelle [*sic*] dining room with its eight spiral columns, its seven and one-half foot oak wainscoting and the beautiful orchestra niche, the ornate splendor of the ebony finish and oriental grandeur of the men's cafe, are all stories in themselves which must be hurried over.

This wonderful hotel was begun last September [1912]. Steel workers are now playing about at a height of several stories, after the entire block had been razed and a 30 foot excavation in rock had been made. . . .

## Building the Hotel,
## The Contractors and Suppliers

A statement in the newspaper just prior to the Davenport Hotel's opening placed its importance to the Inland Northwest second only to the arrival of the first railroad in the early 1880s. The railways, and especially Great Northern Railroad president Louis W. Hill, were among the most fervent proponents and supporters of the new hotel and eagerly followed its development. The primary delay in Hill's development of his Great Northern hotels in Glacier Park, and the local tourist industry in general, had been a lack of adequate hotel facilities at some central point. Hill was certain the park and the hotel together would attract heavy tourist trade through Spokane.

Construction of the hotel, from the ground breaking in 1912 to its completion in 1914, was one of Spokane's major news topics. Throughout the entire project, the newspapers chronicled its progress, providing minute details to an eager public. Two days prior to the hotel's opening on September 1, 1914, the *Spokesman-Review* ran a 10-page section devoted entirely to descriptions of the hotel, with its many unique features, and advertisements placed by the hotel's contractors and suppliers eager to capitalize on the great advertising exposure.

Many of those articles, or excerpts thereof, are included in this publication, not only for their content, but also because the firsthand accounts provide insights into the excitement created by the project and Louie Davenport's personal involvement in the process. They also offer the reader an opportunity to experience the step-by-step progress much the same as Inland Northwest residents did in 1913 and 1914.

As clearly evidenced by the frequent use of adjectives in the following articles, such as "finest," "largest," and "latest," Davenport was committed to applying the most advanced proven technology in the hotel's operational systems and using the best materials and most skilled workmanship money could buy. He sought the advice of experts, all the while conferring with his friend and business associate, architect Kirtland Cutter, whose artistry created a little piece of Europe in the heart of Spokane – where one could be transported to another place or time.

One of Spokane's leading artists, Melville Holmes, instrumentally involved in the present hotel restoration, spoke thoughtfully about the Davenport's role in Spokane and Cutter's involvement. According to Holmes, Cutter drew from his studies abroad, creating room designs reminiscent of Europe, but "combining elements in a unique way that were definitely not reproductions." Regarding the hotel's role, he stated: "There was something this city once was because of the Davenport that it was not able to be without it. Intrinsic humane values are tied up with this institution."

# All the following articles appeared in the *Spokesman-Review*:

July 10, 1913
## AWARDS, $225,000, MADE ON HOTEL
———————

## New Davenport Contracts for Marble, Plastering, Cabinet Features.
———————

### GETS FAMOUS FIRMS

Contracts aggregating $225,000, and including some of the finest features of the new $2,000,000 Davenport hotel . . . have been let within the last few days, according to the announcement yesterday of H.L. Harrison, superintendent of construction for the Brayton Engineering company, which has the general contract for the big hostelry. The latest contracts to be awarded are the interior cabinet finish, the interior marble, the exterior and interior painting, not covered by the cabinet contract, and the plastering and plaster ornament contract.

### Plastering to Cost $85,000.
The largest individual contract in those just awarded is the plastering contract, amounting to approximately $85,000. This job was given to J.J. Tinker of Seattle. The contract takes in the entire plastering of all the walls and ceilings and the modeling of the ornamental plaster. The latter will not be the conventional stock casts, but will be special designs evolved by skilled workmen on the building and molded by them directly on the walls and ceiling or wherever the plans call for them.

### For Interior Painting, $15,000.
The interior painting will be done by D. Zelinsky of San Francisco, reputed to be the greatest mural decorator in western America. The contract runs close to $15,000, including all the interior painting not taken care of by the interior cabinet finish contract. Zelinsky will not do the mural decorations for the big hotel, in fact there will be little of this done, and this will be covered by a separate contract.

### Vermont Marble, $50,000.
The marble contract, amounting to approximately $50,000, has been awarded to the Vermont Marble company of Tacoma, one of the largest marble producers in the world, operating quarries in Vermont, in Alaska and in other sections of the country.

White statuary marble, the most beautiful and most expensive possible to obtain, will be brought from the famous Vermont quarries and will be used in the pilasters and wainscotings on every floor, including the lobby, main corridor, walls and stairways.

The walls of the [Pompeiian] barber shop in the basement will also be of this spotless statuary marble. The steps and stairs and the balcony and ball room will be in light cloud Vermont marble, while the floors will be of pink Tennessee marble, with borders of multi-colored marble from the quarries of the Green Mountain state.

## Cabinet Finish to Cost $75,000

The contract for the interior cabinet finish will run close to $75,000, and has been awarded to Matthews Brothers of Milwaukee, probably the largest cabinet finishing manufacturers in the middle west. . . .

This contract includes all interior cabinet work for the entire building, with the exception of a few serving rooms, which will be done locally by the King Sash & Door company. The woodwork will be in mahogany and gumwood. The office and basement will be finished in oak, the other woods being used in the remaining floors.

Every door, window casing and piece of wood to be used will be completely finished and rubbed in the eastern factory and fitted ready for rapid installation as soon as it arrives in Spokane and the building is ready for it. The unsurpassed facilities of the company at its home plant make it desirable to have as much of the work done there as is feasible to insure the very finest workmanship. As each piece is completed in Milwaukee it will be wrapped in tissue paper and shipped to Spokane in a manner to preclude the possibility of the slightest injury en route.

July 20, 1913
## FOR ICE WATER IN NEW HOTEL, $25,000

### Davenport Contract Let Yesterday Provides for Over 25,000 Feet of Pipe.

#### HAS 25-HORSEPOWER PUMP

### Unique Feature Includes Latest Ideas in Hotel Construction.

. . . the distilled, refrigerated, circulating well water service of the new Davenport hotel will be one of the most unique and also one of the most important features of the many innovations of the hotel service. The service will cost the hotel company $25,000 for its installation alone and the James Smyth Plumbing company of Spokane has been awarded most of the work of installing it . . . .

#### Will Pipe Entire Building.

The company, which is also doing the plumbing work for the entire hotel, will not install the refrigerating machine or the pump and tanks, as these are covered in another contract to be awarded later, but will pipe the entire building for this service and will also install the insulation of the pipes. In this connection some interesting facts are given by Mr. Davenport.

#### To Use 30,000 Feet of Pipe.

To install the service 25,000 to 30,000 feet of pipe will be necessary. Every inch of this will be insulated with a cork casing, an inch and a half in thickness. A 25 horsepower pump will be put in the subbasement, with a capacity of 150 gallons a minute.

This will pump the water from the private well of the hotel into a big tank in the subbasement. This tank will be cooled by ammonia coils to a temperature of 40 degrees. A thermostat will keep the water at an even temperature. The water will then be pumped through a large pipe to the top of the building, where it will pass through a large bypass and from it will be forced into every room of the hotel. So perfect is the insulation to be that the water will return to the subbasement tank only one or two degrees warmer than when it left, or about 41 to 43 degrees.

### Change Supply Every Four Minutes.

The pumps will force water through to change the entire supply every four minutes, the pipes having a capacity of 600 gallons. Fresh ice water will therefore be on tap every minute of each 24 hours.

Specially designed faucets will be in every room so that the guest can have ice water at all times without ringing for a bellboy and paying the customary fee. The service will be instantaneous and there will be no necessity for letting the water run.

. . . Work of drilling the well to supply the system is proceeding. The Keystone Well Drilling company, which is doing the work under the management of J.H. Harris, has already reached a depth of 220 feet through solid rock. The company uses a drill that weighs 2500 pounds. A good supply of water has been obtained already, but drilling will continue to insure an abundant supply for all purposes. [Another account indicated the hotel would use both city and well water.]

July 20, 1913 (the following was a photo caption)
### Steel for Davenport Hotel Goes Up Fast

The skeleton of the new Davenport hotel is rapidly taking shape, and L.M. Davenport of the company announced yesterday that the steel work would be finished within two weeks. The highest columns already reach to the ninth floor and the work is progressing favorably.

On the lower floors carpenters are busy building the forms for the concrete enforcement of the structure. Every column, beam and girder in the entire structure will be covered with cement to a considerable thickness. The cement covering insures the steel against the attacks of moisture and increases its permanency, in addition to giving fire protection. The firm of Gerrick & Gerrick is doing the steel work, under the direction of H.L. Harrison, superintendent of construction of the Brayton Engineering company, which has the general contract.

August 22, 1913
### BALLROOM FLOOR SET ON SPRINGS
———————

### New Hotel to Also Have Roof Garden Ornately Decorated –
### Work Out Details

. . . A swinging, springing ballroom floor [in the Marie Antoinette Room] 85 feet long and 47 feet wide will be one of the most novel features of the new Davenport hotel. A roof garden 200 feet long by 50 feet wide, on the First avenue side, which is three stories high, is another feature announced by L.M. Davenport, president of the hotel company, for the first time yesterday.

Neither feature was included in the original plan of the hotel and both were decided upon yesterday after several of the directors had accompanied Mr. Davenport on their first tour of inspection of the hotel in its present condition. Both ballroom and roof garden will be on the First avenue side, where the steel work and concrete reinforcing is already completed. When the possibilities for the special features were pointed out the directors readily concurred and the details of the new ideas will be worked out immediately.

### Ballroom on Springs.

The ballroom on springs construction is the last word in building construction and is said to lend a buoyancy and exhilaration to the terpsichorean art that is impossible on the ordinary "dead" floor. The "live" floor has been used slightly in the east in private ball rooms, but so far as is known never on so large a scale as is contemplated by the hotel company.

The floor is suspended on resilient steel cables, made of a special steel, and the general principle is along the line of the suspension bridge, common in railroad construction. The floor is perfectly smooth and rigid, but under the rhythmic motions of the dancers gradually adapts itself to the movements and sways slightly, but quite noticeably, with a mild dreamy ocean wave effect.

### Ornate Decoration.

In addition to its novel springing nature the floor will be of the finest selected hardwood, laid in an artistic herringbone pattern. There will not be a post in the entire room to interfere with the dancers. The unique ballroom will be off the mezzanine floor at the southeast corner of the hotel and a balcony will surround it. It will also be the banquet hall when not in use for dancing. The suspended nature of the floor will not be apparent except when dancing is in progress, as the vibration is necessary to produce the right effect.

The formal garden will take up the entire roof over the third floor on the First avenue side. It will be treated in artistic fashion with pergolas, fountains, special lights, flower boxes and vines. It will be reached from the east and west corridors on the fourth floor of the hotel proper. It overlooks the lobby and will be about level with its roof.

Trees and shrubs will be set about the garden and at night ornate lights on pedestals every 15 feet around the edge of the roof will transform it into a fairyland. The garden will be used as a promenade in the open air while dancing is on, as it is easily reached from the ballroom. It will be a general resting spot and also a place for afternoon teas and similar functions in favorable weather.

October 17, 1913
## DAVENPORT HOTEL TILE COSTS $25,000

In the new Davenport hotel 240,000 pounds of tile will be used and the contract for this amount, aggregating approximately $25,000, was awarded yesterday to the Empire Tile and Mantel company, 824 Sprague avenue, directly opposite the new hotel. About six carloads of the very finest tile procurable will be used in the hotel.

The order is the largest tile order ever placed west of the Mississippi river and north of San Francisco. . . .

**Use New Patterns.**
The contract includes all of the tile for the entire hotel with the exception of the tile used in the marble floor of the main lobby. It includes bathrooms, maids' and servants' closets, retiring rooms for men and women on the mezzanine floor, and the dressing rooms on the main floor . . . . In all 350 rooms will be tiled.

In the bathrooms the new herringbone pattern in a ceramic mosaic will be followed. . . . The wainscoting in the bathrooms will be of white tile . . . .

. . . The hotel company is striving to make its bathrooms unsurpassed anywhere in the country and to this end has contracted for the finest tile available.

*The men's room in the basement of the Davenport Hotel in 1915. The September 1915 issue of The Hotel Monthly said the rest rooms included "a feature that no other hotel in the world has adopted, we believe. That is, potted plants and flowers in every public lavatory in the hotel. And in the men's lavatory the north wall is surmounted with an aquarium extending the length of the room . . . ." (EWSHS Libby Studio photo L87-1.11731X-15)*

November 23, 1913
# NOTED DECORATOR FOR LOCAL HOTEL

## E.J. Holslag Gets Contract for Interior Art Work of Davenport . . .

The contract for the interior decorative work of the Davenport hotel was awarded yesterday to Edward J. Holslag of Holslag & Co. of Chicago. Mr. Holslag and his personal representative, J.W.S. Brintnall, were in the city yesterday in conference with L.M. Davenport, president of the hotel company, and K.K. Cutter, architect of the hotel. While the contract figure has not been made public, the prominence of Mr. Holslag in his profession makes the price a fancy one and it will run into the thousands.

Mr. Holslag is a member of the American Society of Mural Painters and was the decorator of the congressional library in Washington, D.C., and also the Congress hotel in Chicago and the Annex hotel. Recently he secured the contract for the decorating of the United States National bank and the Northwestern National bank in Portland. He has decorated many prominent hotels, banks, public buildings and libraries and some of his mural paintings have been widely copied. He worked three years and a half on the congressional library.

### For First Two Floors.
His contract calls for all the decorating on the first two floors of the hotel . . . .

"The lobby of the Davenport hotel will be unique and nothing like it has ever been done in the United States," said Mr. Holslag, yesterday. "It is destined to be the best-known hotel lobby west of Chicago, and none in America will be ahead of it. Even those of New York and Chicago hotels are smaller."

Mr. Holslag will do the lobby in a beautiful treatment, following the Spanish renaissance. The walls will be in Caen stone and the ceiling will be done in soft blues and red and illuminated with gold. It will be artistic and restful. The decorations will accentuate its size. The lighting will be in keeping, of a gold and color combination, with jeweled effects in the lights. The whole will in effect be the transposition to Spokane of an old Spanish baronial castle entrance.

### Blue and Silver Gray.
The walls of the dining room [the Isabella Room] will be in Caen stone also. The frieze and ornamental plaster will be in a color combination of gold and rose. Soft blue will be used against the silver-gray woodwork, in a cameo effect. The ceiling will be in soft ivory and gray, with a mottled effect. The carpet will be old rose, with a rose-gray diaper pattern. The draperies will be of natural linen, with the valances in old rose and bordered with gold appliqued on the valances.

The ladies' waiting room will be finished in mulberry with cameo colorings, and touches of gold. The furniture will be of the Adams period, with the upholstering in keeping with the color scheme.

The buffet will be a Chino-Japanese room, with a Chinese bar, reproducing a Chinese interior [the Chinese Buffet was a men's bar]. Cypress wood will be used and will be illuminated in Chinese interlaced ornaments, in Chinese colors, and embossed gold paper will be used. It will have many unique features and the color detail will be much out of ordinary.

### Ballroom in Gray and Ivory.

The ballroom [the Marie Antoinette Room] will be decorated in a gray and ivory with cameo effects. The balustrade will be of powdered gold. The lights will be crystal glass chandeliers, with as many as 3000 separate pieces of glass in a light.

The committee rooms will be in the Elizabethan period, with finely decorated wainscotings, true to the period. They will have illuminated shields at intervals bearing the arms of Henry VIII. The state suite, the ladies' room, the men's smoking room and the corridors will be decorated in a style harmonizing with the general motif.

Mr. Holslag will personally take charge of the work. It is estimated that its completion will require three months, with from 50 to 100 men working all the time.

*The Old National Bank's "$20 Million" Celebration, October 23, 1919, in the Marie Antoinette Room. The elegant 3108-square-foot ballroom was originally decorated in ivory, French gray, light shades of rose and blue, and accented by the gold and gray mezzanine railing. Below the railing, medallions of court jesters are reflective of the Marie Antoinette period. The huge crystal chandeliers provide a crowning touch. The vibration of dancers on the ballroom floor, which is suspended on cables, creates a slight wave effect. (Libby Studio photo courtesy Walt and Karen Worthy.)*

December 21, 1913
# SILVER FOR HOTEL IS 15,886 PIECES

----------

## Order for Davenport Includes Table Requirements, Candelabras, Tea and Buffet Service.

----------

### ENGRAVED NAME, CREST

. . . In the silver service of the Davenport hotel dining rooms and banquet halls 15,886 separate pieces will be utilized. The contract, one of the largest furnishing contracts, has been awarded to the well-known silversmiths, Reed & Barton of Taunton, Mass., according to the announcement of L.M. Davenport . . .

The service will be one of the most beautiful ever placed in any hotel, and among the pieces are large banquet candelabras, banquet urns and pitchers, special chafing dish service, special five o'clock tea service, buffet service, punch bowls and many magnificent pieces.

### Crest, Name, on Each Piece.

Every one of the 15,886 pieces will be engraved with the crest of the hotel and the name "Davenport." The silversmiths make a specialty of exclusive designs, but the hotel silver service will be a departure from anything yet produced by them. The pieces will be given individual shapes and will all be entirely outside the uniform line of silverware. In some a design similar to that of the Haviland china will be followed.

When the silver service arrives in Spokane Mr. Davenport will arrange to have it on display where citizens and friends and patrons of the hotel company can view it.

The firm of Reed & Barton has made silver services for some of the most exclusive hotels and clubs in the country. Conspicuous in a long list of hotels are: La Touraine, Boston; Belmont, New York; Manhattan, New York; Congress, Chicago; Sherman, Chicago; Hotel Utah, Salt Lake; Palace, San Francisco; St. Francis, San Francisco; Fairmount, San Francisco; Hotel Alexandria, Los Angeles. In addition many railroad and steamship lines, cafes and transportation companies throughout the country have silver services from this firms workshops.

### Elaborate Garden Designs.

Mr. Davenport stated yesterday that a number of elaborate designs for the hotel roof garden have been drawn by James Frederick Dawson of Olmsted Brothers, during a recent visit to the city, and the hotel company has decided to make this one of the distinct features of the hotel.

Mr. Davenport will leave for the east this week on business connected with the hotel and among other things will place the contract for the Haviland china service.

*A typical Davenport Hotel table setting, in this case for a wedding reception in the Elizabethan Banquet Room in 1917, displaying a sampling of the silver and china. The 2250-square-foot banquet hall, located on the mezzanine opposite the Marie Antoinette Room, was designed to be partitioned into two or three rooms by means of accordion doors to accommodate parties of 20 to 150. As the name implies, the artistry in this room represents the Elizabethan era. It is paneled in English oak featuring a frieze of heraldic crest carvings. (Libby photo courtesy Walt and Karen Worthy.)*

December 23, 1913
## TENNIS COURT ON BIG HOTEL ROOF

---

### Only One in World so High Above Ground, Says L.M. Davenport.

---

#### MAY ALSO PLAY HANDBALL

---

### Promenade, Eight Laps to the Mile, Around Edge – Playground for Children.

A tennis court, 48 feet wide and 155 long, a large handball court, a playground for children, with complete apparatus of every kind, including sand piles, and a promenade, eight laps to the mile, will be unique features of the main roof of the Davenport hotel, 12 stories above the street. These will be entirely separate and distinct from the roof garden of the hotel on the First avenue side, which will be three stories from the street.

The tennis court and the handball court, according to L.M. Davenport, will be the only ones in the world on a roof higher than 10 stories. The tennis court will be built on the west wing of the hotel roof.

#### High Netting to Save Balls.

The handball court will be just east of the central penthouse, and the playground will be in the east wing, surrounding the east penthouse. The courts will be surrounded with high netting to keep balls from going over the edge of the roof, and the entire roof edge will be safeguarded with girder rails. The walk around the roof at the edge will provide ample space for an early morning constitutional with an unsurpassed view of the city in every direction.

At night the roof will be illumined with 40 standards, already erected at intervals about the roof edge. These are eight feet high and will be surmounted with ornate post lights. In addition, lights will outline the scallops of the penthouse roof and each point will be capped with a florentine torch.

#### Big Lanterns Around Second Story.

The contract for the exterior lighting fixtures at the second story level has been awarded to the Spokane Ornamental Iron Works. These consist of 41 immense lanterns, spaced about the three street fronts of the hotel at regular intervals on the piers. Each lantern will be 22 inches in diameter and five feet high over all.

The roof lights will be in operation within 10 days. For the first time in over a year the Sprague avenue sidewalk in front of the hotel will be open Christmas eve. The Lincoln street walk is already cleared.

*The Davenport Hotel roof garden, showing the putting green, in 1916. The woman at the far left is Verus Davenport and at the tee is Mrs. Frederick Mason. The other women are Mrs. C.R. Smith of New York, Mrs. Kirtland (Katharine Phillips) Cutter and Mrs. Jerome (Grace Child) Drumheller. In addition to the golf course, the roof garden also had tennis and handball courts, a dance pavilion and a small stage for entertainment. (EWSHS Libby Studio photo L87-1.12424X-16)*

January 9, 1914
## HOTEL ICE PLANT BY SPOKANE FIRM

### Armstrong Company Given Refrigeration Contract at the Davenport After Wide Quest.

### To Provide System for Garbage Freezing Not Used Except in New York.

After considering tenders from ice machine manufacturers all over the country L.M. Davenport . . . announced that the contract for the refrigeration plant of the new hotel had been awarded to the Armstrong Machinery company of Spokane. . . .

The company will install a 40-ton refrigerating plant which will do the refrigerating for the entire hotel, make all the ice, freeze the garbage, cool the water for the circulating ice water system in every room, refrigerate the wines and foods, and generally give the broadest application of the refrigeration idea ever made in connection with a hotel.

**Clarified Water for Ice.**

It will have a capacity to supply and will be connected with the washed air chambers and will cool the lobbies, basement, mezzanine floor, the ballroom, banquet room, committee rooms, billiard rooms, barber shop and women's retiring room. It will also provide cooling facilities for the florist and fur store . . . .

A new system will be introduced whereby air is pumped into the water to be frozen to clarify it, giving a perfectly clear, crystal, slow-melting ice. It will have capacity to care for the extra wing of the hotel when that is built in the future. The ice machine will be operated in the subbasement by four modern, high-power, slow-speed motors.

**To Freeze All Garbage.**

The plant will have the most direct application of power. The tanks will be of heavy steel, one-quarter inch thick, instead of wood, as is often used, and these will be cork insulated. All garbage will be sent out frozen, and this system has been adopted by no hotels in the world outside of New York. By the plan, all fermentation and odors are eliminated.

"We are pleased to think that a home concern could successfully compete against the whole country," said Stanley Mayall, secretary-manager of the Armstrong Machinery company. "We are specializing in this style of ice machine. This year we installed four plants in jails in Oregon and Montana, a number for Swift & Co., and the state agricultural college of Oregon at Corvallis uses one of our machines . . . ."

February 8, 1914
### HOTEL FURNITURE BEING SELECTED

————————

**President Davenport, Architect Cutter and Buying
Commissioner Now at Grand Rapids.**

. . . L.M. Davenport, president of the Davenport hotel building company, and K.K. Cutter, architect of the structure, are in Grand Rapids, Mich., the center of the furniture manufacturing industry of the United States, looking over stocks and making selections for the new hotel. They are accompanied by R.B Paterson, president of the Spokane Dry Goods company [company name was used interchangeably with The Crescent in a future article, but this was the wholesale business and The Crescent its retail store], through which all the furnishings are being bought.

The hotel officials expect to spend approximately $200,000 on furniture and furnishings while in the east. Most of the goods will be bought in New York, where the party will go after finishing their work in Grand Rapids. . . .

The exterior of the hotel is practically finished. All the plate glass windows are in, the Lincoln street entrance ornamental ironwork is in place and the marquises over the Sprague and First avenue entrances have been constructed. The store rooms on the ground floor are ready for occupancy . . . .

February 24, 1914
# RARE FURNITURE TO EQUIP HOTEL

----

## England, Germany, Austria, Ireland Called On by Davenport's.

----

### NEW DESIGNS CREATED

----

## French Curtains and Draperies Coming – Buying Party in New York.

After a month at the New York office, R.B. Paterson, president of the Spokane Dry Goods company, returned Sunday. Mr. Paterson went east with L.M. Davenport, president of the Davenport Hotel Building company; K.K. Cutter, the architect, and Oscar Burg, manager of the carpet department of the Crescent store, in connection with the purchase of the hotel furnishings, all of which are being purchased through the Crescent store [retail store associated with Spokane Dry Goods Company].

"The work of assembling the furnishing for the Davenport hotel is progressing satisfactorily," said Mr. Paterson yesterday, "the facilities of our New York office and our foreign connections being at the command of Mr. Davenport, Mr. Cutter and Mr. Burg. With Mr. Davenport's well known good taste and practical ideas, Mr. Cutter's experience and artistic perceptions, and Mr. Burg's cleverness and knowledge of the best sources of supply, the public may be assured that the Davenport hotel, in it appointments, will present a rare blending of practicability, luxuriousness and elegance.

### New Designs in Furniture.

"The furniture will naturally come principally from Grand Rapids, where the best designers and cabinet makers have worked out some new designs, embodying some of Mr. Cutter's ideas and creating examples of great charm and distinction. Some of the best furniture houses of New York and Boston will also contribute from their collections.

"China and glass will come from England, Germany and Austria, and has been selected with great care and discriminating taste. Linens are already in the looms of two of the best manufacturers of Belfast, weaving a special design, including the hotel crest.

"Curtains and draperies are being supplied by French manufacturers and in part by high-class domestic producers. Carpets are all of special design and colorings, calling out the skill of the best New England makers, while many hand-tufted and other special rugs, designed for various parts of the big hostelry, are being made in Scotland and Austria. The party will doubtless be in New York two weeks more."

. . . "A strong tone of confidence in improving business conditions is now noticeable throughout the east and the same is spreading over the whole country. . . ."

May 9, 1914
## DECORATORS BUSY IN THE DAVENPORT

. . . Twenty-five skilled decorators are busy on the interior of the Davenport hotel. The work is being done under the personal supervision of E.J. Holsclag [*sic,* should be Holslag], one of the foremost mural decorators of the United States. Mr. Holsclag's contract calls for the decorations of all the public rooms, including the lobby, cafe, dining room, ballroom, committee rooms and the women's retiring rooms.

### Color Scheme Determined.
The preliminary work yesterday involved the determination of the color scheme to be followed in the lobby. A small section of one of the big ceilings beams and wall has been selected for this purpose. Various experiments are being made on this section, which has been surrounded by the actual glass and lighting to be used in the finished lobby, that the correct tones may be secured. The beam is heavily ornamented with crests of the Spanish nobility set at intervals. The whole will be treated to give the effect of century old oak beams, colored in rich reds, blues and golds of the Spanish renaissance, with the effect of illuminations on oak beams.

Mr. Holsclag, K.K. Cutter, architect of the hotel, and L.M. Davenport watched the experimental work yesterday and decided on the tones required. Mr. Holsclag decides the color schemes of all the public rooms and will be in the city a great deal of the time the work is under way. Einar Peterson, his assistant, is the foreman in charge. Mr. Holsclag at present is decorating two banks in Portland and a church in Seattle.

*The 3108-square-foot Isabella Dining Room in 1916. The decor was Spanish Renaissance, but without the Moorish influence seen in the Lobby. The decorative frieze encircling the room and across the ceiling beams displayed a continuous array of boys, birds, rabbits, foxes, turtles and other living things. (EWSHS Libby Studio photo L87-1-12479X-16)*

*A view of the lobby, looking north towards the clerk's desk, in 1915. The design was Spanish Renaissance with Moorish influence. Four twisted bronze column lamps, decorated with entwining grapevines and topped with alabaster shells (foreground), were later removed because of the difficulties they presented in arranging tables for banquets held in the lobby. (EWSHS photo L84-207.4.8)*

### Lobby Design Original.

"The lobby of the Davenport hotel is entirely original and unique and no hotel anywhere has the same conception and the same architectural feeling," said Mr. Holsclag. "All the rugs and fabrics are specially designed and manufactured abroad. The covering of the furniture are reproductions of tapestries now being made specially for the hotel. The furniture itself will be an absolute reproduction of antique models in Madrid and other Spanish museums. The lighting fixtures will be of burnished gold, toned down to an antique effect and illuminated. The effect is to give the idea of age rather than of newness.

"The ballroom will be in ivory and gray with old ivory predominating. The draperies will be in antique rose brocaded, with carpet of gray. The balcony rail will be gold, festooned with a silken tassel and rope effect.

"The dining room will be in cerise and ivory. The carpet is of special design, with an allover pattern in cerise and black. The draperies here are of a lighter cerise silk brocade. The banquet hall will be of the early English period, with a high oak wainscoting, emblazoned in the arms of the English nobility. . . .

## May 28, 1914
## COSTLY CARPETS COME FOR HOTEL

---

### Rugs 18 by 35 Feet Woven on Hand Looms in Austria.

---

### WEIGH NEARLY HALF TON

---

### Furnishing of Davenport Hostelry Installed Fast
### as Builders Complete.

The first shipments of the 25,000 yards of carpet required for the new Davenport hotel have been received by the Crescent store, which has the contract for the furnishings and furniture of Spokane's new hostelry.

O.J.W. Burg, manager of the furniture, carpet and drapery sections of the Crescent, who has charge of installing the furnishings, said yesterday: "The carpets and rugs alone amount to two and a half carloads. This first shipment contained the four immense rugs for the lobby. These were made in Austria on hand looms. Each is 18 by 35 feet, and is woven in one piece. Each knot in the pile or surface is hand tied, much after the fashion of oriental rugs. This class of work is not produced in America.

#### Design Is Chinese.
"The design is Chinese fret work, intertwined with floral work on a soft, dark blue background. Both pattern and colorings are designed to blend and harmonize with the general interior scheme of the lobby decorations. The carpets are exceedingly thick and heavy, each one weighing 900 pounds, or nearly half a ton.

"In the same shipment was received the carpet for the state suite. This is a specially woven Austrian axminster in a soft plain pearl gray. This carpet is woven 12 feet wide and is thought to be the first of this width ever brought to the city.

"The first carload of Bigelow carpets for the guest rooms and halls of the hotel has been received and the work of making it up will begin in the Crescent shops this week.

"It is planned to have all the furnishings ready to install as fast as the builders complete their work. This work is being done in the Crescent shops and will give steady employment to a large number of Spokane men and women until the hotel is opened."

Long hours were spent to bring the project to completion and prepare the hotel for its grand opening celebration on September 17-19, 1914. Due to a number of demands, however, the hotel actually opened for business on September 1. Two days prior, a 10-page spread in the newspaper highlighted the many outstanding features of the new hotel. Some of the more interesting items that were not described in the previous articles discussed the operational systems and the emphasis placed on safety measures and the comfort of the guests.

*The Davenport Hotel, from the corner of Sprague Avenue and Lincoln Street, following the hotel's completion in 1914. The hotel, with approximately 400 guest rooms, and Davenport's Restaurant facilities (the Wilson and Pennington buildings) occupied the entire block bounded by Sprague, Lincoln, First and Post. At completion, the hotel stood 12-stories high on the Sprague portion of the block, but, as can be seen at the right, was only three stories on First Avenue. Subsequent additions have altered its appearance along First Avenue. The design is of Italian Renaissance influence, with the upper floors reflective of an Italian Palazzo. The base of the exterior is faced in Boise sandstone and the remaining floors are of red brick with terra cotta trim. (Photo courtesy Spokane Public Library.)*

## Safety, Comfort and Convenience Come First

U pon entering the Davenport Hotel, guests are awed by the expansive beauty and ornamentation that fill their view. Less obvious, but of greater importance, are the features that contribute to functionality, cleanliness and safety.

Fireproofing was of primary importance and the hotel was as fireproof as modern construction could provide. The walls from the basement to the penthouse contained hollow clay partition tile, which had been tested to 3500 degrees without cracking or allowing flames to penetrate, and the floors throughout the building were reinforced concrete. In the subbasement, where the engine rooms, boilers, machinery and flammable materials were located, an automatic sprinkling system was installed that would essentially flood the basement in the event of a fire.

The heating and ventilation systems were state-of-the-art. The Davenport was one of the first hotels to be fully air-conditioned. The ventilation system could produce a complete change of air in the public rooms every six minutes if necessary, which ensured no lingering smells. The ventilation and steam heating systems, automatically controlled by thermostats, were described in some detail in the *Spokesman-Review* on August 30, 1914, an excerpt of which follows:

> The air is brought from the roof to a tunnel in the subbasement. Here it is forced through a strong spray of water and thoroughly cleansed. . . . After being forced through the spray the air passes through eliminators and the water is removed. From the eliminators it passes to the supply fan, capable of handling 80,000 cubic feet of air a minute, and by the fan is shoved through the heating coils and warmed to the desired temperature.

Louis Davenport rigidly adhered to a high standard of cleanliness, so naturally the vacuum cleaning system installed in the hotel was of the highest quality. The newspaper described it as follows:

> It has . . . force sufficient to take the dust off the floor through two thicknesses of heavy wilton carpet. All surfaces will be cleaned by this system, including walls, ceilings, floors, rugs . . . This system is valuable not only because of the magic swiftness and thoroughness with which it snatches away all traces of dust and dirt, but because of its sanitary features. So terrific is the suction exerted that no germs, no matter how small, could cling to fabric or floor where the cleaners have touched.

Two other features were the installation of 450 telephones, resulting in the largest private branch exchange in the Northwest, and the 20 ornamented clocks installed in the various public rooms. Each clock contained a mechanism that operated electrically from a single clock movement in the engine room of the hotel.

*The Sprague Avenue entrance in 1915. A special bus (left), emblazoned with "Davenport Hotel" and the Davenport crest, transported hotel guests to and from the train depot. Although travel by automobile was becoming more commonplace, many patrons arrived by train. When the hotel opened, the city streets were two-way, but subsequent changes resulted in one-way streets bordering the hotel. Passengers being dropped off at the main entrances at Sprague or First exit the vehicle in traffic lanes. (Libby Studio photo courtesy Louis and Nita Davenport III.)*

Only a year and a half after opening the hotel, Louis Davenport was again making improvements. As mentioned earlier, in 1916 the kitchen was remodeled again to make room for the Davenport Delicacy Shop, a charming little restaurant along First Avenue designed by architect G.A. Pehrson. Its focus was catering to the lunch crowd and offering the hotel's "table delicacies of distinctive and appetizing excellence" for "home consumption," as Davenport reported to the newspaper on April 23, 1916.

The need for more guest rooms resulted in the addition of a 13th floor early in 1917, providing another 53 rooms. The 12th floor had been occupied primarily by sample rooms and housekeeping; upon completion of the new addition, the entire housekeeping department was moved to the 13th floor. That year, the hotel also installed an in-house laundry under the direct management of Herbert L. Douglas, who later became the hotel's assistant manager until his retirement in 1945. At the time of setting up the new department, Davenport estimated the laundry, including that of the guests, amounted to 20,000 pieces a day. In addition to the cost savings, this addition represented another way to provide better guest service.

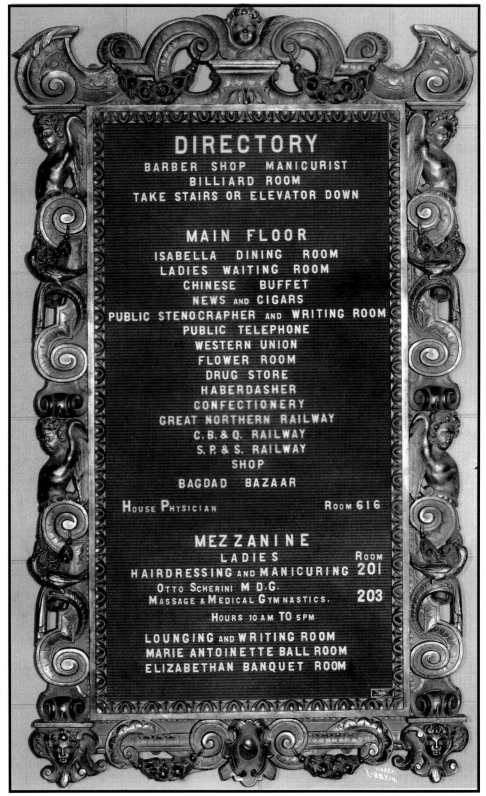

*1914 Davenport Hotel Directory. (Courtesy Walt and Karen Worthy.)*

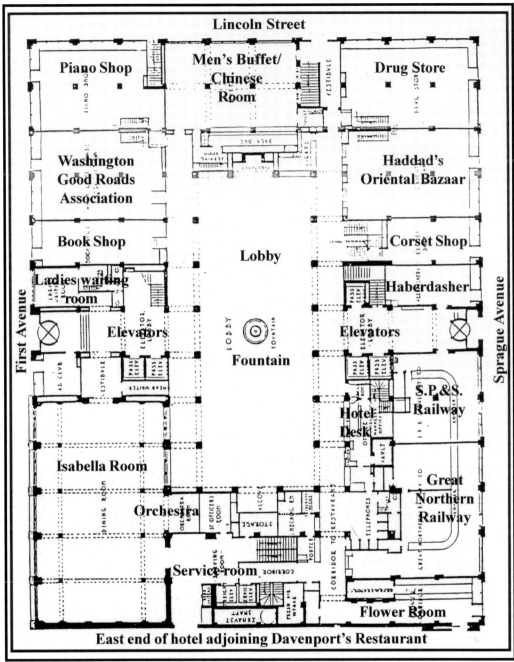

**Lincoln Street**

Piano Shop

Men's Buffet/
Chinese
Room

Drug Store

Washington
Good Roads
Association

Haddad's
Oriental Bazaar

Book Shop

Lobby

Corset Shop

Ladies waiting
room

Haberdasher

Elevators

LOBBY

Fountain

Elevators

First Avenue

Sprague Avenue

Fountain

S.P.&S.
Railway

Hotel
Desk

Isabella Room

Great
Northern
Railway

Orchestra

Service room

Flower Room

**East end of hotel adjoining Davenport's Restaurant**

*A 1914 preliminary floor plan of the Davenport Hotel's main floor with the antici-
pated tenants and some of the hotel facility locations marked. Over the years, there
were many changes in tenants and numerous remodeling projects to accommodate
their needs. Because of their beauty and capacity to accommodate large gatherings
of people, the most popular facilities in the Davenport Hotel on the main floor were
the lobby and Isabella Room. The lobby was used for multiple purposes, as evident
from the following photos. In addition to its primary function, the lobby was also
used for banquets and various types of meetings. (Drawing courtesy Gary Zagelow.)*

*Stoking the fire in the lobby fireplace, March 1919. Except for unusual occurrences, such as back drafts forcing smoke into the lobby, Davenport's standing order to "never let the fire go out" was followed. The fireplace became a common meeting spot; all a person needed to say was "Meet me by the fireplace" and it was understood to be this one. (Libby Studio photo courtesy Louis and Nita Davenport III.)*

*The lobby was a popular meeting spot. (Photo courtesy Spokane Public Library.)*

*This portable grand staircase would be moved into the lobby for style shows and other special events, such as this fashion show in 1924. (Libby Studio photo courtesy Walt and Karen Worthy)*

*Bellman tending one of the many bird cages in the Davenport Hotel lobby. This particular one was designed for lovebirds. (Photo courtesy Walt and Karen Worthy.)*

*Left: Writing desks along the south corridor of the lobby in 1914. (EWSHS Libby Studio photo L87-1.10734X-14) Below: A view of the lobby and the mezzanine looking toward First Avenue. The fountain, made of Italian marble, had goldfish swimming in the base and was often banked with flowers. (Photo courtesy Walt and Karen Worthy.)*

*Some of the birdcages in the lobby of the Davenport Hotel in 1925. Numerous tropical and rare songbirds were a feature in the hotel when it opened, but were removed during World War II. When they became a feature again in 1946, mostly just canaries and parakeets were used. (EWSHS Libby photo L87-1.29360-25)*

# Dining Options

Even in its early days, Davenport's was Spokane's favorite place to dine. The array of choices from the dining and banquet rooms to the Coffee Shop, Delicacy Shop, bars and soda fountains catered to the public's various needs, from a quick snack to elegant, multi-course dinners, all at a surprisingly affordable cost. Summarizing the restaurant facilities is no simple task due to frequent remodeling and renaming, especially in what was originally the lunch counter, the main dining room and the Orange Bower. Changes in the Orange Bower, originally a men's bar turned soda fountain, were driven largely by Prohibition, effective in Washington State on January 1, 1916, and its later repeal. Around 1928 it became the Aladdin Fountain and several years later the Apple Bower. In 1946 it reverted back to a bar, known at the Copper Strike Tap Room, and subsequently the Audubon Room.

*Looking north toward Sprague in the Davenport Hotel Coffee Shop – where it all began. Davenport opened his restaurant in this space, 807-809 Sprague Avenue, in July 1890. Most of the area shown here had been a lunch counter after the restaurant expanded east in the late 1890s. In the teens, it became known as the coffee shop, with the emphasis on quick service, quality food and informality. This photo, taken in 1925, followed a complete renovation, which enlarged the coffee shop to the west, encompassing the former private dining rooms (see floor plan on page 74). Double counters running the length of the room, separated by lighted display cases (left), were installed. Over the years, the coffee shop assumed other appearances, and later was called the Waffle Foundry. It remained open until the hotel's closure in 1985. (Photo courtesy Walt and Karen Worthy.)*

*The Delicacy Shop, looking toward Post Street, shortly after opening in 1917 on the first floor and mezzanine level of the Pennington wing of the hotel. In 1927 it was remodeled and closed in 1952, at which time the space was leased to the McMullen Office Equipment Co. The ten waitresses in this photo illustrated the attention given to service, and the garden effect reflected Louis Davenport's fondness for flowers and plants. (Libby photo courtesy Walt and Karen Worthy.)*

The change that garnered the most attention, however, appears to have been on Louis Davenport's mind as early as 1913, when plans to completely redesign the restaurant dining room were first mentioned in the newspapers. In 1922 Davenport's Restaurant was totally gutted and redesigned by Kirtland Cutter "in the manner of the Italian Renaissance with a beautiful garden effect," appropriately named the Italian Gardens. The seating capacity was doubled and, following the evening meal, tables and chairs were removed from the center section to reveal the new specially-designed dance floor. On Valentine's Day, 1922, Louis Davenport threw a grand party to celebrate the opening of his new restaurant and the 32nd anniversary of the Davenport Institutions, entertaining guests with music and dance. Leonardo Brill and his orchestra, regularly featured entertainers at the Davenport, performed in the lobby. The festivities, as well as descriptions of the main function rooms and brief histories about Spokane and Louis Davenport, were presented in a well illustrated 24-page souvenir program.

Subsequent to the era of the Italian Gardens, the restaurant was remodeled as the Crystal Dining Room, the Matador Room and finally as Louis D's Fine Dining.

*Looking southeast into the main dining room of Davenport's Restaurant in 1919. (Photo courtesy Walt and Karen Worthy)*

*The newly remodeled restaurant in 1922, renamed the Italian Gardens. Both photos were taken from the same position. (Photo courtesy Walt and Karen Worthy.)*

*The Italian Gardens filled with fresh flowers in 1922. This view is looking east from the entrance. (Photo courtesy Walt and Karen Worthy.)*

*The Italian Gardens dining room, hosting a gathering of young people in 1923. (Photo courtesy Walt and Karen Worthy.)*

*A 1922 function in the Marie Antoinette Room, located on the second floor directly above the Isabella Dining Room. (Photo courtesy Walt and Karen Worthy.)*

*The Isabella Room, located off the main lobby at the southeast corner of the Davenport Hotel, hosting the Spokane Credit Women's Breakfast Club, circa 1930. (Photo courtesy Walt and Karen Worthy.)*

*The Davenport Soda Fountain, located two doors west of the Sprague Avenue entrance, circa 1920. This space was originally occupied by a corset shop and later by a Northwest Airlines ticket office. Vernon Hogenson is behind the counter and Ray Johnson on the facing stool. (Photo courtesy Spokane Public Library.)*

*Louis Davenport always believed in using the best that money could buy in everything connected with his establishment, including the food provided by the hotel's various restaurants. His sources to obtain the freshest ingredients were many and varied, and he was directly involved in some of them. He owned a chicken ranch near Deer Park, north of Spokane, shown here in 1915, which supplied the hotel with fresh eggs. Davenport was also heavily invested in and vice-president of a wholesale produce company in Butte, Montana. According to the September 1915 issue of The Hotel Monthly, Davenport occupied a summer home on Hayden Lake in Idaho, where he had several acres of fruit trees and vegetable and flower gardens. (EWSHS Libby Studio photos L87-1.11666X-15 (left) and L87-1.11675-15)*

# The New Davenport Addition

The hotel opened in 1914 with more than 400 guest rooms. Construction of a thirteenth floor in 1917 added another 53, but the hotel still had need for more. In 1929 a $240,000 eleven-story addition was raised atop the three-story wing of the existing hotel, over the Marie Antoinette Room at the southeast corner. This provided the hotel with 80 new guest rooms, all with private bathrooms. (When the hotel opened in 1914, it was a newsworthy item that about 300 rooms had private bathrooms, although all had sinks and ice water on tap.) The plans for this addition were drawn up by Spokane architect G.A. Pehrson and the construction was done by contractors Alloway & Georg, also of Spokane.

Prior to building the new addition, Davenport formed a new corporation, Davenport Hotel, Inc. He announced on December 23, 1928 that he had bought out the remaining stockholders of the Davenport Hotel Company, which owned and operated the hotel, but not the restaurant. Both were then transferred into the new corporation. Of course, Davenport retained the majority interest and control of the business.

**Louis Davenport**

*The Davenport Hotel in 1930, after completion of the new 80-room addition over the Marie Antoinette Room, at the southeast corner of the hotel (see arrow). A few years earlier, KHQ, owned by Louis Wasmer, constructed the radio tower on the roof and began broadcasting from the hotel. (EWSHS Libby photo L87-1.44156-30)*

# A Partial List of Facilities, Function Rooms and Businesses in Davenport's Restaurant and Hotel From Its Inception:

Arabic Tent Room
Archery range
Arena Room
Athletic Round Table
Baker's Oriental Shop
Beauty salon
Betty Bone Boutique
Billiard hall
Blue Bird Gift Shop
Bowling alley
Brass Finders Gift Shop
Brown's Haberdashery
Chinese Buffet
Cigars, newspaper and magazine vendors
Circus Room
Conservatory
Coronet Room
Davenport Coffee Shop
Davenport garages, including Pigeon Hole
    Parking Garage and one in the basement
Davenport Hotel Candy Factory & Shop
Davenport's Restaurant, variously
    remodeled as the Italian Gardens,
    Crystal Dining Room, the Matador
    Room and Louis D's Fine Dining
Davenport Sport Shop
Delicacy Shop
Demert Drug & Chemical Co., later the
    Davenport Pharmacy
Domini Tavern
Early Birds' Club
East Banquet Room, later called the
    Georgian Room
East Banquet Room Annex, later called
    the Scepter Room
Elizabethan Banquet Rooms
Empire Room, later called the Green Room
Filiatrault Book Store (later a gift shop)
Flower Shop
Fountain, The (soda fountain)
G.N., S.P.&S. and Burlington ticket offices
Gage Millinery Shop
Global Travel

Gothic Room
Haddad (exclusive women's apparel)
Haddad's Oriental Bazaar
Hall of the Doges
Hoffman's Cameras and Videos
House physician
Isabella Dining Room
Jewel Box (costume jewelry)
K.H.Q. Broadcasting Studio
Kiddies Toggery
Mandarin Room
Marie Antoinette Ballroom
Milady's Import Shop
Northwest Airlines
Orange Bower, variously remodeled as the
    Aladdin Fountain, Apple Bower, Copper
    Strike Tap Room and the Audubon Room
Peacock Room
Pergola Promenade
Pompeiian Barber Shop (included
    manicurist, massage and water therapy)
Presidential and State Suites
Private dining rooms
Roof Garden with putting green, tennis and
    handball courts
Sample rooms
Serendipity Department for Ladies
Shoe Salon
Spokane Ad Club
Spokane Symphony Office
Stenography Department
Swimming pool
Tailor
Tony's Shoe Shine Parlor
Travel Bureau
United Airlines
Valet and laundry services
Various civic, fraternal & social club offices
Watch repair
Western Union
Wilson Mantor Photography
Women's and men's apparel shops
Yellow Cab Company

*The hotel's huge billboard met travelers as they entered Spokane from the west. The sign says: "Come in just as you are, unusual dining service, very reasonable rates, informal, dinner and after theatre dancing, exceptional music, tourist information." In the early days of automobile travel, it was not unusual for guests to arrive covered with dust from the road and grease from making mechanical repairs on their vehicles along the road. This was the hotel's way of assuring them of their welcome in spite of their appearance. (EWSHS photo L95-97.42)*

# Staff and Services

On August 30, 1914, just prior to the opening of the hotel, the following mission statement of Louis Davenport and his board of directors appeared in the *Spokesman-Review*. Thousands of copies were circulated to potential patrons of the hotel. This statement proved to be a promise that was honored throughout Davenport's tenure.

### An Opening Message
### To the Traveler in the Inland Empire

### An expression of the ideals, ambitions and intentions of the owners
### and management of the Davenport Hotel of Spokane

This hotel, we earnestly believe, typifies all that is best, all that is recognized as desirable, in the most modern hostelries of the highest class the world over. We cannot, however, too strongly impress the thought upon the public that as true as this statement is, the house will be more especially differentiated by the fact that it will be entirely devoid of the oppressive atmosphere of stateliness and the senseless extravagance of tariff which characterize too many of the famous hotels.

Over and above its exceptional beauties and its manifold excellences, moreover, it stands for an ideal, a definite purpose, upon the part of those who have made it possible.

That they have unwavering confidence in the commercial future of the community is self-evident. That they expect the venture to prove reasonably profitable is only natural.

But, at the same time, from its inception to its completion, they have been pleased to look upon it more as a monument to the indomitable spirit, the indefatigable industry, and, above all, to the openhearted manhood and womanhood of those who have made this community what it is.

With this idea in mind, they have not sought to build a mere show place, a mere temple of gorgeous magnificence, but rather a hotel fine enough for the most particular, yet one so free from formality, and so expressive of hospitality, that those finding occasion, from time to time, to sojourn in this city will look forward with pleasure to their stay within its walls.

That they have succeeded admirably is evidenced by the words of approval of those who have inspected the house and who have been kind enough to say that in its arrangement, its ornamentation and its appointments it is truly an unique expression of homelike hospitality.

To the tourist and the traveler from a distance we extend our hearty welcome, well convinced that they will agree with us that the house has few equals, and no superiors, in this country – in fact, that in many respects it strikes an entirely new note in hotel excellence.

To the men and women of the Inland Empire we would say that it is our ambition and intention to make of this hotel a community center, a social and business focal point. We recognize that to accomplish that object we must make them feel perfectly comfortable and absolutely "at home." To that end we shall bend every effort, and will heartily welcome any suggestion that may result in the improvement of our service and consequent enhancing of the satisfaction given.

To all we give the assurance that, while the house ranks with the most noted in this country, the rates decided upon are moderate and within the reach of persons of modest means. We offer forty rooms at $1.50; forty rooms with shower baths at $2.00; sixty-nine rooms with private baths at $2.50; seventy rooms with private baths at $3.00. Other large rooms and suites from $3.50 up. Commercial display rooms [the sample rooms], all with private baths, from $2.50 up.

**Davenport Hotel Company**
**Spokane, U.S.A.**

S ome measure of a man is in his words, but a greater measure is his actions. Through his words and actions, Louis Davenport created a welcoming atmosphere in his hotel and backed it with excellent service. The importance Davenport placed on service cannot be overly emphasized. His directive to employees was, "Whatever your job is, do it better than it has ever been done before." He counseled his staff on what was expected, with attention placed on the finest details, emphasizing that their job security was directly related to success of the hotel. The hotel published an 18-page booklet for employees, entitled *What SERVICE Means at the Davenport Hotel, Spokane, U.S.A.,* highlighting ways to offer exceptional service. It included general tips for all employees, as well as specific ones for the desk clerks, bellmen, elevator and telephone operators. It stated that employees unwilling to put forth every effort in following the guidelines "will have to make way for those who can and who will help us to 'make good' to the fullest extent with our guests." Marjorie Douglas Rowe, whose father, Herbert L. Douglas, worked at the Davenport for 29 years and was an assistant manager under Louis Davenport, wrote in a paper: ". . . Mr. Davenport wanted my father to be on the lookout for ways to provide memorable services to the guests." No detail was too small for either staff members or Davenport himself to attend to on behalf of the establishment's guests.

Although Davenport was exacting in his expectations, he treated others with respect – and received it in return. A deferential attitude toward one's "superior" may have been more prevalent than in today's workplace, but comments about Louis Davenport as an employer did not convey merely a sense of dutiful respect; they spoke of high regards for a man who conducted himself in a manner deserving of respect. It is also not unusual to find references to employees who worked at the Davenport for decades. Although some of the loyalty may have been in response to a scarcity of secure, good-paying jobs in pleasant environments and a strong work ethic intensified by the Depression years, people were proud to work for and be a part of the company. Davenport treated his employees well, and rewarded them with decent wages and benefits.

Davenport made it his practice to welcome guests in the lobby and other public rooms of the hotel, expressing his appreciation for their visit. His objective was for guests to "be glad they came, sorry to leave and eager to return." An example of how his actions spoke louder than words was related to the authors by his only grandson, Louie Davenport III. The following story was told to him by Mrs. Mary H. Haddad, the owner of Haddad, a women's apparel shop in the Davenport Hotel. As the story goes, one day an older couple came into the hotel with a brown bag, sat down at one of the tables in the lobby and proceeded to eat their lunch. Mrs. Haddad watched as Mr. Davenport, who had just stepped out of his office on the south side of the mezzanine, observed the couple for a few moments with a look of consternation. Mrs. Haddad relayed to the grandson that her heart sank and she thought, "Oh, I just hate to see this." But to her relief, two waiters suddenly appeared carrying tablecloths, china, crystal and silverware, and set up the couple's table so they could eat in style.

From the hotel's inception until his retirement, Davenport made every effort to uphold his ideal, as was quoted in the September 1915 issue of *The Hotel Monthly:*

> I consider, first, Utility; second, Life; third, Beauty. I place "utility" first, for the reason that Service is the keynote of successful hotel keeping. I put "life" next, because I look upon this structure and its mission as an investment for all time. I consider "beauty" after the other qualities, for the reason that, when you have accomplished the useful and the lasting, it is largely a matter of taste to produce the harmonies – the restful, relaxing, home-like atmosphere. And when you get that "home" feeling in the hotel, you get all that can be attained.

While interviewing people for this publication, a recurring theme about what made the Davenport Hotel so special was that people felt "at home." The attachment people feel for the hotel spans the generations. Dorothy Rochon Powers, retired longtime columnist and associate editor for the *Spokesman-Review*, summed it up: "There are many good hotels in Spokane, but none will ever replace peoples' affections for the Davenport. It became a second home, it was everybody's house." Because of Louis Davenport's welcoming attitude and attention to detail, it became the heart and pulse of Spokane. He set a standard by which all future activity throughout the hotel's history would be measured, even long after his retirement. It was a tough standard to meet.

***Bellmen waiting to greet and assist guests lined the great hallway to the Davenport lobby from Sprague Avenue. The fountain in the center of the lobby is slightly visible at the center of the photo. (Photo courtesy Walt and Karen Worthy.)***

In 1919 Louis Davenport wrote a five-page article, called "**It Pays Us To Give A Little More**," for a business journal, called *System,* published in Muskegon, Michigan, from 1916 to 1927. In effect, it was Davenport's blueprint for his success in the hospitality business. The following excerpt, under the subheading "**It's A Hard Task – But Worth Doing**," emphasizes the importance of training employees:

> You can plan to make your mechanical equipment practically foolproof, but it is very much harder to train employees always to express the house policy. Yet in the last analysis it is through employees that the house policy must be principally expressed. A surly look or discourteous word is more than enough to banish in a second all memory a guest may have of a comfortable bed or an exceptional meal.
>
> We feel that we cannot expect our employees to express the policy of the house unless they understand it and appreciate the reasons for it. We spare no pains to make them understand it. If, then, understanding it, they are unable or unwilling to maintain our standards without being held arbitrarily to the line by cast-iron rules, we feel that they are a liability. The sooner they are eliminated, the better for us and the less likely our customers will be to form false ineradicable impressions of our hotel.
>
> This is actually the line of least resistance. For the employee usually finds his work easier and more pleasant if he knows that he is functioning properly in the general scheme of the house policy.
>
> However, even employees with the best intentions will fall down occasionally – perhaps not in what they actually say to customers, but in the implications of their tones, carriage, inflection, and gestures – unless they are carefully trained. We are not content with merely telling employees what our house policy is; what they are to do, or why; we tell them how.
>
> Our school is quite informal. But our teachers of expression are devoting much time and thought to commercial phases of their work, and as a result our instruction is different from ordinary elocution. The instructors lay down fundamentals in the use of inflections, the significance of tones, the impressions given by certain postures and gestures. But they go much further, and study individuals to note handicapping peculiarities, which, it is their business gently and delicately to remedy.
>
> Relaxation is an art. We try to make the entire atmosphere of our hotel one in which guests can relax and refresh themselves. And we insist upon the need for relaxation among our employees, particularly those who are under the great strain through being constantly in touch with guests and through having to deal with all kinds.
>
> It is really remarkable the difference it sometimes makes to teach a nervous man to relax. In his work he is perhaps rubbed the wrong way by a gruff guest. If he is at the end of a series of such incidents and his nerves are frayed, he may start out with the next customer by being tense not deliberately discourteous, but seemingly so, to the travel-tired guest.

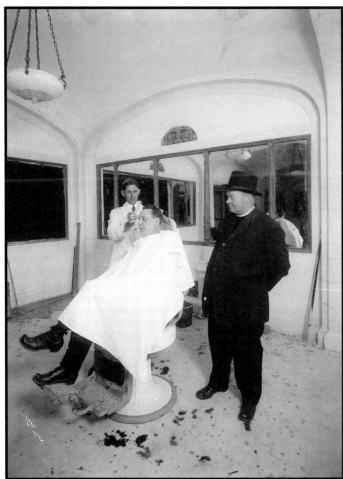

*A corner section of the Pompeiian Barber Shop in the basement of the Davenport Hotel in 1914. The white statuary marble walls, elliptical ceiling arches and columns were accented by red mosaic wall decorations. Eight red leather barber chairs sat on white enamel bases. The manicure tables were tucked in an alcove. Later, a 60x30 foot "swimming tank," Pompeiian baths, steam room and water therapy equipment were added, as well as a hair bobbing salon (in addition to a beauty salon off the lobby mezzanine). (EWSHS Libby Studio photo L87-1.10710X-14A)*

*Guest rooms, as shown in 1915 (left), were simply but tastefully appointed, using the finest quality furnishings. With an emphasis on restfulness, they were free of the busy ornamentation found in the public rooms. (EWSHS Libby Studio photo L87-1.11496X-15) Right: Special corner guest suite in 1915. Most of the rooms could be converted into suites of varying sizes in order to accommodate almost every need. (EWSHS photo L84-207.4.7)*

*The Davenport Hotel flower shop, at the east end of the hotel adjacent to the restaurant, remained in the same location from 1914 until the hotel closed in 1985. It was originally a branch store of The Spokane Florist Company, whose main store was on Riverside. (EWSHS Libby Studio photo L87-1.1152X-15)*

*On December 20, 1917, these women became part of the first all-female crew of hotel elevator operators anywhere in the country. Due to World War I, the shortage of men in the labor force created many job opportunities previously unavailable to women. (EWSHS Libby Studio photo L87-1.14434-17)*

*A sample room in the Davenport Hotel in 1921, with a display of the current fashions in women's hats. To attract the patronage of commercial travelers, there were sample rooms on every floor above the mezzanine level, located near the freight elevator. (Libby Studio photo courtesy Walt and Karen Worthy.)*

*Over the years, numerous shops were located in the Davenport Hotel. About the time the hotel opened, the Blue Bird Gift Shop, shown here in 1917, began as a gift shop (under another name) and remained at the hotel until the mid-1960s. The shop was just west of the First Avenue entrance. (Photo courtesy Gary Zagelow.)*

A 1914 newspaper advertisement from the Hawkins Motor Car Company, advertising the Davenport Hotel's new buses. It appeared in the Spokesman-Review on August 30, 1914 in a 10-page section of the newspaper that described the new hotel in detail. Most of the advertising space in this section was occupied by the hotel's contractors and suppliers, who took advantage of the great advertising exposure.

*One of two Federal Hotel buses purchased from the Hawkins Motor Car Company, located at 1128-1130 East Sprague Avenue, for the new hotel when it opened in 1914. The price was $1800 F.O.B. from Detroit, Michigan. At the time, many people traveled to Spokane by train. These buses transported guests to and from the train depot. (Photo courtesy Louie and Nita Davenport III.)*

*The parking garage, designed by G.A. Pehrson and located directly across from the First Avenue entrance to the hotel, in 1941. To increase capacity, a pigeon hole parking machine (a Spokane invention) was installed in the 1950s. The garage was demolished around 1970 to make way for another Davenport Hotel project, which never materialized, leaving an empty lot. (EWSHS photo L88-404-21b)*

As fascination with and reliance on the automobile grew, hotel parking became an ever increasing problem. In 1939 construction began on a basement garage, as well as a new 4560-square-foot facility for the Inland Empire Early Birds' Breakfast Club, all designed by G.A. Pehrson, in the area formerly occupied by the laundry department, carpenter shop, baggage storage area, billiard hall and part of the candy factory. The billiard tables were sold and everything else repositioned in the basement of the restaurant (Wilson Block), formerly occupied by the bowling alleys.

When completed in August 1940, the new garage provided parking spaces for about 75 to 80 cars, a total area of 18,750 square feet. Entrance to this garage was on First Avenue near Lincoln Street, where cars were lowered into the basement by an electric elevator. In the basement, a balanced turntable, easily operated by hand, pointed the cars in the direction of where they were to be parked. Two gas pumps, a lubrication area and wash racks were also installed. Unfortunately, this parking garage was never adequate; tight quarters, regardless of the care taken, resulted in too many scrapes and dents in patrons' cars. The basement garage closed prior to 1947, and the popular Early Birds' Club took over most of the space to expand their club facilities. The remodel project was the design of architect Harold C. Whitehouse, who was also the Early Birds' president. Part of this area later became the Arena Room.

*Doormen, bellmen and elevator operators on the roof of the Davenport Hotel in 1920. The hotel's publication "What Service Means" given to all employees stated: "We cannot impress upon you too emphatically that every employee is expected to preserve absolute silence as to anything he may see, hear or learn relative to the affairs of any guest." (EWSHS Libby Studio photo L87-1.18784-20)*

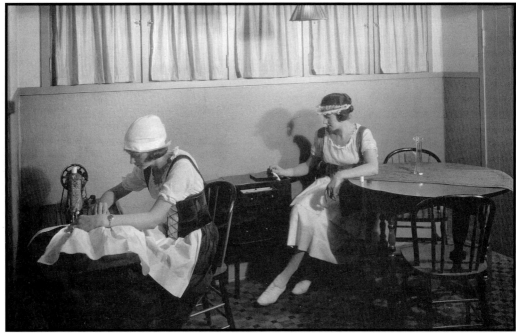

*The hotel's sewing room in 1922. (Libby Studio photo courtesy Gary Zagelow.)*

*Hotel personnel taking a break in the staff lounge. Previously the Conservatory, this room was remodeled in 1922 for the staff. The "What Service Means" publication directed employees to "always make the guest to whom you are attending feel that you have nothing more important to do, that there is no one to whom you would rather speak or attend to at that particular moment" and to be on guard for "any defect in any part of our service." (Photo courtesy Walt and Karen Worthy.)*

*Left: A waitress in uniform tending a flower arrangement. (Photo courtesy Walt and Karen Worthy.) Right: Marceil "Marcy" Williams, who worked in the housekeeping department at the Davenport Hotel from the mid-1970s to mid-1980s. (Photo courtesy Howard Williams.)*

*Davenport Hotel employees, probably from the housekeeping and maintenance departments, in 1918. (Photo courtesy Walt & Karen Worthy.)*

*Chef Edward Mathieu teaching a class to his Davenport Hotel staff in 1922. (Libby Studio photo courtesy Walt and Karen Worthy.)*

## Chef Edward Mathieu, "Chef Supreme," the Davenport Hotel's Longest Tenured and Most Famous Chef

Dining at the Davenport was a special affair or, at least, treated as such by the hotel's management. There were a large number of restaurants in Spokane during Davenport's glory days, but none in the entire Inland Northwest could match the Davenport's pristine environment and elegant ambiance. The quality of the meals was consistently excellent, the service unsurpassed and the prices were surprisingly reasonable. Louis Davenport's philosophy was to make a little money from a lot of people, rather than a lot of money from a few. Every effort was made to please both hotel patrons and the general public alike.

From his early beginnings in the hospitality business, Louis Davenport fully recognized the importance of having the right chef in order to accomplish his high aspirations and realized how that one key person could greatly influence his success. To that end, he sought out Edward F. Mathieu, a skilled French chef, to head this most important department. Prior to hiring Chef Mathieu in late 1917, Davenport had the unfortunate experience of three head chefs who proved unsatisfactory in the three years since the hotel opened. But Davenport was a determined man and, with Chef Mathieu, the selection could not have been more satisfying. Mathieu worked for the Davenport for 30 years.

Mathieu was born in the province of Savoy in southeastern France in January 1882. At age 16 he apprenticed as a cook in a hotel at Savoy. Before he left France in 1907 for the United States, he worked for the Aix-les-Bains' Bristol Hotel, Hotel de l'Europe, Grand Hotel in Monte Carlo, Pavillon Royal Restaurant and the Hotel Ritz in Paris. At the Ritz, he was trained in the art of "haute cuisine" (a style of cooking featuring artfully prepared, often elaborate, cuisine). With the exception of a three year period in his life, during which time he served in the French cavalry, Mathieu devoted his entire life to cooking. His life's dream was to become a master chef.

After his arrival in the United States in 1907, he began working in the kitchens of the Hotel St. Regis in New York, followed by San Francisco's Fairmont Hotel, where he was the executive chef. After four years, when the hotel changed hands, he was replaced by a chef the new owner brought with him. It was then that Louis Davenport learned of his availability through the membership rolls of the Chefs de Cuisine Association of America. This was an organization of master chefs associated with the American Culinary Federation of Chefs.

In 1958 Mathieu published his autobiography entitled, *The Life of a Chef,* recounting his experiences as a master chef for, as he put it, "Spokane's famous Davenport Hotel and of San Francisco's select Fairmont Hotel." The following quote describes his first contact with Louis Davenport and his thoughts about moving to Spokane:

> . . . Magazines for hotels and restaurants carried articles referring to my leaving the Fairmont since the position of Executive Chef is of considerable importance in the hotel field. The article did not make agreeable reading to me but it was of interest to hotel managers who might be in need of a chef.
>
> I received a letter from Mr. Alexander, the owner of a fleet of steamers and hotels in Honolulu, but I was not interested in leaving the continental limits of the United States. A few days later I received a letter from Spokane containing a picture of the Davenport Hotel.
>
> Of all the places I had in mind, Spokane was the last. I had no desire whatever to go North. After working in Paris, New York and San Francisco, New York and Los Angeles seemed to be more to my liking. Naturally, curious and happy with the thought that perhaps someone wanted me, I opened the letter. It was from Mr. L. M. Davenport, president and owner of the Davenport Hotel. It is surprising how an unexpected letter can change our perspective. The thoughts expressed went directly not only to my brain but to my heart. He said he would like to meet me the next Monday at 8:00 p.m. at the Palace Hotel in San Francisco.
>
> Already at our first meeting I had the conviction that my future was sealed with this man, and that we had a common bond.

*These two photos were taken at a 1937 Christmas banquet in the Marie Antoinette Room for Louis Davenport's employees. Approximately 300 employees were in attendance at this function. (Photo courtesy Walt and Karen Worthy.)*

*Edward Mathieu, Chef de Cuisine, and his staff in the Marie Antoinette Room of the Davenport Hotel in 1919. Mathieu is the man in the center with the goatee. (Libby Studio photo courtesy Walt and Karen Worthy.)*

In the following quote from his book, Mathieu described his arrival in Spokane, some of his first impressions of his new position, and his thoughts concerning others on Louis Davenport's management team:

> It was dark when I arrived in Spokane but I was anxious to report to Mr. Davenport, so I went directly to his office. There I was received with informal cordiality which later on I found was a part of the great Northwest, and our bond of friendship was confirmed. In a comfortable large room, prepared for my arrival, already on this first night, I had the conviction that I was in good company. Mr. Davenport asked me to stay at the hotel until my wife arrived; I would be too busy to find a house or apartment.

**James McCluskey and Chef Edward Mathieu, 1939.**

> Early the next morning I went to the roof overlooking the city and surrounding country. From there I could see the downtown as well as the commercial district and the North side residential district. The South side, which is built on a plateau above the city, could not be seen. It is there that I built my home [504 West 24th Avenue] in which I am living today. It was a clear day and I could see the chain of mountains which separate the frontier of the United States from Canada. As far as I could see there was a tremendous area of natural beauty. Spokane appeared to be a new, progressive city built on a solid foundation.

> . . . Previously I had no reason to be interested in the State of Washington and I intended to study the situation carefully to form a just opinion of my new position. New York City was not completely out of my mind since it was the city of opportunity for the young and enterprising. With the little I had learned and seen of the country I felt that I had made no mistake. . . . it looked like a good place in which to live.

> My greatest interest was the hotel. Would it justify my ambitions? I was soon to learn that I was in the right place and in a great hotel rightfully advertised as "America's Exceptional Hotel." The great American poet Vachel Lindsay lived at the hotel and we became great friends. He once told me that the hotel gave him a great deal of creative imagination, and the immensity and beauty of the surrounding country did lift a weight. It gave him great pleasure to see a smiling face everywhere he turned in the hotel.

> Quickly I learned that the hotel was the pride of the city. It covers a square block, facing on four streets and has about 500 rooms, many suites and is an imposing structure for a city the size of Spokane. . . .

> . . . while it [the Davenport Hotel] was the best hotel in the Northwest and offered the best accommodations for people who demand special service, it also has to cater to the traveling public, tourists and those engaged in the development of the natural resources who make their homes in small communities.

Among the notables I served there were many Presidents, the Queen of Roumania [*sic*], the ex-Empress of Austria and her family of princes and princesses, great divas, Marshal Foch, governors, senators, Supreme Court judges, and government secretaries who occupied the most ornate and elegant suites. At one time there were eighteen bishops and archbishops staying at the hotel for the consecration of two bishops, where they also celebrated the Mass, each one in his own apartment in a dignified atmosphere.

The greatest of all prima donnas [actress Sarah Bernhardt] sent me this note [in 1918], written in her own hand [in French], of which I am very proud. . . . Translated it reads: "I want to thank you before leaving the hotel and tell you how much I appreciate your culinary art, so delicate. This is rather rare in this magnificent America. . . ."

The hotel could not have survived with this kind of patronage solely. . . . Only forty per cent of the clientele of the dining rooms came from the hotel and sixty percent came from people of the city and surrounding areas, affectionately known as the Inland Empire. Amongst our customers were society matrons, doctors, lawyers, merchants and well-to-do farmers. They demanded not only good food but fast service at a moderate price. It was necessary to have widely diversified menus with a large volume and catering to people with such a large variety of tastes. I began to realize that my position as Executive Chef was more difficult than I had expected.

In a city of this size I knew that the people, especially women would be quickly responsive to good performance and cordial treatment. Three of my predecessors had been unsuccessful. The dining rooms do not compare in seating capacity to those at the Waldorf in New York City or the Palmer House in Chicago, but we had a seating capacity of 2300 without counting the lobby and mezzanine floor, where

*Some of the Davenport Hotel restaurant waitresses, circa 1915, showing their Swiss and Dutch style uniforms. (Photo courtesy Walt and Karen Worthy.)*

*A luncheon in 1937 in the Circus Room on the seventh floor in Room 730. Verus Davenport is seated third from the right. Other names listed with the photo, though not specifically identified, were Mrs. Walter Merryweather, Mrs. August Paulsen, Mrs. James G. Matthews, Mrs. John A. Reinhardt, Mrs. Frank Gibbs and Mrs. William H. Farnham. The centerpiece was an array of fruits and vegetables and, of note, an ashtray was placed at each table setting. Until the health risk became more apparent in recent years, smoking was in vogue and it was typical after meals to light up cigarettes and cigars. Over the years, a smoke residue built up on the walls and ceilings of the Davenport, dulling the gleam of its interior. (EWSHS Libby Studio photo L87-1.12614-37)*

another 1,000 could be accommodated for special occasions. We had four dining rooms serving the public for breakfast, luncheon and dinner.

Naturally, I was anxious to meet Mrs. Davenport, especially since Mr. Davenport had told me I must take special care of her entertaining. She was a dignified and gracious hostess and I had the pleasure to serve her on thousands of special occasions. Even with a great desire to please her and her guests, no doubt she was not always entirely satisfied, but she never at any time made a complaint. She very considerately thanked me after each one of her social functions. When she did not come, I knew that something had displeased her which made me very unhappy.

Before giving a party, she would call me to her apartment where we would discuss every detail of cuisine and service. In a short while I knew her specialties and how she liked them served which made things easier and contributed much to the success of her functions. Like Mr. Davenport, she had the superlative quality of remembering friends who experienced misfortune.

Then I met Harry Wraight, the Catering Manager. In San Francisco I was told that he was hard to get along with, and that I would have to use patience and diplomacy. . . . Mr. Davenport told me that he was a little high tempered, but to pay no attention to it and just do a good job. Wraight could calculate sales and profit with great precision, and I learned a great deal from him.

The Maitre d'hotel was Lee Chandler, who was in charge of all the dining rooms. . . .

Mrs. Jackson was the head of the auditing department and it took me some time before we could be really good friends. Some days are not profitable in the hotel business and on such a day she would come to me with a sad look to tell me how bad business was and that we should do better – always using the word "we" to show  her importance. She was very successful in making me feel down-hearted. One day I got tired of her admonitions and asked her to stop it. My short speech must have been effective for that was the end of those very unpleasant reproofs.

I was sensitive in all of my relations with heads of departments and I was careful not to intrude in their duties. I resolved that it was important and I did not interfere in Mrs. Jackson's business and I did not want her to interfere in mine.

One day in the banquet kitchen on the second floor I was annoyed with the nauseating smell of some boiling concoction and I was naturally concerned. I learned quickly that it was a scientific product being manufactured by the head hairdresser. I did not like this deliberate intrusion in my department without my permission. The hairdresser informed me that Mrs. Jackson had given permission and told her she did not have to ask the chef.

I was very much piqued at this incident and I told the hairdresser that this was not Mrs. Jackson's department and that she had no such authority. A few days later at luncheon time the same ingredients were boiling again in the banquet service kitchen with the unsavory odor. That was such defiance that I threw the concoction into the garbage can.

An hour later Mrs. Jackson came to the kitchen so much agitated that I thought she was walking on electric wires. I told her, "Mrs. Jackson, you have overstepped your authority so greatly that I have lost all my patience with you. I must ask you to keep out of my department." To this she replied, "You are looking for trouble, so you will have trouble. I am going to talk to Mr. Davenport immediately." The next day I discussed the incident with Mr. Davenport and he advised me to pay no attention to it. For some time she would not speak to me, but later we became very friendly and she came to our home many times.

The resident manager was Guy Toombes with whom I had few dealings, and I found him to be an attractive person. . . . In his position he saw life as a big parade and in his own words: "To please with a thank you, where the word "service" calls for action." He became a great success at the Hotel Utah in Salt Lake City after he left Spokane. He was a good friend and a connoisseur of good food.

When he left, James McCluskey became resident manager. He was an agreeable companion and many times we went hunting together.

Herbert Douglas was assistant manager in charge of the laundry and building maintenance. He was a trusted friend, very quiet and unassuming, with a fine sense of humor and respectability. . . .

Over the many years that Davenport and Mathieu worked together, they cultivated a close friendship. In his book, *The Life of A Chef,* Mathieu often expressed his affection and respect for Louis Davenport:

Mr. L.M. Davenport was a man with exceptional intelligence and ability in the hotel business. He was a man of refinement. In our thirty years of association, I had the privilege of knowing him well. In fact, we took our luncheons together almost every day during the last fifteen I was with him. I owe much to him.

Clinging to the simple things in life, there were to him no trivial matters. Everything had its own weight. He had such a suave and intelligent way of dealing with heads of departments and employees that they realized that their own welfare was dependent upon the prosperity of the hotel and he felt their cooperation was assured. He was an example of neatness.

An amusing, little-known secret was revealed to the authors by retired dentist George Wood of Spokane. Although the cuisine was almost entirely Chef Mathieu's creation, one particular item would occasionally be ordered that the kitchen did not produce – chili. Whenever such an order was received, the chef sent someone down the street to Bob's Chili Parlor! Apparently it was hard to improve on Bob's chili.

In a large restaurant, the success of a chef depends on both his talent and organizational skills. A first-class chef is a often a bit of a prima donna. He commands a high salary and usually demands total dominance over the kitchen, which is typically divided into departments, each with their own duties. In addition to being responsible for all the meals, their principal duties of the head chef include creating menus; stocking the storerooms, insuring proper storage and quality control; supervising the food preparation; hiring, training and discharging staff; inspecting kitchen equipment; and maintaining steam tables, dishes and refrigeration at the right temperature. Mathieu's kitchen and restaurant staff consisted of about 75 employees.

Chef Mathieu was the head chef at the Davenport during its most prosperous years and was a major player in the success of the hotel, contributing to the hotel's legend. In addition to being one of the best chefs in the nation, he gave Louis Davenport his utmost loyalty, and was an intelligent and diplomatic leader.

## A Selection of Other Notable Employees

Over the years, the Davenport has employed thousands of hard-working, dedicated people. In the hotel's heyday, there were upwards of 600 at a time. Obviously, it would be impossible to do more than present a brief mention of a few whose names are familiar or responsibilities were unique.

**Clarence A. Chase, (First manager of the Davenport):** One of Louis Davenport's first employee searches involved the pursuit of a general manager. His search culminated in the employment of Clarence Chase, who had been the manager of the renowned La Salle Hotel in Chicago. Originally from New England, Chase had received his early hotel training and experience at the famous Tremont House of Boston, noted for its hospitality and cuisine.

**James A. "Jim" McCluskey, (Most noted manager of the Davenport):** McCluskey came to Spokane with his family in 1904 at the age of nine. His father, a former sheriff in Colorado, joined the Spokane Police Department and later became its chief. Jim's first job in Spokane was selling newspapers on the corner of Riverside and Washington. Following a number of part- and full-time jobs while in high school, just days before the formal opening of the Davenport Hotel in September 1914, McCluskey was hired by Manager Chase.

**Jim McCluskey**

McCluskey's first job at the Davenport was opening crates and screwing light bulbs into all the new sockets. But his most memorable assignment occurred the final evening before the grand opening. He was put in charge of removing the hundreds of cats, which had been given free room and board in exchange for ridding the new hotel of the rats and mice that had taken up residence during the construction.

When the hotel officially opened, McCluskey was assigned a 12-hour shift as an elevator operator. This was the start of his long and successful career. He worked in nearly every position and department, becoming general manager of the hotel in 1935 and later vice president. He was truly Louis Davenport's right-hand man. Next to Davenport, McCluskey was probably the most recognized and popular man in the company, known for his kindness, generosity and friendly manner. He had an uncanny ability to recall people's names, even though years may have elapsed between visits. After 39 years of faithful service, he retired in 1953. In 1970, some years after his wife Susie's death, McCluskey married Augusta "Gussie" LaLone, who had become the assistant managing director of the hotel in 1947. At the time, she was only the second woman in the United States to hold an executive hotel position. Prior to this position, she had also served as private secretary to both McCluskey and Davenport.

**John Ungari (aka "Silver John"):** Ungari, who worked for the hotel for over half

**Silver John**

a century, was in charge of cleaning all the silver in the Davenport, including the silverware, silver servings and the silver coins that passed through the hotel on a daily basis. When Davenport began the unique tradition of washing the coins, a dollar purchased a lot more than it does today and the use of coins, which then were pure silver, was more prevalent. The average coinage Ungari washed each day amounted to between $6,000 to $10,000. In addition to the clean and shiny coins, the paper currency Davenport patrons received in change was new. Although washing the coins was a clever, memorable gimmick, it may also have been a sanitation measure. Louis Davenport had a reputation for his meticulous attention to cleanliness, and it is a known fact that money is one of the world's most significant carriers of germs. Consequently, the clean money set the tone for the sanitary conditions one could expect at the Davenport.

**William "Dad" Jones, (Keeper of the fireplace):** Another Davenport Hotel tradition that added to its legend was the fire in the lobby fireplace that was never allowed to go out. For over 27 years, beginning in 1923, William Jones was the keeper of the fire that was famous for having cheered thousands of visitors, including United States' presidents, diplomats and celebrities from around the world.

After the first fire was lit at 2:00 a.m. on the morning of September 13, 1914, it has been said that one of Louis Davenport's standing orders was to keep a constant fire in this fireplace. According to news accounts, the only time it was extinguished was in 1947, when the entire chimney and fireplace was rebuilt with a more modern firebrick. Although fire adds a welcoming glow and warmth on a chilly day, being the practical man he was, it did not seem reasonable that Davenport would greet guests with a blazing fire in the heat of a Spokane summer. In 1919, Louis Davenport wrote an article for a publication called *System*, in which he said, "The fire is never allowed to go out **in the winter** [emphasis added] . . ." Also, according to John Reed, one of the Davenport Hotel's longest tenured employees, who began working at the Davenport in 1942, back drafts would occasionally force smoke into the lobby and the fire would have to be put out immediately.

**Marion L. "Mike" Piper, (Keeper of the birds):** Almost from the inception of the hotel in 1914, both the lobby and the main restaurant were home for a various assortment of birds. At times there were hundreds of tropical birds – mostly canaries and parakeets. Few guests typically ever left the hotel without the pleasant memory of the tropical atmosphere provided by the sounds of the birds singing.

By the time Louis Davenport sold the hotel in 1945, the bird population had decreased to 14 and there was no permanently assigned person to care for what few were left. Since the presence of caged birds in the Davenport was part of its legend, a search was made for an expert bird-keeper. In 1945, Mike Piper, formerly from Mullan, Idaho, responded to a "help wanted" ad in the local newspaper Known as one of the best canary breeders in the Inland Northwest, Mike naturally got the job. Within a short time, Mike had the bird population in the Davenport up to 150. The various birds were shuttled between the lobby, Italian Gardens and the aviary, located above the Hall of the Doges, where they were kept at night. In general, Mike was quite successful with his various bird displays, with the one exception of a parrot who had to be retired because of his offensive language.

**Robert "Bob" Harris, (Head bellman):** Bob Harris's career spanned 68 years in the hotel service business, serving 19 of those years at the Davenport Hotel. During

his time at the Davenport, he served many famous people, including Bing Crosby, Jack Benny, Richard and Pat Nixon, and Tom Foley (at that time, a student at Gonzaga University, he later became majority leader of the U.S. House of Representatives). At the time of this writing, Harris is 93 years old and still lives in Spokane. In an interview with Grayden Jones of the Spokane Teachers Credit Union, Harris stated: "Service is all we have to offer." The photo to the right shows Harris with an earlier photo of bellmen lining the grand entry to the hotel lobby from Sprague Avenue. Harris was proud to relate that his uncle, with his two teams of horses, was involved in the 1913 construction of the hotel.

**Bob Harris (Photo courtesy Grayden Jones, Spokane Teachers Credit Union)**

**Tony Giannou (Photo courtesy Tony Giannou Jr.)**

**Tony Giannou, (Davenport Shoe Shine Parlor):** Tony Giannou came to the United States from Greece in 1912, at the age of 18. In 1944 he went to work for Louis Davenport, a year prior to Davenport's sale of the hotel. When Giannou first opened his shop in the basement of the Davenport, he worked a 13-hour day, seven days a week, and charged 25 cents a shine. With tips, he averaged about $300 a month. He shined the shoes of many notables who stayed at the hotel, including a U.S. president. During the prime of Giannou's shoe shining career, even the young people were conscientious about their appearance. By 1978, when he retired, his business had fallen off considerably, which he attributed to the changing dress codes.

**James Hamilton "Ham" LaFar, (Page boy for the hotel in its heyday):** LaFar went to work for the Davenport in 1923 as a page boy and, until he left in 1942 to take another job, was among the hotel's most popular employees. At a reunion in 1970 for former employees, LaFar was quoted as saying: "Everything that happened in Spokane happened at the Davenport Hotel." LaFar died in 1982 at the age of 83.

*Left: Newspaper clipping of Ham LaFar (center) with Herbert L. Douglas, assistant manager, and Chef Mathieu in 1942. This photo was taken during LaFar's last shift at the Davenport. Douglas, who was hired by Louis Davenport in 1917 to head the laundry department when the new facilities were installed, later became the hotel's assistant manager. He worked for the Davenport for 29 years. Right: LaFar and Douglas in 1924. (EWSHS Libby Studio photo L87-1.28024.24)*

*Hamilton LaFar, sixth from the left, playing the saxophone with the Mel Butler Orchestra in the Marie Antoinette Room in 1923. (EWSHS photo L84-174.245.24)*

*John Reed, one of the Davenport Hotel's longest tenured employees, pauses during an interview in July 2001 with Robin Briley and Jim Bolser of Peak Video Productions, on the lobby balcony of the Davenport Hotel. Even though the hotel closed in 1985, John has continued his employment there. (Bamonte photo.)*

In 1942, John Reed went to work as a busboy in the Davenport Hotel at the young age of 13. This was during World War II, when there was a severe shortage of manpower throughout the entire United States. To fill this shortage, employers were able to obtain special permits to allow young people to work certain low-risk jobs. John was in the seventh grade at the time and was able to work in the evenings and on weekends. His first job consisted of setting and clearing tables. He made 35 cents an hour, plus whatever tips the waitresses would split with him. John only worked there about a year, but returned in 1958, this time a college graduate, and began working as a bellman. When the hotel closed in 1985, John retained his employment as head of maintenance for the various owners of the hotel. He probably knows every nook and cranny of the hotel better than anyone.

John fondly remembers Louis Davenport as a gentleman and perfectionist in everything he did. He wanted his guests to have the best of everything a hotel could offer – excellent cuisine, perfect presentation and outstanding service.

## Music and Dance

Louis Davenport loved music and his hotel was always filled with it, frequently with live music in several rooms at the same time. There was almost always dinner music in the restaurant and the dining room, followed by dancing into the night. Afternoon teas and tea dances were popular weekly functions. According to pianist Arthur Zepp, who was employed by the hotel in the 1930s, the Davenport was "the very center of the social and musical life of Spokane." After the KHQ radio broadcasting tower was built on the roof of the hotel in the mid-1920s, music was often broadcast over the air live from the Davenport, rooms 427 and 428.

Numerous well-known and little-known musicians entertained guests of the Davenport and, during Louis Davenport's years, he was often directly involved with the selection process. Before the hotel opened, he traveled to New York to scout a competent orchestra conductor. He hired the talented violinist, Leonardo Brill, who later formed Spokane's first symphony orchestra. Generally, after the initial screening and auditions, potential employees were required to perform for Davenport, upon whom the final decision rested. Tension was high in those auditions, as he would often listen quietly, and then leave the room without saying a word. It was generally left to a manager to give the musicians the good or bad news. Once hired, the musicians were expected to provide the same excellence in performance and appearance demanded of all the staff. The result was a quality of music and entertainment that attracted and delighted the public.

*Mel Butler and his orchestra in the Marie Antoinette Room of the Davenport Hotel in 1922. (Photo courtesy Walt and Karen Worthy.)*

*Mel Butler's Orchestra members in 1924 in the Marie Antoinette Room. From left:*
*Chet Cederholm, Mahlon Nerrick, Ernest Reid, George Scott, Mel Butler, Harold*
*Grief, Clayton Goff and Byron McCoy. (Photo courtesy Walt and Karen Worthy.)*

*All female orchestra, in 1927, entertaining in the Italian Gardens, where there*
*was live music every night of the week. (Photo courtesy Walt and Karen Worthy.)*

*The Fred Hartley Orchestra in 1926. From left: Fred Hartley, Ben Lenue, Edna Berkle, Lyle Chasse, Ben Krause and Florence Waterhouse Wasmer. Hartley was the band director at the Davenport in the 1920s and 1930s. This popular dance band also played regularly at the Garden Dancing Palace. (Photo courtesy Jamie Baker.)*

*Jim Baker (standing at center) and his orchestra were the feature group from 1955 to 1968 in the Early Birds' Club, where they broadcast live over the air. Jim played saxophone, clarinet and flute, and in addition to performing at the Davenport six nights a week, he also taught school. He played for the Friday afternoon Tea Dances from the late 1970s through the 1990s, and for various other special occasions, including New Year's Eve 1998, at age 84. During Baker's career, which spanned from age 16 to his death in 1999, he wrote 4,000 musical arrangements. His son Jamie, also a talented musician, is second from left in the above photo, which was taken in 1974. (Photo courtesy Jamie Baker.)*

# Chapter 5

## People and Events

*Louis Davenport welcomed the local Indian tribes as guests of his hotel on numerous occasions. The first guests of the Davenport Hotel were members of the Blackfeet Tribe. In June 1913, while the hotel was still under construction, Spokane hosted a week-long pow wow. During that time, the Blackfeet set their tepees up under the shelter of the hotel's steel framework and ate their meals in Davenport's Restaurant. Before leaving, they performed a special dance to personally thank the Davenports for their hospitality and persuaded Verus Davenport to join in the dance. Following Louis Davenport's death in 1951, his obituary stated that members of the Blackfeet Tribe pitched their tepees on the roof during the hotel's grand opening and, dressed in full regalia, mingled with the crowd. Unfortunately, no reference to this was found in the newspapers at the time of the opening nor was any other evidence found to support it, leading to a conclusion of just another myth associated with the great old hotel. (Photo courtesy J.J. Hill Manuscript Collection of the James Jerome Hill Reference Library in St. Paul, Minnesota.)*

The Davenport Hotel's grand opening was held on September 17-19, 1914, but the hotel actually opened for business on September 1st. The demand for services, especially banquet facilities, overwhelmed the planned schedule. Consequently, the hotel unofficially opened 16 days ahead of its formal opening. The first banquet held at the Davenport Hotel was the Pacific Northwest Library Association, followed by the Druggists and Physicians of the Pacific Northwest, and the American Institute of Electrical Engineers.

Typical of Louis Davenport, in spite of the premature opening, he was able to smoothly accommodate his first guests and visitors. Some of the mezzanine furniture, held up en route by a railway accident, was not yet in place and a few auxiliary facilities unfinished, such as the barber shop, billiard room and the men's cafe, but the lobby and the luxurious Isabella Dining Room were ready for guests.

---

### Davenport Hotel Guest Register
### September 1, 1914:

Charles R. Sligh of Grand Rapids, Michigan, whose company was the hotel's furniture and drapes supplier, had the distinction of being the first guest to register at the Davenport Hotel on its opening day. Other guests on the opening night, in the order they registered, were listed in the *Spokesman-Review*, as follows:

Mr. and Mrs. Adolph Galland, Spokane; Mrs. R. Andreet and son of Spangle; J.R. Fullinwider, Spokane; T.J. Flavin, Butte, Montana; A.P. Nox, Portland; Mr. and Mrs. L.R. Mason, Portland; C.A. Richards, San Francisco; Charles Graham, Corbin, B.C.; Mrs. Louis Heitman, Helena, Montana.; Mr. and Mrs. W.M. Leuthold, Deer Park, Washington; H.A. Hover, Helena; R.H. Bailey, Pierce, Idaho; Alexander Saslavsky, New York; Alfred DeVoto, Boston; William Horn and Everett Horn, Ritzville, Washington; Mr. and Mrs. H.S. Kurtz, Chicago; Charles Thanauer, Berlin, Germany; August Obst, Budapest; J.H. Mittendorf, Philadelphia; Robert Lewers, Reno, Nevada; A.W. Hendrick, Portland; Mr. and Mrs. George N. Billings, Delphos, Kansas; Winifred R. Smith, Seattle; F.O. Field, Conkling Park, Idaho; A. Urbohn, Laredo, Texas; J.S. Cohen, Los Angeles; Samuel Eckstein, Chicago; Maude E. Nelson and Mabel E. Sellers, Calgary, Alberta; Mr. and Mrs. S.R. Stern, Spokane; Mr. and Mrs. L.E. Mark, Edwall, Washington; Mr. and Mrs. F.E. Parks, Deer Park; A.E. Campbell, Malden, Washington; Mr. and Mrs. James Raflery, St. Joe, Idaho; A.W. Peterson, Seattle; Mr. and Mrs. L.L. Boyd, Henderson; Miss M. Dowlon, St. Paul, Minnesota.; D.F. Staley, Pullman, Washington; Mr. and Mrs. O.L. Waller, Miss Gladys Waller and Miss Louella Egge, Pullman; Y.B. Brisendine, Spokane; R.W. Green, Snohomish; C.B. McNeeley, Cleveland, Ohio; W.H. Laversky, Chicago; B.E. Rowdon, New York; C.S. Irvin, Vancouver; and A.L. Oliver, Spokane.

At 5:00 p.m. on September 1, 1914, the doors of the Davenport hotel opened to the public. Within 20 minutes, 54 guests had registered to stay in the hotel. By midnight, an estimated 10,000 people had visited the hotel, and the throngs of visitors continued throughout the following day. The majority of the crowd was made up of townspeople eager to examine Spokane's magnificent new landmark.

Guests that evening were entertained by a variety of musical and dance performances. Leonardo Brill and his orchestra played throughout the evening. A male chorus of about 100 voices performed under the direction of H.W. Newton and F.W. King. Over 400 guests dined in the Isabella Room that first evening, reportedly, with flawless service.

Prior to opening, the new Davenport Hotel and Davenport's Restaurant received the first saloon license for the year 1914, at an annual fee of $2,200. At the time, the city was pursuing a policy of issuing licenses only to hotels of over 50 rooms. Davenport's license was approved and issued by the Commissioner of Public Safety, Charles Fleming. Fleming, who later became Spokane's mayor, had just assumed that office the first of the year. Just over a year later, on January 1, 1916, prohibition went into effect in Washington State. Davenport made it very clear to his employees that his establishment would uphold both the spirit and the letter of the law, and any violation would be grounds for immediate discharge. Further, employees were informed that the hotel's management would notify the authorities of any infraction and cooperate in bringing about a conviction.

## Preparation for the Grand Opening

The grand opening ceremonies for the Davenport Hotel, on September 17-19, 1914, were a fitting welcome for one of the most celebrated and appreciated projects in Spokane's history. In keeping with its physical magnificence, the festivities would set the tone for the better part of the hotel's history. To mark this special occasion, elaborate plans were made under the direction of the planning committee comprised of R.L. Rutter, Thaddeus S. Lane, Samuel Galland, R.E. Bigelow, Thomas S. Griffith and F.H. Lloyd. A reception committee of about 350 representatives from local civic organizations was also formed.

The first evening was devoted to the formal presentation of the hotel. A banquet on the second night, which hosted over 1,000 guests, was the largest banquet ever held in the Inland Northwest up to that time. It was primarily to honor the mayors and other ambassadors of the Inland Northwest. Guests were seated in the Marie Antoinette Ballroom, the Isabella Dining Room and the Elizabethan Banquet Room, where they were entertained by musical performances. The grand finale, on September 19th, was marked by a formal ball.

Advanced reservations were taken for the grand opening celebrations. The planning committee telephoned nearly a thousand prominent citizens, urging them to make their reservations early. Among those who did were: Harry L. Day and his guests from Wallace, Idaho, who reserved six rooms for the entire week and 20 tables for the opening banquet; Thaddeus S. Lane and party of 12; J.D. Sherwood and party of ten; Marion E. Hay (Washington governor, 1909-1913) and party of ten; Jay P. Graves and party of 14; Will H. Ziegler; A.L. Flewelling; Clyde Graves; T.F. Spencer; Harry Holland; M. Oppenheimer; L.J. McAtee; Dan R. Brown; Dr. H.S. Clemmer; E. Clark Walker; Jake Hill; E.T. Coman; Leo Greenough; C.M. Fassett; and Charles P. Lund.

The August 30, 1914 issue of the *Spokesman-Review,* with its detailed description of the new hotel, mentioned that Louis W. Hill, president of the Great Northern Railroad and friend of Louis Davenport, had plans to bring a contingency of railroad and financial businessmen from St. Paul for the formal opening. However, accounts at the time of the opening, which covered in detail the names of the prominent attendees, made no mention of Hill. In the 1940s, an article in the *Spokesman-Review* on the history of the Davenport Hotel's state suite claimed its first guest was James J. Hill, allegedly on opening night of this grand celebration. The origin of this information is a mystery and appears to be unfounded. James Hill was the nationally known railroad magnate who founded the Great Northern and built a railroad empire from coast to coast. His presence – or that of his son Louis – would have created a certain newsworthy item. Present on the Davenports' table the last evening of the festivities was a replica of the Northern Pacific Railway's "Great Big Baked Potato," a symbol adopted for a promotion of the Northwest. If this seemed noteworthy enough to report, certainly the attendance of James or Louis Hill would have been even more so.

It appears, according to another article written sometime later, that Ernest Lister, Washington State's governor, was the first to occupy the state suite. This account is more credible as Governor Lister was named as a participant in the festivities.

---

**Announces Staff Personnel**

On September 1, 1914, hotel manager, Clarence A. Chase, announced his lead staff as follows: Oriel Smith, M.J. Briggs and Harold Johnson, room clerks; Thomas E. Hines, auditor; A.A. Morse and Volney Shepard, mail clerks; Grace Simpson and Selma Engstrom, front-office cashiers; Helen Whitmore, manager's private secretary; Charles McBride, chief engineer; Walter Stevenson, chief electrician; Mrs. A. Smith, housekeeper; Mrs. E.W. Lansing, chief telephone operator, and Clara Yenney, Belle Warner, Jane Murray and Hazel Stack, assistants; John Bausman, superintendent of service; Fred Scudder and Frank Fiddler, bell captains; L. Marsh, ex-Chicago detective, house officer; James F. Derbis, head porter; Albert Kelley, assistant porter; and Frank Brown, head bartender.

*The grand opening banquet in the Marie Antoinette Room on September 18, 1914, hosting the mayors of the Inland Northwest communities and other ambassadors from Washington, Idaho and Montana. (Photo courtesy Walt and Karen Worthy.)*

## Davenport Presents His Grand Hotel

The September 18, 1914 edition of the *Spokane Daily Chronicle* carried the following story of the first evening of the grand opening celebration, the hotel's first major event.

### OPEN GREAT HOTEL
### Many Notables Present at Formal Ceremonies in the Davenport.

Spokane last evening underwent the transition from a big country town into a metropolis. The traditional marks of the mining camp and the frontier were formally discarded and tailored ennoblements became the convention, replacing the bandana handkerchief and the flannel shirt of early days.

Such was the change effected by the opening of the new Davenport hotel, declared Mayor W.J. Hindley as he introduced the formal program presenting the hotel to Spokane and to representatives of the northwestern commonwealths.

Among the several thousand citizens and visitors who packed the lobby and balconies were scores whose memory could recall the beginnings of Spokane and who had known the hospitality of the California House at Howard and Main, the city's first hostelry. [Spokane's first hostelry was actually the rudimentary Western Hotel, with the California House being its first upscale hotel.] The spirit of western good fellowship which they had instilled into the life of Spokane would not pass away, stated the mayor, but was combined with the magnificence and splendor of the metropolis as represented by the new hotel.

Depicting social progress and wealth, the ceremony and scenes of the evening were probably the most resplendent and luxurious of the city's history. The great Spanish lobby, with its beams and pillars of soft, intricate colorings, afforded a fitting setting for the gay lustre of evening gowns, the wealth of floral pieces of bright autumn blossoms and the happy activity of the groups and crowds.

### Crowds See Ceremony.

With a bugle call from the brass quartet, the ceremonies opened at 7:30 o'clock. The first notes brought conversations to a close, the mezzanine railings became suddenly packed, and on the main floor the hundreds surged together to gain a better view of the procession.

In military processional came the ceremonial party, led by the quartet. At the head were the official representatives of Washington, Idaho and Montana and Miss Marguerite Motie, costumed as Miss Spokane.

Thirty one society girls of the city acted as escorts and in occupying the platform at the east end of the lobby formed a semi-circle behind the seated guests. They were: Carol Rutter, Helen Grinnell, Kathleen Kimball, Francis Rutter, Evelyn Dillingham, Elizabeth Dillingham, Marion Luhn, Abbie Boggs, Rita Ballinger, Marion Howell, Norma McCuaig, Helen Gentsch, Bernice Winter, Virginia Riblet, Rachel Hutchinson, Gladene Rankin, Rhea Clark, Katherine Clark, Helen Sengfelder, Josephine Murphey, Virginia Murphey, Ramona Ham, Katherine Williams, Margaret Jensen, Sybil Spencer, Marion Gentsch, Jean Porter, Florence Humbird, Marie Oudin, Josephine Oudin, Augusta Howell.

### Seated on Platform.

Seated on the platform were Governor Lister, Lieutenant Governor Taylor of Idaho; J.F. Davies, official representative of Governor Stewart of Montana; Mayor Hindley; Miss Spokane; Dr. Frederick Smith of Rochester, N.Y., imperial potentate of the Nobles of the Mystic Shrine; William A. Huneke, presiding judge of the Spokane county superior court and C.H. James, chairman of the board of county commissioners.

Above the platform, worked in white, yellow and red blossoms, was the inscription: "Good luck and good cheer to all who enter here."

Introducing the presentation ceremony, Mayor Hindley reviewed briefly the progress of Spokane. "Tonight we are celebrating the transition of Spokane from a camp to a metropolis," said the mayor. "We have become a great, big country town, growing so rapidly that we have hardly had time to adopt the ways and marks of city life. The opening of this magnificent structure represents our change into a city of the first class."

**Miss Spokane Speaks.**

Behind the seated guests stood three miniature reproductions of the hotel building, covered with American flags. Signaling to the standing escorts to uncover one of the tokens, Miss Spokane addressed Governor Lister, presenting "the tiny model of a great building as an expression of a Spokane hospitality that is all-embracing."

In replying, the governor expressed the interest of the entire state in Spokane's magnificent hotel building. Following his brief word of acceptance, the brass quartet played the air of the Washington state song.

The second model of the building then was presented by Miss Spokane to Lieutenant Governor Taylor of Idaho, asking that the token be accepted as a "remembrance and symbol of continued good-will from the people of Spokane to the Gem state."

The air of the Idaho state song followed Mr. Taylor's reply.

**Appears for Montana.**

The third reproduction of the building was presented to Mr. Davies, representing Montana. "Montana owns a part of this hotel," declared Mr. Davies. "We feel proud of your accomplishment in the completion of such an edifice and claim a share of the ownership and interest in the institution."

The air of "Dixie," adopted by Montana for its state song, then was played, closing the ceremony.

With the quartet and orchestra playing in unison, the possession moved from the platform to the Isabella dining room, where tables were set for the speakers and official guests.

For an hour following the ceremony the male chorus under the direction of H.W. Newton entertained the crowds in the lobby and balconies. . . .

On the final evening, the festivities began with private dinner parties at 7:30 p.m. in the Isabella Dining Room, followed by a formal ball in the Marie Antoinette Room. Society was well represented in all their finery. The dancing was interspersed by various dance performances. A group of dancers, dressed in courtly 18th century French costumes, danced a minuet in the Marie Antoinette Room, followed by a contemporary ballet performance around the fountain in the lobby. Moving back into the Marie Antoinette Room, the younger society set entertained the guests by dancing the tango. Prior to the grand opening, the entertainment committee had hired a dance instructor from back East to teach a large class how to dance the tango and other popular dances expressly for this event. The dancing continued until midnight, at which time, guests were ushered into the dining room and supper was served. With the conclusion of the grand ceremonies and celebration, the hotel was ready to assume its position as the heart of the community.

## Miss Spokane

The honor of formally presenting the Davenport Hotel to the attending public and dignitaries was given to Miss Spokane, Marguerite Motie. "Miss Spokane" was considered the official city hostess, a position held with great pride and dignity. The program began in 1912 with the objective of producing a symbol to represent Spokane and the Inland Northwest, some sort of unique emblem that could be used on promotional materials. To that end, the Spokane Advertising Club sponsored a contest among local artists to submit their ideas. The **Marguerite** winning entry depicted an Indian princess with a sheaf of wheat **Motie** in one hand representing the agricultural wealth of the area and, in the other hand, a vessel from which water was being poured, a symbol of the region's abundant water supply. Immediately following this contest, a second one was held to choose the photograph of a young Spokane woman's face to superimpose on the sketch to bring this Indian princess to life.

The comely face of 17-year-old Marguerite Motie was chosen from 138 entries. The original intent of the contest, that of producing just an inanimate symbol, quickly changed when the Ad Club discovered Marguerite's charm, poise and oratory talents. In keeping with the original winning drawing, she was outfitted in replicated native dress and introduced as a living symbol to represent the region. Thus, the official city hostess position was born. Marguerite would become the most publicized woman in Spokane's history and truly Spokane's first ambassador, who played a significant role in its early 20th century history. She spoke at almost every important function, often as the featured attraction, and represented the city at many events throughout the West Coast region.

She was venerated in almost every conceivable way. Postcards and brochures were printed with her image. Poems and songs were written about her. There were Miss Spokane buttons, medals, statues, fountains, spoons, candy, perfume and even a license-plate bracket. In 1917 a steamship on Lake Coeur d'Alene and, two years later, the first airplane of the Northwest Aircraft Company in Spokane were christened *Miss Spokane*. A huge stained-glass likeness of her hung in the entry way of the Cheney Cowles Museum for many years.

According to the rules of the contest, Marguerite was to reign until she married. However, even after marrying Walter Shiel in 1920, moving to Seattle and starting her family, Spokane periodically requested her presence at special events. During the Depression years, the role of Miss Spokane essentially fell into obscurity, but Marguerite Motie held the title until the second Miss Spokane, Catherine (Betts) Williams, was chosen in 1939.

The manner in which Miss Spokane was presented brought pride to the greater Spokane area community. The local Indian tribes were willing participants in the program, despite the fact that over the life of the program (which ended January 1, 1976), none of the Miss Spokanes were Native American. Many of the city hostesses were adopted into the local tribes as honorary members, and tribal members participated in creating the native dress the women wore (except for Marguerite Motie's). They endorsed having their heritage represented in this way. Although the issue of the native dress fell under attack at various times, generally from those who advocated wearing contemporary street clothes, many of the most vocal proponents of retaining the Indian dress came from the tribes. On December 5, 1947, Joseph T. Seltice was quoted in the *Spokesman-Review* as follows:

As chief of the Coeur d'Alene Indians and chairman of the tribal council I wish to point out that Spokane was named for an Indian tribe and should be proud of its traditions associated with the earliest inhabitants of this area. A change in costume would lower Miss Spokane to cheap showmanship. It would obliterate her as a representative of the spirit of the west. . . Why shouldn't Miss Spokane continue wearing a garb which represents the west more truly than changing fashions?

*This photo, taken after Miss Spokane Marguerite Motie was inducted into the Blackfeet Indian Tribe of Glacier National Park, was in a photo album presented to her by Louis and Verus Davenport. Marguerite officiated at many functions held at the Davenport Hotel. Louis Davenport is standing at the far right. (Libby Studio photo courtesy Dorothy and Bob Capeloto, Marguerite's daughter and son-in-law.)*

"The bonfire we had built on the beach in the early evening was all but out, and the red embers glowed in the velvety darkness. Then over the mountains across the lake rose the moon, full and glorious, first a mere silver tip behind the jagged pines of the sky line, then mounting into the heavens, until the bright radiance streamed in a brilliant path across the water, the shore line clear cut in silhouette. Diana is splendid anywhere, but she is magnificent on these mountain lakes."—LOG OF THE SUNSET TRAIL.

A COMFORTABLE place in which to live makes a lot of difference when you are traveling. In Spokane there is a hotel home to suit any purse and taste. The new Davenport has been completed at a cost of $2,500,000 for the comfort of those who travel.

There are other reasons why you should make Spokane your objective for your western trip. It is the center of the great Inland Empire, the green summer playground of America, where the railroads of the Pacific Northwest all meet. These converging lines will bring you into Spokane from any quarter of the compass.

Side trips by automobile or electric train will take you into a land of beauty and plenty, where orchard and field reflect the bounty and wonders of nature; where lake, mountain and valley offer you a delightful outing and relief from summer's heat.

Come—let Spokane greet you within her gates. Plan your western trip along the routes of the National Parks.

**VIA SPOKANE**

Write to Travel Service Bureau, Chamber of Commerce Building, Spokane, Washington.

The new $2,500,000 Davenport Hotel invites you to Spokane.

*This advertising brochure featuring Miss Spokane welcoming guests was designed in 1915 especially for Louis Davenport and the promotion of his new Davenport Hotel. At the time, Miss Spokane, Marguerite Motie, was in demand for numerous functions and promotions, where she was often the featured attraction. She drew crowds wherever she was advertised as the scheduled speaker. (Courtesy Dorothy and Bob Capeloto, daughter and son-in-law of Marguerite Motie.)*

Festivities continued at the hotel following the grand finale on September 19th. A formal tea, the first of many, was held two days later. Women filled the Marie Antoinette Room, the mezzanine and the Elizabethan Room, bedecked in their "new fall gowns." According to a newspaper article a week later, the festivities at the formal opening marked the start of the 1914-1915 "social season." Plans for a winter series of weekly dances at the Davenport were made public. They were to be held every Saturday night from 8:00 until midnight, followed by supper in the Hall of the Doges. Once a month, the dance would be a formal affair beginning at 9:00 p.m. and continuing after the midnight meal was served.

As Louis Davenport had hoped, the hotel became the center of the community. Men and women from Spokane and the surrounding communities gathered to conduct business and to hold their annual business meetings. Civic, social, fraternal and business organizations met at the Davenport, some even establishing their offices in the hotel. It was the location of banquets and conventions for miners, loggers, educators, law enforcement and more. All sorts of social functions were celebrated there – weddings, graduations, birthdays and various holiday parties. Of course, for Easter and Christmas, the hotel was a mass of flowers and decorations. Trade shows – from cars to cattle – were held there. Fashion shows, political rallies, proms and other dances were regular events, and if you cared what others thought, you had better be seen at these dances. The teas and tea dances were heavily attended, and there was always music in the lobby, especially organ or piano (if not live, a player piano entertained), as well as in the dining areas and other public rooms. Visiting dignitaries and celebrities were hosted at the hotel, as were participants in the Indian Congresses. Parents brought their young children to the Davenport to teach them social graces, and friends would meet around the fireplace. Others might sit at the desks placed along the mezzanine to write letters or just watch the activity below. During World War II, the lobby and mezzanine even provided a place for servicemen to spend the night. Plans for Grand Coulee Dam were drawn up at the Davenport. And the list goes on. The small sampling of photographs that follow give an idea of how the hotel has been patronized over the years.

*A Maypole Dance in the lobby of the Davenport Hotel in 1915. (Photo courtesy Dorothy and Bob Capeloto.)*

*Preparing for an automobile trade show (top) in the Davenport Lobby in 1915 and the final staging. At the time, being able to claim that Louis Davenport purchased a vehicle from them was a good endorsement for the dealer. (EWSHS Libby Studio photos L87-1.11587X-15 and L87-1.11605x-15)*

THE PRICE—IN SIX STAGES

*This 1912 cartoon from the Spokesman-Review provides a humorous perspective of a situation that probably mirrored Louis Davenport's experience in many ways. At the time of the first frame, in 1874, Davenport would have been six years old. In 1912, the year construction began on the hotel, there were less than 1,000 cars in all of Spokane County and over 100 different automobile manufacturers in the United States. The automobile was far from being perfected and still not widely available to the average family. However, by the time the hotel opened in 1914, cars were becoming somewhat more dependable and popular.*

This cartoon from the February 16, 1912, edition of the Spokesman-Review showed a typical response from the public, especially in light of the vast volume of horse transportation that was soon to be replaced by motorized vehicles.

Two of Louis Davenport's cars. On the left is his 1912 Stevens Duryea, with Lewis Jr. at the wheel, accompanied by his mother, Verus Davenport. (Photo courtesy Louis and Nita Davenport III)  The other car is his 1926 Cadillac Coupe. (EWSHS Libby Studio photo L87-1.31255-26)

*A 1915 wedding party in the Marie Antoinette Room of the Davenport Hotel. (Libby Studio photo courtesy Walt and Karen Worthy.)*

*A dining party in the Elizabethan Room in 1921. Note the silver food-warming cart and the silver chandeliers. (Libby Studio photo courtesy Walt and Karen Worthy.)*

*The Glacier National Park Juvenile Band at the Sprague Avenue entrance to the Davenport Hotel in 1915. (Libby Studio photo courtesy Walt and Karen Worthy.)*

*A 1916 appreciation event for the Davenports from the Northern Pacific Railway. The book-shaped cakes were compliments of the railway's dining car department. The center cake was inscribed: "A Book Full of Good Wishes for the Success and Future of Mr. & Mrs. Louis M. Davenport and the Davenport Hotel." The "baked potato" behind the cakes and the advertising on the boy's apron were part of their "Great Big Baked Potato" promotion of the Northwest. (Libby Studio photo courtesy Walt and Karen Worthy)*

*The 15th anniversary of the El Mabarraz Temple No. 92 in the Hall of the Doges on April 26, 1915. (Photo courtesy Walt and Karen Worthy.)*

*Nurses' banquet in the Annex Room of Davenport's Restaurant in 1918. (Libby Studio photo Walt and Karen Worthy.)*

*A dance in the Hall of the Doges in 1918, sponsored by the National League of Women's Service, for the military men stationed in the Inland Northwest during World War I. (Libby Studio photo courtesy Walt and Karen Worthy.)*

*A banquet for Electrolux personnel on November 9, 1935, held in the Georgian Room of Davenport's Restaurant.. (Libby Studio photo courtesy John Tuft.)*

*Davenport Sport Shop models in the Marie Antoinette Room in 1923. The young boy in the golfing clothes is Warn Winston, who became an outstanding amateur golfer. (EWSHS Libby Studio photo L87-1.22926-23)*

*The Davenport Sport Shop, which opened in 1919, was located at the corner of Sprague and Lincoln (shown here in 1923). It later expanded along the Lincoln Street side. Several years later, it moved farther east, where it remained until the hotel closed. Haddad took over this space. (EWSHS Libby photo L87-1.24367-23)*

*A comedy act in the Marie Antoinette Room in 1924. (Libby Studio photo Walt and Karen Worthy.)*

*A 1950 banquet in the Davenport lobby. Hotel manager, Jim McCluskey, said it took a lot of convincing to get Louis Davenport to agree to host banquets in the lobby. Obviously, it greatly increased the total banquet space. EWSHS Libby Studio photo L87-1.62513.50)*

*A parade during the 1926 Indian Congress passing the Sprague Avenue side of the Davenport Hotel. Princess America Jessie Jim and her entourage are on the float, followed by members of the Blackfeet Indian Tribe from Browning, Montana. A total of 28 tribes took part in this celebration. (EWSHS photo L97-13.24)*

*A group of Indian women in the Davenport Hotel on September 10, 1932, during the Inland Empire Jamboree. (EWSHS photo L93-69.11.5)*

*Admiring a 1932 Chevrolet sedan in the Marie Antoinette Room of the Davenport Hotel. Louis Davenport loved cars and went to great lengths in accommodating dealerships with displays in his hotel. (EWSHS Libby Studio photo L87-1.937.32)*

*The Washington State Patrol's ninth annual conference in the Hall of the Doges, November 16, 1934. (Photo courtesy Walt and Karen Worthy.)*

*A montage of floor shows in the Marie Antoinette Room of the Davenport Hotel in 1923. The bottom photo was for the New Year's Eve celebration. (Libby Studio photos courtesy Walt and Karen Worthy.)*

*The wedding party of Thoburn C. Brown and Edna Mae Endslow, during their wedding reception on September 4, 1940, in the Elizabethan Room of the Davenport Hotel. From left: Eugene Endslow, Edna Mae's brother; Steve Shrock; Dean Eshelman; William R. Brown, Thoburn's brother; Arthur Kinley; Thoburn and Edna Mae; Gunvor Endslow; Rosabelle Brown, Thoburn's sister; Maybelle Brown, Thoburn's; and Ahdee Kinley. Young girls in front are Virginia Endslow (left) and Elizabeth Endslow. (Photo courtesy Thoburn and Edna Mae Brown.)*

Edna Mae and Thoburn Brown were both raised in Spokane. After graduating from Washington State College, Edna Mae attended Indianapolis University Medical School for a year to become a dietician. She stayed in that area, working for the Eli Lilly Company in her chosen profession. In the mid-1930s, she returned to Spokane to take the "Dorothy Dean" position with the *Spokesman-Review*, which she held for over five years. One of her responsibilities was a regular weekly program on home and cooking topics. These programs, held in the Chronicle Building auditorium, had an average attendance of 300. On one occasion, Chef Edward Mathieu of the Davenport Hotel was the guest speaker. Through him, Edna Mae met Louis Davenport and was frequently invited to join him, Chef Mathieu, Jim McCluskey and Herbert Douglas for lunch. Chef Mathieu would ask her to critique new menu items. She always graciously complied, but said she "really couldn't 'touch' his cooking!" In the mid-1980s, Edna Mae, who is a longtime member and on the board of the Friends of the Davenport, served as the decorating chairman on a refurbishing project of the Davenports' former Flowerfield house at St. George's School.

Thoburn, who owned his own businesses – Clark Equipment, Brown Trailers, and Brown Industries – usually ate lunch at the Davenport Coffee Shop. After seeing Edna Mae there, he became smitten and devised a plan to meet her. One day he approached her with a request to help him plan a kitchen for his mother. That evening, when Edna Mae excitedly told her mother about this "cute boy's" request, her mother said, "Why, I know Mrs. Brown. She wouldn't want you to plan her kitchen – she'd plan it herself!" Edna Mae decided to just play along. After going over the plans, Thoburn asked if he could drive her home. When she answered "yes," he decided to take the next step and invited her to dinner. That was the first of many evenings dining and dancing at Davenport's. The couple has four children and have been married for over 61 years.

*The Circus Room (#730), located just north of the service elevators on the Seventh Floor of the Davenport, was decorated in a circus theme around 1935 for businessman Harper Joy, a friend of Louis Davenport, who had a passion for the circus. Whenever Joy could get away, he would join the Ringling Brothers Circus as a clown. A. Rutgers "Van" VanderLoeff (left), owner of a sign and show car business, was hired by Davenport and Joy to paint the room. Contrary to some written accounts, this room was not a play room for Lewis Davenport Jr. He was a grown man when it became the circus room. (Photo courtesy Spokane Public Library.)*

*Left: Ethel VanderLoeff (center), wife of "Van" VanderLoeff, shown here with Don Haffner (third from left) and Carl Krageland (in the suspenders), Van's assistants on the Circus Room project (above). The other men are unidentified. (Photo courtesy Spokane Public Library.)*

*A wedding photo of Elwood Powers and Dorothy Rochon Powers taken on November 19, 1945. (Photo courtesy Dorothy and Elwood Powers.)*

Few who have lived in Spokane for any length of time would not recognize the name Dorothy Rochon Powers. She had a lengthy career with the *Spokesman-Review* as a columnist and associate editor, and since retirement has written two books. Although she wrote about every imaginable subject during her career, her articles about the Davenport Hotel, especially after word of possible demolition reached her ears, helped raise community awareness about the pending fate of its historic gem. In no small part, she contributed to its survival.

Much of Dorothy and Elwood Powers's personal lives have been intertwined with the Davenport. During an interview with Dorothy in May 2001, she related early Davenport memories with a story-telling ability that can only be defined as a natural-born gift. Following the interview, she compiled several pages of notes reiterating some of her recollections. She graciously granted permission to print her firsthand account verbatim:

Throughout my life, professional and personal, the Davenport was the scene of wonderful happenings to me that I think are rare: I met my future husband there, spent my wedding night there, was honored at awards banquets there, the *Spokesman-Review* honored me at my retirement with a party for 400 in 1988 after the Davenport had closed and, now, I'll be at its glorious reopening! What a life we've had together, since 1943 – from WWII through Korea, Vietnam, the Gulf War. For all of this time, the Davenport was "home" to thousands of servicemen and women either "passing through" Spokane or stationed here. It was "everybody's house."

That summer day, more than half a century ago, I "met" the famed Davenport Hotel when friends visiting from Montana invited me to dinner there. At their table when I arrived on my dinner break from the *Spokesman-Review* – where I'd just been hired a few weeks earlier – was a handsome young B-17 bomber pilot, due to leave soon for the European Theater in WWII.

That was 1943; I was 21 years old and new to Spokane. Now I'm 79.

From 1943 until I retired in 1988, I wrote hundreds of thousands of words about the Davenport Hotel for the Spokesman-Review – as a news reporter, feature writer, columnist and editor.

In addition to my professional memories of news events, there are countless personal memories. Two years after the 1943 introduction to the handsome bomber pilot, Elwood Powers, I married him. We spent our wedding night, of course, at the Davenport. Throughout our courting that summer of '43, we had, along with others of his crew, feasted late almost every date night on spaghetti and meatballs in silver casseroles in the Davenport coffee shop – for only 50 cents! Through our hundreds of letters during his tour of duty in Europe, Elwood would frequently recall the Davenport meals.

For those of us lucky enough to know Louis Davenport, his graciousness never will be forgotten. Always handsomely dressed in a three-piece suit, he "presided" from the mezzanine throughout the day, and walked in the main floor lobby and in the various dining rooms to greet guests personally. He was geniality personified. "He never saw a stranger," people said of him. That undoubtedly was because he instantly introduced himself and shook hands when he encountered new faces in his hotel. Mr. Davenport welcomed the world to the edifice he considered as a "home" to which they were welcome.

In WWII, he allowed stranded (or financially embarrassed) servicemen and women to sleep in the lobby. Often, the many richly carpeted staircases had a sailor or airman stretched full length on each step.

The Davenport was unquestionably the "heart" of Spokane. Civic clubs staged their luncheon sessions there, and filled the lobby. Worthwhile projects for the city were planned there and many charity causes were able to raise large amounts of money because elegant balls could take over the lobby, Isabella, Elizabethan and Marie Antoinette rooms, using several bands.

Education also was aided. After five years of beseeching the popular late journalist and author Erma Bombeck to speak here free on behalf of establishing scholarships, I received word that she had managed to get permission from her lecture bureau. What a coup! Her fame filled the Davenport lobby and mezzanine to overflowing. A profit of several thousand dollars enabled Women in Communications, a journalism group, to help high school students go to college.

When I recall the remarkable people who worked there and about whom I wrote columns, . . . then I know another reason the hotel was great.

Spokane must <u>never</u> forget that others saved this jewel for us. It was tended and preserved. Lomas and Nettleton cared for it and so did the entire Ng family of Sun International. Now Spokane's gifted entrepreneur, Walt Worthy, daily enhances our city's jewel. All of us should appreciate the legacy of loveliness he gives us. Bless 'em all – those who over all the years preserved and cherished the Davenport, who danced there, hosted the world there, dined there, cried over wartime farewells there and, yes, laughed with joy there. The "heart" of Spokane is beating again!

*Alfred W. "Al" and Mae I. Schaeffer enjoying a social hour hosted by Elwood Powers' company during the annual Northwest Mining Convention at the Davenport Hotel, circa 1950. The convention, always held the first weekend of December, drew participants from a wide radius. Schaeffer was the Metaline Falls plant manager of the Lehigh Portland Cement Company. The small community of Metaline Falls, located about 95 miles north of Spokane, was built on the mining industry, which included the cement plant. (Photo courtesy Al and Mae Schaeffer.)*

*A meeting of friends in the early 1950s in front of the Davenport Delicacy Shop in the Pennington Building, at First and Post. From left: Ann Butterfield Dralle, Lois Robinson Hogan, Maxine Lee Heath. (Photo courtesy Lois Hogan.)*

# Davenport's Notable Guests

The following is a partial list of notable guests at Louis Davenport's establishments:

**Anderson, Marian -** One of the 20th century's most celebrated opera singers. She was the first African-American singer to perform with the Metropolitan Opera. At Eleanor Roosevelt's invitation, she sang at the Lincoln Memorial on Easter 1939, to a crowd of 75,000.

**Arnold, Eddy** – Country Western singer.

**Autry, Gene** – Movie actor.

**Barker, Bob** – Television celebrity.

**Barrymore, Ethel** – American actress.

**Belafonte, Harry** – American singer.

**Benny, Jack** – World-famous comedian.

**Bernhardt, Sarah** – Most well-known French stage actress in the early 1900s.

**Borge, Victor** – Nationally-known pianist, comedian and movie actor.

**Brown, Les** – Big Band leader during the Golden Age of Swing. His group was called the Band of Renown.

**Burr, Raymond** – Television and movie actor.

**Calhoun, Rory** – Movie actor.

**Carnera, Primo** – Heavyweight champion.

**Carradine, John** – Movie actor.

**Carter, June** – Country Western singer.

**Cash, Johnny** – Country Western singer.

**Cliburn, Van** – World-renowned pianist who caused a sensation in both the United States and Russia by winning the First Tchaikovsky International Piano Competition in Moscow.

**Cole, Nat King** – Famous American singer.

**Coolidge, Calvin** – Thirteenth president of the United States (1923-1929).

**Corbett, "Gentleman" Jim** – American prizefighter, whose first notable fight, in 1891, was a four-hour heavyweight contest, resulting in a draw after 61 rounds. In 1892 he became the first heavyweight champion of the world when he knocked out John L. Sullivan in the 21st round.

**Cosby, Bill** – Famous American comedian.

**Cox, Will** – President of the Brooklyn Dodgers.

**Crosby, Bing** – World-famous singer and actor.

**Davis Jr., Sammy** – World-famous singer and actor.

**Day, Dennis** – World-famous actor.

**Dean, Jimmy** – World-famous singer and actor.

**DeMille, Cecil** – American film director and producer in the late 1920s to 1950s. Among the films he produced are: *The Ten Commandments* (1923 and 1956), *The King of Kings* (1927), *Cleopatra* (1934), *The Plainsman* (1936), *Unconquered* (1947), *Sampson and Delilah* (1946) and the *Greatest Show on Earth* (1952).

**Dempsey, Jack** – Dempsey became world heavyweight boxing champion in 1919.

**Dewey, Governor and Mrs. Thomas E.** - New York City governor, political leader and attorney. Two-time contender for U.S. president: 1944 against Franklin Roosevelt and 1948 against Harry Truman.

**Donlevy, Brian** – Popular movie actor during the 1950s to 1970s.

**Drew, Ellen** – A second-echelon leading lady in movies during in the 1930s to 1950s.

**Durante, Jimmy** – Famous American comedian.

**Earhart, Amelia** – World-famous aviatrix. First woman to fly solo across the Atlantic, establishing a new record for the crossing: 13.5 hours. In 1935, she became the first woman to cross fly across the Pacific Ocean, crossing from Hawaii to California. In June 1937, she began a flight around the world, accompanied by navigator Frederick Noonan. Their plane disappeared on July 3, while en route from New Guinea to Howland Island.

**Eddy, Nelson** – Popular actor and singer with a rich baritone voice. He began his career in the early 1920s.

**Elgart, Les** – Along with his brother Larry, Les competed with many top-name bands of the 1950s.

**Fairbanks, Douglas** – American movie actor and producer who began his movie career in 1915. He became one of the most popular actors of his times and was known for his daring athletic feats and swordsmanship. His second wife was movie actress Mary Pickford. He founded the film production company, United Artists, Inc., in 1919. His movies included: *The Mark of Zorro, The Three Musketeers, Robin Hood, The Thief of Bagdad, Don Q, Son of Zorro, The Black Pirate, The Gaucho, The Iron Mask,* and *The Taming of the Shrew.* The listed movies were all made in the 1920s.

**Flaherty, Ray** – Professional football coach.

**Foch, Marshal Ferdinand** – French marshal who commanded the Allied Armies on the Western Front during the final campaigns of World War I.

**Fontanne, Lynn** – Movie actress who was born in and, in 1905, made her debut in London. Often toured the United States with her husband, actor Alfred Lunt. One of the films they starred in was *The Taming of the Shrew.* Fontanne was honored for lifetime achievement by the Kennedy Center in Washington D.C.

**Ford, Glen** – Popular movie actor.

**Ford, Tennessee Ernie** – Popular nationally-known singer.

**Gable, Clark** – Famous American movie actor, often referred to as the "King of Hollywood." He was the leading man in *Gone With the Wind.* Stationed at Ft. Wright during WWII, he was a frequent guest at the Davenport.

**Gadski, Madame Johanna** – Famous opera singer in the early 1900s.

**Goodman, Benny** – Famous clarinetist and band leader who made his professional debut in 1921 at Central Park Theater in Chicago.

**Gray, Gilda** – Inventor of the shimmy dance and also a longtime member of the Ziegfeld Follies.

**Grey, Zane** – World-famous author, often referred to as the all-time greatest storyteller of the American West. By the time he died in 1939, Grey had written almost 90 books, 60 of them Westerns. He had become the bestselling Western writer of all time. The Davenport Hotel was used as a setting in one of his novels.

**Guitar, Bonnie** – Singer/musician.

**Guthrie, Woody** – The Nation's original folk hero. In the 1930s and 1940s, he transformed the folk ballad into a vehicle for social protest, paving the way for other social protest singers and song writers.

**Hammett, Dashiell** – American novelist who gained fame during the mid 1920s to 1930s. Wrote detective fiction, including: *Red Harvest, The Dain Curse, The Maltese Falcon* (a scene was set in the Davenport), *The Glass Key* and *The Thin Man.*

*Hall of the Doges prepared for a banquet in 1908 honoring Louis Davenport's friend, railroad magnate James J. Hill. (EWSHS Libby Studio photo L93-68.9-16)*

*Banquet in honor of President William H. Taft's visit in September 1909. President Taft is seated at the head table beneath his portrait and the United States flag. Decorations in the Hall of the Doges included apple trees laden with ripe apples. (EWSHS Libby Studio photo L93-68.9-43)*

**Harding, Warren G**. – 29th president of the United States (1921-1923).

**Harlem Globetrotters** – Famous national basketball team, who put on exhibitions throughout the United States.

**Harris, Phil** – Radio bandleader and comic on *The Jack Benny Program* from 1936 to 1952. He also had his own radio show with his wife, Faye.

**Hill, James Jerome** – American railroad "Empire Builder" and financier. Founded the Great Northern Railroad and had many mining and banking investments.

**Hoover, Herbert** – 35th president of the United States (1929-1933).

**Hope, Bob** – World-famous comedian.

**Howard, John** – Popular politician from Australia who later became its Prime Minister.

**Hubbard, Elbert** – Famous American writer and founder of the Roycrofters. He was the first journalist to give Davenport's Restaurant a national review.

**Hudson, Rock** – Nationally-famous movie actor.

**Humphrey, Hubert H.** – 38th vice-president of the United States.

**Hutton, Betty** – World-famous movie actress and singer. Often referred to as the "Blond Bombshell," she was one of the most original and colorful singers of 20th century American pop music.

**James, Harry** – Most famous trumpet player during the swing era. In 1939 he formed his own "big band" and had a hit with the song *You Made Me Love You*. By the early 1940s, James's band was the most popular in the world.

**Jessel, George** – Big-time entertainer and song writer in nightclubs and on Broadway. Began producing musical films for Fox in 1945. Often entertained troops over-seas and was known for his charity work.

**Johnson, Lyndon B.** – 36th president of the United States.

**Kennedy, John F.** – 35th president of the United States (1961-1963).

**Kennedy, Robert** – United States political leader and attorney general, and brother of former president John Kennedy.

**Kingston Trio** – Nationally-famous singing group.

**Lauder, Sir Harry** – popular international singer, song writer and comedian in the early 1900s. He gave much of his time to charitable causes.

**Lee, Peggy** – Nationally-famous singer

**Lennon Sisters** – Nationally-famous four-sister singing act.

**Lewis, Jerry** – Nationally-famous comedian, best known for his charitable causes, especially in the fight against muscular dystrophy.

**Liberace, Wladziu Valentino** – World-famous pianist and entertainer, known to the public as just "Liberace," and also referred to as "Mr. Showmanship."

**Lindbergh, Charles** – World-famous aviator who, on May 20, 1927, completed the first nonstop flight across the Atlantic.

**Lindsay, Vachel** – World-famous poet who lived in the Davenport Hotel for a number of years.

**Louis, Joe** – World heavyweight champion boxer from June 1937 to March 1949.

**Lunt, Alfred** – One of America's foremost stage actors. In 1922 he married British actress Lynn Fontanne and, for 35 years, they were the most popular married couple in the entertainment world.

**MacDonald, Jeannette** – Singer and actress. Was Nelson Eddy's singing partner. She appeared in 28 films, numerous musicals and almost 200 radio talk shows.

**Marshall, General George** – A principal military strategist for the Allied operations in Europe during WWII. Following the war, he was responsible for the Marshall Plan, under which the United States built up European economies.

**McIntire, John** – Popular television star, known primarily for his role as the wagon master in *Wagon Train*. During his career, which was at its pinnacle in the 1960s, he appeared in almost 90 movies.

**McQueen, Steve** – Considered by many to be one of the greatest movie stars in the world, maintaining a superstar status throughout his career. Some of his movies include *The Great Escape*, *The Sand Pebbles*, *Nevada Smith*, *The Getaway* and *Papillon*.

**Moss, Stirling** – Famous British race car driver.

**Nabors, Jim** – Nationally known actor, singer and comedian.

**Nelson, Ricky** – A teenage movie actor and singer. He became an idol to thousands of teenage girls in the 1950s. He is best known for his role as Ricky Nelson (played himself) in *The Adventures of Ozzie and Harriet.*

**Nixon, Richard M.** – 37th president of the United States ( 1967-1974). Officially opened Expo '74, the 1974 world's fair held in Spokane.

**Nolan, Jeanette** – Began her early career in the 1930s on radio and stage, and later became a movie actress. Her final film appearance was in 1998, playing the mother of Robert Redford's character in *The Horse Whisperer.*

**Pavlova, Anna** – Considered to be the greatest 20th century ballet dancer. The Russian-born dancer traveled worldwide in the early 1900s, including the United States, introducing audiences in many countries to ballet for the first time. She is credited with doing more to popularize ballet than any other dancer

**Peary, Robert E.** – On April 7, 1909, Peary and five other men were the first known human beings to set foot on the North Pole. Peary also proved Greenland was an island, not a continent.

**Pershing, General John J.** – The American general who led the American Expeditionary Force in Europe during WWI.

**Pickford, Mary** – The most popular female actress during the silent-film era. She was married to Douglas Fairbanks and one of the founders of United Artists. She was both physically beautiful and an exceptionally astute businesswoman.

**Pons, Lilly** – Born in France in 1904, Pons made her opera singing debut in America in 1929. The majority of her performances were with the Metropolitan Opera and the Chicago Civic Opera.

**Power, Tyrone Sr.** – Well-respected and talented stage and silent movie actor. He was the father of Tyrone Power Jr., the 1940s and 1950s movie superstar. Power was responsible for Spokane's first movie studio, built at Minnehaha Park.

**Price, Vincent** – Nationally-known movie actor during the 1940s through the 1960s. He became famous for his roles in horror movies and thrillers.

**Prince Olav and Princess Martha of Norway** - Crown royalty of Norway. Prince Olav became King Olav V in 1957. Martha came from a royal family in Sweden. They married in 1929, but Martha died before Olav became king. While in Spokane in May 1939, the local Lutheran churches held a special church service at the Davenport Hotel for the Royal Party.

**Queen Marie of Romania** – Born in 1875 in Kent, England, to Alfred, Duke of Edinburgh and the former Grand Duchess Marie Alexandrovna of Russia. She was the granddaughter of Queen Victoria. In 1893 she married Ferdinand of Romania and became Queen of the Romanians in 1914. During WWI, she volunteered as a Red Cross nurse serving sick and wounded Romanian soldiers.

**Ray, Johnny** – Nationally-known singer and actor. Became famous for the songs *Walking in the Rain*, *Cry,* and *Little White Cloud That Cried.*

**Rickenbacker, Captain Eddie** – American aviator who served in the United States Air Force in France during WWI. While there, he became the leading American combat pilot receiving many decorations, including the Congressional Medal of Honor. In 1938 he became president of Eastern Airlines and served as the chairman of its board, 1954-1963. He is also the author of three books.

**Ritter, Tex** – Popular county folk musician who began his career in 1929. Ritter acted in 85 movies, 78 of which were Westerns. Some of his hits include *You Are My Sunshine*, *Hillbilly Heaven*, *High Noon,* and W*ayward Wind*.

**Roberts, Oral** – Evangelist, educator, businessman, author and television personality, 1960s through the 1990s.

**Rogers, Will** – Known as the "Indian Cowboy" from the Cherokee Nation, Rogers became one of the most popular and beloved Americans of his time. He was born in 1879 and died in a plane accident in Alaska in 1935.

**Roosevelt, Theodore** – 26th president of the United States (1901-1909).

**Ruth, George Herman "Babe"** – Ruth began his career in 1914 and became one of the most gifted and popular players in the history of baseball. He was in Spokane for his own vaudeville show at the Pantages Theatre.

**Schumann-Heink, Ernestine** – German-born opera singer. Became a U.S. citizen in 1908 and later known for her radio broadcasts.

**Selassie, Haile** – Became the emperor of Ethiopia in 1930. Several failed attempts were made to overthrow him, the first of which was led by his son. In 1974 his military forces revolted against him because he failed to do anything to prevent the corruption, starvation and drought within his country. He died in 1975.

**Shipman, Nell** – Canada's first silent screen movie actress. Shipman moved to Spokane in 1922 with her cast and crew, and lived in the Davenport while directing and starring in silent movies produced at Minnehaha Park. She later established Lionhead Lodge, her movie studio on the northeast shore of Priest Lake.

**Sousa, John Philip** – Famous American bandmaster and composer, known as the "march king." In 1880 he was appointed leader of the United States Marine Corps Band. In 1892 he resigned that position and formed his own band. His most well-known march is *The Stars and Stripes Forever*. He was among Louis Davenport's favorite guests. During his visit in 1915, he gave a concert under the stars on the roof garden.

**Symington, Stuart** – Secretary of the United States Air Force, 1947-1950.

**Taft, William Howard** – 27th president of the United States (1909-1913).

**Taylor, Robert** – Famous movie actor who began his career in 1934. His good looks soon made him a matinee idol. His first wife was actress Barbara Stanwyck.

**Tibbett, Lawrence** – Opera star, who began singing with the Metropolitan Opera in the early 1920s.

**Truman, Harry S.** – 33rd President of the United States (1945-1953)

**Tunney, Gene** – Won the world heavyweight boxing title in 1926 when he defeated Jack Dempsey. He retired undefeated in 1928.

**Warfield, David** – Popular America actor born in 1866. He was popular during the music-halls era.

**Welk, Lawrence** – Popular American musician and band director, who gained national fame with his television program, *The Lawrence Show*.

**White, Betty** – Emmy award winning actress who was popular from the 1950s to the 1990s. She was a lifelong supporter of anything to do with animal rights.

**Wolfe, Thomas** – One of the great writers of the 20th century. His first novel, *Look Homeward, Angel*, was published in 1929. Other novels include *Of Time and the River*, *From Death to the Morning* and *The Story of a Novel*.

**Yogananda, Paramahansa** – A noted spiritual leader from India who founded the worldwide organization of Self-Realization Fellowship. Arrived in the United States in 1920 and conducted a series of national lecture tours to overflowing audiences between 1925 and 1936.

**Ziegfeld Jr., Florenz** – Founder of the Ziegfeld Follies and one of Broadway's greatest producers and most intriguing characters. He spared no expense in making his shows glittering extravaganzas. He permanently transformed musical theater by employing and furnishing the best of talent and materials.

*A Knights of Columbus banquet in the Hall of the Doges in 1911. (EWSHS Libby Studio photo L93-68.9-57)*

# NO TRICK AT ALL TO CLIMB WALL

## "Human Spider" Makes It to Top of the Davenport in Twenty Minutes.

Scaling the Lincoln street side of the Davenport hotel with the apparent ease of the ordinary man climbing a ladder, Bill Strother, "the human spider," Monday night gave thousands of Spokane people another hair-raising exhibition of skill and nerve.

Incidentally, Bill put about $500 into the treasury of the Spokane home of the Washington Children's Home Finding society, and added that much to his own resources as a result of collections taken through the crowds by some 20 members of the Elks' lodge and girls from the Y. W. C. A.

Bill went up the side of the building in 20 minutes, causing breathless gasps by his daring, when he purpusely allowed his feet to slip at times, and when he stood on his head on a window sill on the ninth floor level.

Going over the cornice at the top a rope was passed about his body for safety, but he did not even tighten the rope. On the top he rode a bicycle around the cornice rim, at one time letting the front wheel slip over the edge while the crowd groaned.

### Wonderful, Says Jones.

"Mr. Strother has given us the most wonderful exhibition of nerve that I have ever witnessed," stated the Rev. Hugh W. Jones, superintendent of the local Washington Children's Home Finding society. "He is a most marvelous man, and a gentleman. I sincerely hope that he will come to our city again and give us another exhibition.

"So great was his feat that I felt that he had more than earned the entire collection taken up, and I urged him to accept all the proceeds, but he indignantly refused, insisting that the children's home accept its share.

"At this time, also, I wish to express my deep appreciation of the fa-

This news clipping appeared in the August 23, 1921 edition of the Spokesman-Review. Bill Strother, the "human spider," climbed the Lincoln Street side of the Davenport Hotel.

After reaching the top of the hotel, Strother excited the crowd even more by riding a bicycle around the cornice rim. At one point, he purposely let the bicycle wheel slip over the edge.

Two days prior to his Davenport climb, Strother was almost killed in Coeur d'Alene. After riding his bicycle around the rim of the city hall building, he was descending the fire escape when someone handed him his bicycle. As he reached for it, the other person let go and the bicycle came in contact with some live electrical wires. If the bicycle hadn't fallen from his grasp, he would have been electrocuted.

*(Photo of the Davenport Hotel courtesy Dorothy and Bob Capeloto.)*

West side

Complimentary Dinner
Tendered by Citizens of Spokane, Washington, to

Mr. Tyrone Power

in the Marie Antoinette Room, Davenport Hotel
Thursday Evening, August 23, 1917

*On August 3, 1917, a group of citizens sponsored a complimentary dinner in honor of the famous movie actor Tyrone Power II. This is a photo of the menu cover.*

On August 19, 1917, movie actor Tyrone Power II arrived at the Great Northern Railroad Depot on Trent Avenue (now Spokane Falls Boulevard). Miss Spokane Marguerite Motie and representatives of the Spokane Ad Club, who were largely instrumental in bringing Mr. Power to Spokane, greeted him. He was honored with a dinner in the Marie Antoinette Room of the Davenport Hotel.

Following a six-day survey of Spokane's scenic possibilities, Power made the decision to establish a movie studio in Spokane. The site he chose, Minnehaha Park, was owned by the city and under the control of the Spokane Park Board. Members of the park board were eager for the opportunity to attract a movie studio to the Spokane area and quickly signed a lease providing the entire Minnehaha Park area for this venture. In early August 1917, preliminary incorporation papers, with capitalization of $500,000, were signed for a film production studio to be established at Spokane. On August 24, 1917, the Spokane newspapers announced that the new company would be called Washington Motion Picture Corporation. Tyrone Power had signed a three-year retainer with the company. The studio was intended to be a reproduction of the famous Universal City Studios at Los Angeles, California.

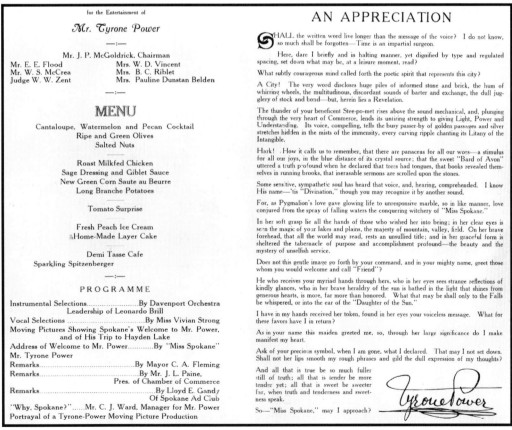

*The menu, prepared especially for Tyrone Power's visit to Spokane, included a prose written by Mr. Power in appreciation for the kindness he was shown while in Spokane. (Menu courtesy Spokane Public Library.)*

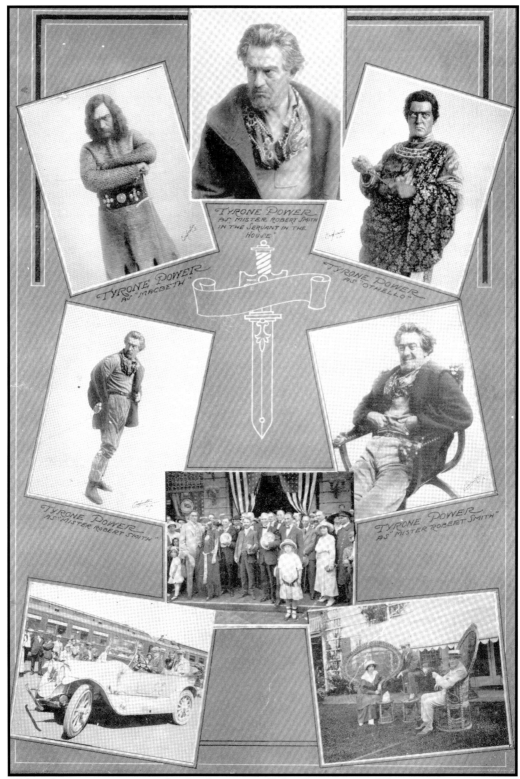

*This photo montage on the back cover of the Davenport "Tyrone Power menu"*
*depicted some scenes from Power's career. (Photo courtesy Spokane Public Library.)*

# Nell Shipman, Silent Movie Screen Actress, Stays at the Davenport Hotel – Takes Over Tyrone Power's Studio

During her earlier vaudeville and theater days, Nell Shipman had visited the Inland Northwest on many occasions and was familiar with the area's beauty and pristine wilderness. It was ideal for the type of outdoor movies she produced. Nell contacted Wellington Playter, a former movie actor who played a lecherous old fool in Nell's movie *Back to God's Country*. Playter was now living in Spokane and had a lease on the former Washington Motion Picture Corporation's studio at Minnehaha Park. This was perfect for Nell. She had accumulated a private zoo consisting of over 70 animal actors and was ready to take a break from the Hollywood scene.

Nell arrived in Spokane with her cast and crew in the early spring of 1922. She described their accommodations in the following manner: "The Cast lived at Louis Davenport's lovely hotel and ate high on the hog. I marched in and out of an expensive suite in my leather coat, carrying my briefcase, playing Madame Producer to the hilt but scared cold-silly inside. Could *The Grub Stake* carry the load?" One of Nell's first challenges was raising money for the production and to tailor the Minnehaha studio to her needs. Within a short time, they raised $180,000 to film a feature called *The Grub Stake*. She immediately hired three local men to begin construction of the necessary changes and accommodations she would need for her productions and animals. The men she hired were Paul Peters, a skilled carpenter and two of his sons, Lloyd and Ray. (Both sons had a desire to be movie actors and worked for Nell as carpenters and actors for the duration of her stay in the Inland Northwest.) Filming began almost immediately, with some of the first scenes being shot during March of 1922 near Tiger, Ione and upper Lake Thomas in Pend Oreille County. Other scenes were shot at the Minnehaha studio and on Mt. Spokane.

After a few months in Spokane, Nell moved her production company and zoo to the northeastern shore of Priest Lake, where she built a studio and movie camp called Lionhead Lodge. She lived there from 1922 to 1925, where she experienced some of the greatest highs and lows of her life. *The Grub Stake* was finished, but the American distributor who purchased it soon declared bankruptcy, tying the film up in legal actions. Unable to pay her investors and creditors, her quality of life began to decline. Although Shipman continued to produce other small films, she left Priest Lake, never to return. What remained of her animal actors were donated to a zoo in San Diego. During her time in the Inland Northwest, Nell gained tremendous notoriety and made a memor- **Nell Shipman** able mark on those she touched. *(EWSHS photo)*

# Davenport's Restaurant Hosts North Central's First Graduating Class.

This group photo of the first graduating class of North Central High School appeared in the Spokesman-Review on Sunday, February 4, 1912. Top row, from left: Maude Stiles, Flossie Settlemire, Leroy Trager, Francis Fuller, Douglas Parker, Verona Lange and Edith McDonald. Middle row: Esther Nelson, Mildred Moran, Maude Herrington, Ruth Maurer, Bertha Jones, Gertrude Hall and Mabel Jones. Bottom row: Bernice Lucas, Mae Wallace, Florence Steffer, Francis McKenzie, Louis Seagrave, Arthur Jeffrey, Elizabeth Stone and Kathleen Stout.

The first class to graduate from North Central High School, which was in 1912, held their graduation banquet in the East Banquet Room of Davenport's Restaurant. For three hours, the 22 graduates sat at the banquet table while they listened to addresses by their classmates and guests.

Following the evening program, the class drank a toast to North Central's principal, R. T. Hargraves. For ten minutes he spoke to his first graduates on "Auf Wiedersehen" (till we meet again). In part, he said:

> We talk about getting character, but there are other things of importance. Personality counts for a great deal. A great deal is gift, but personality can be developed. I mean that when you meet people try to treat them so that they wish to meet you again.

*On November 29, 1921, a banquet was held in the Marie Antoinette at the Daven-port Hotel to honor Marshal Ferdinand Foch during his visit to Spokane. Miss Spokane Marguerite Motie offered the official greeting from Spokane. Trees laden with apples provided the decorations at the head table. Because of the season, the apples had to be attached by hand, unlike during President Taft's visit, when live apple trees were brought in. (Libby Studio photo courtesy Dorothy and Bob Capeloto.)*

French Marshal Ferdinand Foch was the supreme commander of the Allied Armies, including the American forces, on the Western front during the final campaign of World War I. As such, he led a series of counteroffensives resulting in the final victory that brought the war to an end. He was honored far and wide for this accomplishment.

Present at this event were some of the era's most prominent men from Spokane, Washington State and the Nation. A partial list (some of who are in the above photo) includes: Col. Frank Parker, Leo Duffy, Col. John D. Markey, Col. Francis E. Drake, Spokane Mayor Charles A. Fleming, General James Drain, C.D. Cunningham, General Desticker, Washington Governor Louis F. Hart, Hanford McNider, Robert Insinger, Lt. Gov. W.J. Coyle, Col. G.S. Albert, Major de Mierry, George A. Phillips, E.D. Potvin, M.B. Connolly, Alan Toplet, Frank P. Motie, Miles Cahill, W.S. Gilbert, Waldo G. Paine, E.K. Erwin, E.P. Chapin, Harry Heylman, Frank T. McCollough, A.B. Fosseen, H.T. Anthony, Arthur D. Jones, Charles Dilio, G.H. Ellis, Lester M. Livengood, W.P. Hopkins, Roy R. Gill, Walter Hogan, Dr. H.L. Moorehouse, George H. Keith, B.Gard Ewing, H.M. Blakely, Harry Olive, Major Bidds, C. Herbert Moore, William Beardsmore, Dr. C.O. Liner, Grant Ware, C.L. King, Thomas Keene, Al Ware, and Dr. C.E. Grove.

# Vachel Lindsay
## The Davenport Hotel's World-Famous Poet in Residence

***Vachel Lindsay posing with his family, circa 1930. His wife, Elisabeth (Conner) Lindsay, is seated between him and their daughter, Susan Doniphan Lindsay. Vachel is holding their son, Nicholas Cave Lindsay. (EWSHS photo L94-9.61)***

Nicholas Vachel Lindsay was a gifted and nationally-recognized American writer and poet during the early 1920s. His fame began in 1913, when he published one of his best works, *General William Booth Enters Heaven*. Shortly after, a national magazine called *Poetry* began printing his poems.

Spokane attorney, Ben H. Kizer, was an admirer of Lindsay's work and began corresponding with him. Kizer eventually convinced the poet to move to Spokane. In the summer of 1924, with the ongoing financial assistance from Ben Kizer and Louis Davenport, he established residency on the 11th floor of the Davenport Hotel (room 1129). Louis Davenport reasoned that the prestige of having a nationally-famous poet in residency would attract guests.

Lindsay quickly made himself at home at the Davenport and was seen on a daily basis in the lobby, writing or reciting poetry, mingling with guests or simply lounging by the fireplace. Lindsay's presence did provide an attraction. For those familiar with his fame and reputation, it was exciting to be in his company. However, his eccentricities also made some guests feel uncomfortable.

One his many most talked about antics involved two cloth French-boudoir dolls, which were popular at the time. They had long arms and legs, with peculiar faces and dazzling attire. His first doll was originally intended as a model to sketch, but upon realizing the attention it attracted, he purchased a second one. The dolls became his frequent "companions" in public places. He would typically reserve a table at the far end of the restaurant, thus having to walk the full length of it carrying his dolls, which maximized the attention he received. The waiters had been instructed to immediately place high chairs at his table when he showed up with his dolls and were expected to take the "dolls' orders" with complete seriousness and respect. Following the first introduction to this behavior, most of the hotel employees served Mr. Lindsay and his companions with friendly interest. In her book, *Vachel Lindsay, Poet in Exile*, Mildred Weston stated: "The dolls might take tea or lemonade or some other light refreshment; and they sat with cups and plates before them while Lindsay solemnly ate his dinner." Weston summed up his behavior as follows:

> It was plain that a wish for attention was almost always in his mind. His costume, too, suggested this: a raincoat or overcoat when others were coatless, or a black shirt when black shirts were not common. Some time later the carrying of his baby daughter in the manner of an Indian papoose was simply one more of his whimsical notions.

On May 19, 1925, at age 45, Lindsay married Elisabeth Conner, a 23-year-old teacher at Lewis and Clark High School. The ceremony was performed by Rev. Charles Pease in Vachel's room at the Davenport. Their daughter, Susan, was born May 28 the following year. With a child to raise, the couple moved into an apartment at 2318 West Pacific in Browne's Addition, where they were remembered by their wild parties. Their second child, Nicholas, joined the family on September 16, 1927.

Although Vachel retained his suite at the hotel for work, by the time he moved to Browne's Addition, his welcome at the Davenport Hotel was beginning to wear thin and the public's interest in him waning. In 1929 he moved the family to Springfield, Illinois, his boyhood home. Suffering from depression and a lot of inner turmoil, Vachel Lindsay ended his own life on December 5, 1931. In spite of his eccentricities and notoriety, Spokane's recollections of the once-famous poet quickly faded.

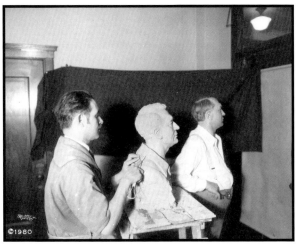

**Vachel Lindsay posing for a sculpture in 1929. (EWSHS Libby Studio photo L87-1.38935-29)**

*A class in the Masonic Temple on September 24, 1925 on the principles of yoga was taught by Paramahansa Yogananda (front center), a yogi from India. (Libby Studio photo courtesy Spokane Meditation Group of Self-Realization Fellowship.)*

A rumor that Mahatma Gandhi had stayed at the Davenport Hotel was easy to dispel because he was never in the United States. However, another revered spiritual leader from India, a contemporary of Gandhi, was a guest of the hotel in 1925. Perhaps he was mistaken by some to be Gandhi? Paramahansa Yogananda came to the United States in 1920 and founded Self-Realization Fellowship, a worldwide nonsectarian religious organization with international headquarters in Los Angeles. During the organization's early years, Yogananda traveled the country on lecture tours, which included Spokane in September 1925. For a couple of weeks, thousands of people were drawn to the Masonic Temple to attend his free lectures and private classes on spiritual matters. During this time, he stayed at the Davenport.

The instructions and teachings offered in his classes were later compiled into a series of lessons, available through his organization. His *Autobiography of a Yogi,* now considered a spiritual classic, is available in 18 languages. Collections of his talks and other writings have also been compiled into numerous books. His spiritual teachings are a blending of East and West, based on the teachings of Jesus Christ and the principles of yoga. The monastic order established by Yogananda is dedicated to the dissemination of his teachings and carrying on the humanitarian and charitable work of the organization, including the Worldwide Prayer Circle. Thousands of members around the world pray daily for those requesting prayers and for world peace. Of note, the only ashes of the Mahatma Gandhi enshrined outside of India are at Self-Realization Fellowship's Lake Shrine in Pacific Palisades, California.

# Queen Marie of Romania and Her Children Visit Spokane in 1926 ~ Guests at the Davenport Hotel

*Queen Marie Alexandra Victoria of Romania (center) with Princess Ileana and Prince Nicholas, in 1926. Queen Marie is holding a large bouquet of orchids that was a gift from the City of Spokane. (EWSHS Libby Studio photo L87-1.32264-26)*

Queen Marie was the first royal guest to visit the city of Spokane. She was the granddaughter of Queen Victoria of Great Britain and the wife of King Ferdinand I of Romania, whom she married when she was 17 years old. When he succeeded to the throne in 1914, Queen Marie became a major influence on Romanian politics. Her eldest son eventually became King Carol II of Romania.

The Queen and her children stopped in Spokane on November 2, 1926, en route to dedicate Sam Hill's still unfinished Maryhill Art Museum in southern Washington, a gesture of appreciation for Hill's generous aid to Romania following World War I. The royal party arrived at the Northern Pacific Depot at 7:30 p.m. and was greeted by an enormous crowd. After a brief rest, Queen Marie emerged from the train to the strains the Romanian national anthem, played by the Fort Wright Military band. An estimated 40,000 to 50,000 people lined the streets to greet the Queen and applauded as over 250 marching military men and the 17-car caravan carrying the royalty and numerous city officials made its way to the Davenport Hotel. The parade traveled north on Browne Street to Riverside Avenue, west on Riverside to Madison Street, south on Madison to Sprague Avenue, then east on Sprague to Post Street and, finally, south on Post to First Avenue, where they stopped at the entrance to the hotel.

The *Spokane Daily Chronicle* recorded the event on November 3, 1926. The following excerpt made reference to their arrival at the Davenport Hotel, where they were guests for the evening:

### Enters Davenport

Marie alighted with Mayor Fleming, graciously accepted the greeting of Guy Toombes, assistant manger of the Davenport, and stood nodding to the cheering, surging throng until the second and third cars arrived and her two children, Ileana and Nicholas, stepped to her side. Then she turned and entered the hotel.

Hung with Rumanian [old spelling] and American flags, the corridor leading to the lobby gave the appearance of a fairy tunnel. The queen walked majestically forward, smiling at the group of maids and young matrons who lined either side of the corridor. She hesitated a moment as she entered the lobby, where she was greeted by a roar of applause and the strains of the Rumanian national anthem.

While at the Davenport, the royal party was also greeted by members of the Coeur d'Alene and Nez Perce tribes, as well as Princess America II, Jessie Jim. Princess Illeana and Prince Nicholas were initiated into the tribes as honorary members. These ceremonies were followed by tribal dances in honor of the royal party.

Following the public reception at the Davenport, the royal party rested for a brief time in the State Suite, which was simply, but tastefully, decorated for the occasion with black Japanese bowls of Premier roses.

From the hotel, the royal party made a brief stop at the Review Building. Following an appearance on the balcony, where Queen Marie spoke a few words of appreciation to the crowd, the royals were returned to the train depot. Their train departed at 10:30 p.m. The three-hour visit was a memorable occasion for the citizenry of Spokane.

# Charles Lindbergh
## Overnight Guest at Davenport Hotel

*Charles Lindbergh giving a speech at the Spokane Fairgrounds in 1927. (EWSHS Libby Studio photo L87-1.34192.29)*

On September 12, 1927, Colonel Charles Lindbergh flew into Spokane in his *Spirit of St. Louis* as part of his nationwide tour to promote aviation. This tour, which started in New York on July 20, 1927, included 75 cities in the United States.

Lindbergh's visit to Spokane was of such significance that all the schools closed at noon so the children could participate in the event. They gathered at the fairgrounds to listen to him speak. As Lindbergh entered Spokane, he flew low over the fairgrounds to give the children a thrill. After landing at Buell Felts Airfield (now known as Felts Field) at Parkwater, he was paraded to the fairgrounds, where the children awaited.

Leaving the fairgrounds, Lindbergh was escorted to the Davenport Hotel, where he was the guest of honor. He arrived at the Davenport about 4:30 p.m., with a little time to rest in the State Suite, prepared especially for him, before the evening banquet in his honor. Tickets for the banquet in the Marie Antoinette Room were $4.00 per plate, with limited seating for 525 people. The banquet program consisted of a number of speeches and entertainment by Lillian Frederick's orchestra.

The following day, after departing Spokane en route to Seattle, Lindbergh had two scheduled fly-overs at Walla Walla and Yakima.

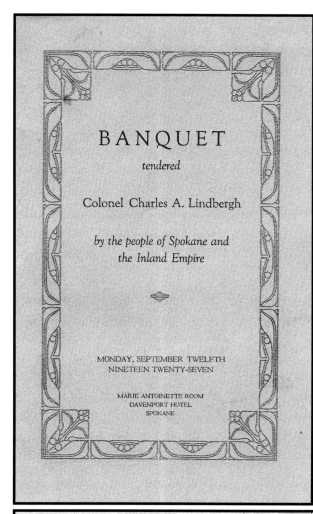

*The special banquet menu and program prepared by the Davenport Hotel for Lindbergh's banquet on September 12, 1927.*

*During Lindbergh's visit, Mayor Charles Fleming asked if he had ever eaten moose meat. He replied that he had not. The following morning Mayor Fleming delivered a generous piece of moose meat to Davenport's kitchen, which was prepared for Lindbergh's breakfast. The meat Fleming provided was from a hunting trip in Canada.*

*Jim McCluskey, who became the hotel manager, recalled that whenever Lindbergh was asked what he would like to eat, he always requested the hotel's chocolate eclairs.*

*(Menu courtesy EWSHS)*

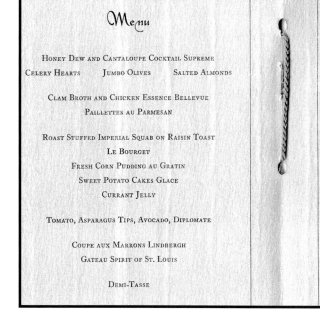

## Amelia Earhart Stays in Davenport's State Suite

*A headline in the Spokane Press announcing the departure of Amelia Earhart from Spokane during a blinding snowstorm on January 31, 1933, proved to be false. When Earhart and her party arrived at Felts Field that afternoon, visibility was at 200 feet. After waiting several hours, they returned to the Davenport Hotel and Earhart left by train that evening.*

On January 30, 1933, the world's most famous aviatrix, Amelia Earhart, flew into Spokane. However, her arrival was as a guest passenger, not the pilot, of a trimotor Ford airplane belonging to Northwest Airways. The purpose of the flight and Earhart's visit was as a test run on a proposed northern cross-country air mail route. Earhart was along primarily for the publicity of the flight, which originated in St. Paul, Minnesota. Her party consisted of Colonel L.H. Brittin, general manager and vice president of Northwest Airways, two pilots, some airplane mechanics and a steward. En route they made stops at Bismarck, Billings and Helena.

Earhart was one of the nation's early feminists. A *Spokesman-Review* reporter interviewed Earhart in the State Suite at the Davenport, but seemed more preoccupied with how feminine she appeared and what she wore than what she had accomplished. The following quote was taken from the January 31, 1933 newspaper:

> . . . you discover in Miss Earhart merely an attractive young women of gentle and gracious kindliness who seems to belong more to the hearthside than in the history of courageous world achievements. And that is probably as it should be, for Miss Earhart was saying . . . "I didn't add anything to the science of flying in my flight across the Atlantic, but I did show that a woman could do it." . . . she stated that she didn't see any use of women being afraid of rats and snakes and bugs and things, or anything, for that matter. Although to behold, Miss Earhart is feminine enough to look as though she might not enjoy meeting a mouse. ..."

See **SKY**

**BETTY and BENNY**

**DANCERS**

Dance on a 24-Inch Platform
50 Feet Above the Roof of
the Davenport Hotel

They've Thrilled
Thousands With
Their
"DANCE in The
CLOUDS"

Betty and Benny in Person!!!
Come and meet them . . . talk with them
. . . ask them questions!!

**Extra!! Extra!!**

**Sensation!!**

Come and

**·DANCE·**

With
**BETTY & BENNY**
in person and

**Mann Bros.**
Greater Orchestra
(14–Artists–14)
TOMORROW

**Monday Night**
Sept. 17th
at the

**·GARDEN·**
DANCING PALACE
335 SPRAGUE.

NOTE—You will have an opportunity to dance on
the same little platform on which you saw Betty and
Benny dancing on the Davenport Hotel roof.
Entire Public Invited.
Admission, per person, 25¢.

*On September 1, 1934, the above ad appeared in the Spokane Daily Chronicle.*

*The couple pictured are Benny and Betty Fox, who performed two 12-hour marathon dance performances atop a 50-foot pole on the roof of the Davenport Hotel. The platform they danced on was only 24 inches in diameter. The first performance was on Friday, September 14th from 8:00 am until 8:00 p.m. and the second one the following day, from 7:00 a.m. to 7:00 p.m.*

*The news clipping on the right was taken in the morning, just after mounting the pole they danced on.*

*Among those in this photo at the Davenport Hotel in the 1940s are: Joel E. Ferris (front left); Louis M. Davenport (back left, with glasses); the next three men to the right of Davenport are R.L. Rutter, W.M. Marshall and Ellsworth French; Aubrey L. White is at the far right. (EWSHS photo L93-66.104)*

*Left: Washington governor, Dixie Lee Ray, who had an office on the third floor, and United States congressman, Tom Foley, making a toast at the Davenport Hotel in late 1970s. Right: Colonel Sanders, the founder of Colonel Sanders' Kentucky-Fried Chicken, standing beside a cardboard cutout of himself in the lobby of the Davenport Hotel. (Photos courtesy Walt and Karen Worthy.)*

# Chapter 6

## The Davenport Family

L ouis Davenport loved to promote his restaurant and hotel, but was a private man who spoke little about himself and disliked drawing attention to his personal life. Piecing together a profile of him and his family history required researching archives from coast to coast. The urban legend about Louis Davenport (discussed in Chapter 1), which many local residents easily recite – arrived in Spokane by chance, already an experienced restaurateur, with only $1.25 in his pocket and dug ditches to scrape together $125 to start his first restaurant in a tent – did not hold up under scrutiny. Although Davenport still remains somewhat of an enigma, new information about his personal life now fills a certain void. Louis Davenport was truly a genius in his chosen field and, from middle-class beginnings, became a wealthy man, but the original simplistic summation can now be augmented by what has been learned about his earlier circumstances.

Louis Davenport came from a large clan (references to families with 10 to 12 children were not unusual) and a long line of Davenports in England, who began emigrating to this continent around 1670. A significant volume of genealogical information on the line of Davenports from which Louis Davenport descended was compiled in a book and subsequent supplements entitled *Thomas Davenport, Philipstown Pioneer, 1682-1759, and His Descendants*. Although it appears he was preceded by two generations in this country, Thomas Davenport was the first of this line to have been born on American soil. Upon reaching manhood, he settled along the Hudson River in what became Philipstown, a township that extends the entire length of the Hudson in Putnam County, New York. The area in which he settled became known as Davenport's Landing, until the West Point Foundry was established there in 1818, giving rise to the village of Cold Spring. The foundry, located across the river from the West Point Academy, was built in response to the War of 1812, primarily to produce munitions. However, it also manufactured a variety of other metal products and, in 1831, built the original DeWitt engine, which was one of the first railroad engines constructed in the United States.

The connection Louis Davenport had to Thomas Davenport was as follows: The first born son of Thomas, also named Thomas, had a son Isaac, one of 11 children. Isaac married Elizabeth Hustis and they had ten children, the eldest of whom was Louis's great grandfather, John Davenport. Interestingly, for a period of time, his great grandfather was in the hotel business in Philipstown. During the founding years of Cold Spring, he was one of the most prominent residents and occupied most of the farmland around the village. Widowed by his first two wives, Mary Snook and Mary (Nelson) Haight, he married Mary (Lobdell) Weeks, who outlived him. He fathered 12 children, including a set of twins, Elijah John and Susan Davenport, born to Mary Snook on February 28, 1915. This Elijah was Louis's grandfather.

## Elijah and Phebe Davenport's Family

Although an impressive amount of data was compiled in the *Thomas Davenport* publications, the information concerning Louis's grandparents and their off-spring was rather sketchy and incomplete, especially from the time family members began moving west from the ancestral home of Cold Spring. Through a great deal of research, documents were located to confirm, correct or add to the existing information, resulting in a more complete family tree, beginning with Louis's grandparents.

On February 28, 1836, Elijah Davenport married Phebe A. Haight (the most frequent spelling was "Phebe," but "Phoebe" was also noted), born February 2, 1818. According to Phebe's obituary in 1881, the couple bore nine children, but this number is a point of confusion, the variance being from four to eight depending on the source. Because the information for the obituary most likely came from the family, it is deemed to be the most reliable. Louis's father, John S. Davenport, born June 8, 1836, was the eldest. The other children, in what is presently thought to be the correct birth order, were: Laura Jane (born circa 1838, married name Massee), Milton (born 1839 or 1840), Mary E. (also "Molly," born 1841 or 1842, married Edmund J. Shellhorn), George W. (April 13, 1843, married Mary J. Shellhorn), Charles W. (May 1844), Isaac (March 7, 1845–August 3, 1846) and Elijah John (March 8, 1850). There is an unresolved mystery, however, about the ninth child. One source lists "Daughter Davenport," born about 1854. It appears she died before being named, which may explain the lack of any additional information.

## The Davenports Begin Moving West

Elijah and Phebe were both natives of New York. Following their marriage, they settled in the village of Cold Spring, where their children were born and Elijah had a harness shop. Around the mid-1850s, shortly after Nebraska became a territory and was opened for homesteading, Elijah and Phebe moved the family to Richardson County, Nebraska, where Elijah took up farming. It appears that John (Louis's father), now a grown man, remained in Cold Spring.

Life dealt many heartbreaking blows to this family. While still living in Cold Spring, the couple's 17-month old Isaac died and, if the conclusion about "Daughter Davenport" is correct, they endured the death of another baby, perhaps at birth. A few years after moving away from family and familiar surroundings to homestead in Nebraska, Phebe watched as her husband and four sons – John, Milton, George and Charles – set off to fight for the Union in the Civil War. (Elijah Jr., still a child at the time of the Civil War, served as a scout against the Indians in the Kansas Cavalry in 1867 and in the army during the Spanish-American War of 1898.) September 1863 was most certainly a dark time for the family; Charles was killed in action and, on the 13th of that month, John was taken prisoner and later interned at Andersonville, the Confederate's worst prison. Before being paroled in May 1864, John experienced some of the war's greatest horrors and atrocities as thousands of men died from disease and starvation. He was one of the fortunate ones – over 13,000 men died during the prison's 15-month existence.

## Young Louis Davenport and His Uncle Elijah

Following the war, John joined the family in Nebraska and, for a period of time, many family members settled in and around Pawnee City in Pawnee County. On January 19, 1867, John married Amelia E. "Minnie" Taylor, who was born in New York on January 7, 1848. They made their home in Pawnee City and the following year, on July 14, 1868, their first child was born, a son named Llewellyn Marks "Louis" (or "Louie") Davenport. His brother, Arthur J., was born on January 4, 1874. During this time, Elijah Jr. (John's youngest brother, Louie's uncle), who appeared to be a restless man ever in search of adventure and opportunity, had moved to California in 1870 and was working for a friend of his father. Around 1876, John and his family joined Elijah in California, where daughter Jessie D. Davenport was born in July 1877. They soon settled in Red Bluff in Tehama County, and John opened a mercantile business in partnership with his brother Elijah.

Elijah operated the mercantile with John for a period of time, but by the fall of 1882, Elijah and Eva, his wife of six months, were headed north to Spokane, a new frontier of opportunity. Over the next decade, Elijah became the proprietor of four hotels and a restaurant, as well as a partner in a meat market. In March 1889, after Elijah had become quite well established in business, his nephew Louie arrived in Spokane and began working in Elijah's restaurant, the Pride of Spokane. This was a new experience for Louie, as his prior work history had been as a clerk. An 1885 California directory listed him as a clerk for John Clements, the postmaster, who also sold "stationary and varieties" in Red Bluff, and San Francisco city directories for 1887 and 1888 listed him as a clerk for the Del Monte Milling Company (a flour mill). According to his son, Louie also attended a business school in San Francisco. While his prior work experience and schooling may have prepared him for handling business matters, it did not provide him with restaurant experience. He quickly learned enough of the trade while working in his Uncle Elijah's Pride of Spokane Restaurant, however, to take over as proprietor of the restaurant just before it was destroyed by

Spokane's big fire of 1889. The fire leveled Spokane's business district, but seemed to fuel a desire in Louis to become a part of its reconstruction and future development, and he immediately opened another restaurant. (The details about Louis and Elijah's business ventures in Spokane, having been thoroughly covered in earlier chapters, will not be repeated here.)

According to Elijah's great-grandson, Larry Davenport of Spokane, a bit of a conflict developed between Louie and Elijah after the 1889 fire. As the story was told, Louie wanted Elijah to go into business with him, but Elijah rejected the idea. (A minor observation, however, is that Elijah's businesses, being outside of the fire district were unaffected, so the likelihood is that Louie actually wanted to go into business with Elijah, not have Elijah go into business with him.) At any rate, Louie allegedly felt rebuffed by Elijah – although Elijah did loan his nephew some money to get started – and it created, as Larry put it, "a little bad blood." Over the years, however, some amends were made.

Elijah and his family apparently were hit hard by the Economic Panic of 1893 and, around that time, left Spokane for Rossland, B.C., in search of new opportunities. By 1903, Elijah was living in Butte, Montana, and working as a watchman for the Ryan & Newton, a wholesale produce company of which Louis Davenport was vice president. Farming later became his primary occupation and references were made to farms in Montana and Chewelah, Washington. Until his dying day, however, Elijah must have considered himself a "hotel man," as that was the occupation listed by the family on his death certificate. On July 12, 1927, Elijah and Eva moved into a veteran's retirement home in Retsil, Washington, where they spent their final years. Elijah died on January 12, 1929, at age 78, and Eva on February 24, 1937, at age 74. The couple had three children: Clifford, Leo and Freddie.

*Larry Davenport (center), great-grandson of Elijah and Eva Davenport, with wife Bernice (left) and mother, Maxine (Ickes) Rolie, all of Spokane, in August 2001. Maxine was married to Leo Davenport Jr., son of Elijah and Eva's son Leo, until his death in 1985. Larry has an older sister, Phyllis Koplin of Beaverton, Oregon; a younger sister, Carol Butler of Tacoma; and a younger brother, Richard Davenport of Bryce, Utah. (Bamonte photo.)*

## Louis Davenport's Family Joins Him in Spokane

In 1891, after Louie was solidly situated in his restaurant, his mother Minnie, brother Arthur and sister Jessie joined him in Spokane and established residency in the Great Eastern Block (rebuilt as the Peyton Building after a tragic fire in 1898). For a few years, Minnie was listed in the city directories as "Mrs.," but beginning around 1895, a notation followed her name indicating she was the widow of John. Interestingly, John did not die until 1909, and had remained in Red Bluff until his death, at age 73. His obituary noted he was survived by two sons and a daughter, but did not mention a wife, nor did his Civil War pension file, in which the "marital status" box was left blank. (The file also indicated his pension was $12 a month. According to the obituary, John had "disposed of his store nearly twenty-one years ago," although voter registrations in 1892 and 1896 still listed him as a merchant.) Apparently, John and Minnie remained separated, but did not divorce. Minnie lived in Spokane until her death, at age 76, on July 20, 1924, and is buried at Riverside Memorial Park.

During most of Louie's early years, he lived above his restaurant in a rented room. Around 1900, Mrs. Maud C. Pennington's name began to be associated with the furnished rooms listed at this location, S. 6 Post (the building entrance on Post). Most likely, it was through Maud that Louie met her sister, his future wife, Verus E. Smith, who was listed in the city directory as a student. Louie and Verus married on August 30, 1906. Verus, the daughter of John C. and Martha (Erans) Smith, was born in Roseburg, Oregon, on July 12, 1878, and Maud in Wilbur, Oregon, on June 1, 1879.

On June 4, 1907, the Davenports were blessed by the birth of their only child, Llewellyn Marks "Lewis" Davenport II. By this time, Davenport's Restaurant had become nationally known and was enjoying a booming business. In March 1908, the Davenports purchased land on the north-facing slope of the South Hill, the city's most desirable place to live, and began construction of their new $225,000 home at 34 West Eighth Avenue. (Detailed description of this home appears in Chapter 3.) About six months after making this significant financial commitment, Louie was approached by a group of businessmen and investors to become the key man of a new hotel they hoped to build. Acceptance of this position was given with his full devotion to the project. The hotel would require a financial commitment on the Davenports' part and, as a result, within a short time of completing construction on their home, they sold it to raise capital for the hotel. The Davenports had moved into their new home on Eighth at least by April 1910, when the census was taken, but in October 1912, they negotiated a sale agreement with the Richard B. Porter family. The sale involved an exchange of residences, plus some land in the Rockwood area and a remaining cash payment from Porter. After living in the former Porter residence at 221 West Sumner for a period of time, the Davenports decided to make the new hotel their primary residence. In October 1916, they sold the Sumner house.

*Llewellyn M. "Louie" Davenport reading to his young son, Llewellyn M. "Lewis" Davenport II (left) and Lewis being read to by his mother, Verus E. Davenport.*

*Verus and Lewis at their home at 34 West Eighth (left) and Louie admiring his son (right), circa 1912. (All photos courtesy Louis and Nita Davenport III.)*

*Lewis Jr. sharing his fifth birthday with his dog in 1912, and Rex Davenport's trophy. The Davenports had a number of dogs over the years, but Rex, a Newfoundland, was a favored one. In 1910 he won this trophy at the Spokane Kennel Club's Seventh Annual Show. (Photos courtesy Louie and Nita Davenport III.)*

*Left: Lewis Jr., delighted by a monkey the man on the right is holding, circa 1915. No other identities known. (Photo courtesy Louie and Nita Davenport III.) Right: The Davenports' summer home, Flowerfield, circa 1930. (EWSHS photo L88.404.19b.15)*

*A rare shot of Louis Davenport (second from left) without a hat or his wig, swimming with Lewis Jr., circa 1915. Other two people not identified, but possibly the man was Louis's brother. (Photo courtesy Louie and Nita Davenport III.) A cartoon drawn for Davenport in 1922. (EWSHS "Tribute to Louis Davenport" Album.)*

During Lewis Jr.'s years in the Davenport Hotel, the family lived on the 10th floor. After Lewis graduated from Lewis and Clark High School in 1928 and set out on his own, Louie and Verus moved to the northeast corner of the 11th floor (room 1128), overlooking the restaurant, where they lived for the rest of their lives.

## Flowerfield

The Davenports had enjoyed their beautifully landscaped grounds and gardens surrounding their home on Eighth and, after making the decision to move into the hotel, wanted a place where they could still have gardens and escape the city in the summer. At first, they rented a place on Hayden Lake in Idaho, but their attention soon turned to the Little Spokane River, about 10 miles north of downtown Spokane. A number of written references were made to purchasing land in 1921 and spending several summers in a small cottage, which later became their gardener's cottage, before building their summer home, aptly named Flowerfield. However, Warranty Deed 883287 for the purchase of the 22.4-acre parcel on which they built the house was entered into on September 16, 1925. (Perhaps they had rented a cottage before buying?) Spokane County records indicate the house was built the following year, corroborated by a guest book with entries first appearing in 1926. The Davenports enjoyed entertaining and many prominent names appeared in this guest book, including a number of Davenport's business colleagues, who also owned estates in the vicinity, such as Aubrey White and Jay P. Graves. An amusing aside, upon one visit, Graves jotted in the remarks column "swell groceries!"

The house was situated on a knoll overlooking the river and was designed by architect G.A. Pehrson to take advantage of the beautiful woodland scenery. Expansive windows, a sunroom and an enclosed porch helped to bring the outdoors into their living spaces. A gazebo was located in the gardens, where Louie enjoyed his after dinner cigar; according to their grandson, Verus absolutely hated cigar smoke and would not allow her husband to smoke in the house. The Olmsted Brothers firm landscaped the grounds, which included magnificent flower gardens that stretched to the river. Many of the fresh flowers used in the hotel and restaurant during the summers came from Flowerfield. A staff of about a dozen assisted the Davenports in caring for their home and gardens. Flowerfield was another Inland Northwest showplace, and was recognized by a 1933 *National Geographic,* which featured a picture of it.

Over the years, the Davenports continued to purchase adjoining property, eventually accumulating over 450 acres. In 1943, they sold their summer home at 2929 West Waikiki Road, to Donald G. Corbett, a prominent Spokane physician, and his wife, Georgia. Albert P. Lewis purchased it in 1949 and, in 1955, it became the property of the new St. George's School, which opened that fall with 45 students. It is presently used primarily for special school functions and meetings.

## Growing Up in the Shadow of the Davenport Hotel

As the young son of Louie and Verus Davenport, growing up in Spokane's grand hotel during its heydays must have been exciting for Lewis Jr. The lobby was filled with chirping birds and huge tanks of colorful fish were positioned in various spots throughout the hotel and restaurant. The food choices were, no doubt, to any little boy's delight and the entertainment flowed freely with a fascinating procession

of celebrities, dignitaries and other interesting guests, to say nothing of being able to ride one's bicycle on the roof of one of the tallest buildings in the city. But the expectations were also high that one day Lewis would assume his father's position in the great hotel. According to his son, Lewis also had a lot of medical problems in his youth and, from his perspective, felt his grandparents were overly protective of their son and "micromanaged" his life. During his senior year in high school, he was the business manager for the school's annual, *The Tiger*, and it is quite interesting to note that the Davenport Hotel had placed the majority of the advertisements.

**Lewis Davenport, 1928**

Fully seasoned to life in the splendor of his parents' hotel, Lewis had ideas of his own. Following graduation from high school, he attended Pomona College in Southern California, and did some traveling in Europe. On April 9, 1937, he married Mary Kathleen McHugh, who was born and raised in Bertrand, Nebraska. Kathleen, who was born on August 23, 1907, had attended Nebraska State Teachers' College and majored in music. According to the couple's only son, Llewellyn Marks "Louie" Davenport III, born on September 13, 1941, she was an accomplished pianist. The couple settled down in LaHabra, California, where they purchased a 38-acre citrus

and avocado ranch. Lewis maintained strong ties with Spokane, but returned only for visits, and, obviously, never assumed his father's business. In 1939, Lewis and Kathleen built a new $25,000 home in LaHabra, designed by G.A. Pehrson, the same Spokane architect who designed Flowerfield and many of the new additions and remodeling projects in the Davenport Hotel. Both Kathleen and Lewis were active in various civic organizations.

**Kathleen Davenport**

**Lewis Davenport**

*(Photos courtesy Louie and Nita Davenport III)*

Some of Lewis's attraction to Southern California may have been the presence of other familiar family members. References were found to at least three aunts (Verus's sister, Maud; Louie's sister, Jessie; and an Aunt Alice) living in the Los Angeles area. Louie's sister, who had married a Dr. Robins, was still living in Spokane for several years after Lewis was born, but eventually settled in San Pedro, California. Aunt Maud, who had managed the Pennington Hotel (the building Louie owned that adjoined his restaurant), was, according to his son Louie Davenport III, Lewis's favorite aunt. She married Harry W. Hollis in 1908 and left the Spokane area around 1912. An entry in the Flowerfield guest register in April 1930 read "Harry W. Hollis, Los Angeles." Louie III recalled his father's "Aunt Alice," who lived in Los Angeles when he was growing up, who lived to be 101. Louie thought Alice may have been his grandmother's oldest sister.

At some point, Louie's brother, Arthur, who had been living in Chicago, also relocated to Southern California; the location given at the time of his death, on October 7, 1941, was Los Angeles. According to Red Bluff's Oak Hill Cemetery records, Arthur was cremated at the time of his death and, on December 23, 1941, his remains were buried next to his father, John Davenport; they are the only two Davenports buried in that cemetery. It appears from John's will that Arthur was the favored son (or perhaps more in need of the financial help, as Louie was doing extremely well financially). When John died in 1909, he bequeathed equals share of his estate to his children and his siblings, with the exception of Arthur, who also received his father's real estate holdings in Red Bluff.

## Louis Davenport Retires

In 1945, after 56 years of providing the best hospitality services money could buy, Louie's health began to fail and he made the decision to sell his hotel and retire. Davenport had always been active in civic affairs and continued to be after his retirement at age 77. He had been an active supporter of organizations dedicated to the growth and betterment of Spokane and the Inland Northwest. His role in the campaign to purchase Geiger Field and Galena acreage was instrumental in allowed the Air Force to establish a base on the outskirts of Spokane. He was a member of the Spokane Park Board from 1908, the year after it was formed, until his death in 1951, and for many years was the Board's vice president. He was one of the incorporators of the Spokane United Railways Company in May 1922. In addition, he had been a director of Spokane and Eastern Trust Company, Washington Water Power, Western Life Insurance Company, as well as a director and vice president of the Old National Bank and the Old National Bank Building, and vice president of the Ryan & Newton Company. He was a member of the Masons, Elks, the Spokane Club, Spokane Country Club, and Spokane Amateur Athletic Club. In 1950, Washington State College (now University) awarded him a certificate of merit for his contribution to the state.

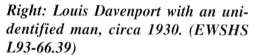

*Above: Lewis and Kathleen Davenport at a Kiwanis convention held in Reno in October 1954. (EWSHS photo MSSC 396-b)*

*Right: Louis Davenport with an unidentified man, circa 1930. (EWSHS L93-66.39)*

*A group of businessmen dedicating the Vista House on Mt. Spokane, designed by Spokane architect Henry Bertleson, in 1934. Louis Davenport is third from the right.. (EWSHS Frank Gilbert photo L95-111.354)*

On July 28, 1951, at age 83, Louie Davenport died in his suite in his beloved Davenport Hotel, with Verus, his wife of 45 years, at his side. Although he only stood 5'4½", Louis Davenport cast a giant shadow. Mourners from around the world sent messages of condolences, while hundreds gathered at the Cathedral of St. John to mourn the passing of one of Spokane's greatest entrepreneurs, who did more than any other single person to put the Inland Northwest on the map. Lengthy newspaper articles extolled his accomplishments, one of which stated many people far and wide "knew the name of the hotel but not that of the town in which it was located." It was often said that people would come to Spokane just to see or stay at the Davenport Hotel. Louie was survived by his wife, son, daughter-in-law, grandson and his sister, and provisions were made for each in his will. He established a trust for his sister, Jessie, which provided her with $4,000 a year until her death (one unconfirmed source gave the date of her death as January 13,1958). Verus outlived

her husband by 16 years and, following a long illness, passed away on October 11, 1967, at the age of 89 (the newspaper accounts of her death erroneously reported age 86). She had always loved gardening and had been one of the founders of the Landscape Association of St. John's Cathedral.

The Davenports were remembered and memorialized in many ways. People spoke of them with respect, pointing out that both were soft spoken, never indulged in gossip and were very friendly. Louie's character, much of which was revealed in his business dealings, has been discussed in earlier chapters, but little has been said about Verus. Comments picked up from various sources about Verus included, "She was a lady," "the sweetest person," "an angel," – and apparently modest, as well. According to her grandson, Louie Davenport III, she hated to have her picture taken. When a camera came out, she would quietly disappear! The picture to the left was a rare exception; she obviously wanted this photo with her grandson. Equally as obvious is the grandson's discomfort with the suit she made him wear!

**Verus Davenport and her only grandchild, Louie Davenport III, circa 1950. (Photo courtesy Louie and Nita Davenport III.)**

Another one of Louie III's recollections spoke volumes about his grandfather. Louie was only ten when his grandfather died, but the following incident gave him an insight into his grandfather's business mind:

I have nothing but fond memories. My grandfolks would spend the winter in Southern California, so I spent some time with them when he was still alive. We just had fun. We didn't do anything specific – it was just a good time together. I remember one instance in Spokane that was kind of an important lesson for me. We were just walking down the street and passed this toy store. I looked in and a little toy road grader really caught my eye, because I just loved construction equipment. I stopped and said, "Boy, I would really like to have that!" He said, "Well, I'll buy it for you, or we can take that amount of money, put it in the bank, save it and let it grow, then someday you'll be able to buy something that's much more valuable to you that you'll need much worse than you do this." He gave me the choice and I took [the latter] choice. I don't know if it was to please him or if he really convinced me that was the better choice. I don't remember him putting any pressure on me. I think that's probably how he approached a lot of things in life.

## Most Generous With Spokane

In 1956, Verus and Lewis donated a beautiful fountain to the Parks Department in Louis Davenport's memory. It became the focal point of the Duncan Gardens in Manito Park, Spokane's favorite park. The granite Louis M. Davenport Memorial Fountain was designed by the architectural firm of Whitehouse & Price. The contractor was Henry George & Sons. Following Kathleen's death on April 10, 1986 and Lewis Jr.'s death on July 9, 1987, just a month after his 80th birthday, Lewis's will bequeathed to Spokane Parks and Recreation Foundation $25,000, which essentially ensured the maintenance and preservation of the fountain.

Even though Lewis had not lived in Spokane for over 50 years, he loved his hometown. This was demonstrated by the desire to be buried in Spokane, along with his wife, parents, paternal grandmother Minnie and Aunt Maud, and the bequests in his will that left a majority of the Davenport estate to Spokane. Eastern Washington State Historical Society was

**Lewis Davenport Jr. by the Davenport fountain in Manito Park, during his last visit to Spokane just months before his death in 1987. (Photo courtesy Louie and Nita Davenport III)**

given nearly a million dollars for a Davenport wing or gallery to display the many valuable family heirlooms in the museum's possession. In addition to the historical society and the parks department, St. George's School, the Crosby Library at Gonzaga University, and the Cathedral of St. John all benefited from Lewis's will.

In 1924, following the death of Louis Davenport's mother Minnie, the Davenports dedicated a stained glass window to her memory in the Cathedral of St. John, where they were longtime members. According to a bequest in Lewis's will, three additional stained glass memorial windows, all depicting major events in the life of Jesus, were installed in the chancel in 1992: the Ascension window, a memorial to Louis Davenport, and the Resurrection window, a memorial to Verus, are both on the north side; the Crucifixion window on the south side is a memorial to Lewis and Kathleen.

The Davenport plot occupies a small, inconspicuous section in Riverside Memorial Park. Louis and Verus Davenport are buried in the middle, along with Lewis and Kathleen; Louis's mother, Minnie Davenport; and Verus's sister Maud (Smith Pennington) Hollis. Maud had returned to Spokane about nine months before her death on December 9, 1935, possibly due to illness. She was only 56 years old. Each grave is marked with a simple flat headstone engraved only with names and dates. The modest appearance of the family plot is reflective of the Louis Davenport, who in spite of his fame and fortune, retained his humble demeanor.

## Carrying on the Name

Lewis and Kathleen Davenport's only child, Louie Davenport III, was born on September 13, 1941, and grew up in LaHabra in Los Angeles County. As a young boy, Louie knew he wanted to become a farmer and was involved in Future Farmers of America (FFA). Following graduation from high school, he attended California State Polytechnic College in Pomona, California. He soon began his first farming enterprise, located in Moreno Valley, California. Since 1974 he has had a large agricultural operation in Gooding, Idaho, where his primary focus is raising and processing pinto beans. It was here he met Nita, his lovely wife of 16 years, who manages her own business in Gooding. They have a blended family of six children and four grandchildren. Louie has two sons and two daughters; Nita has two daughters.

Although their careers followed different paths, in regards to character traits, Louie III is certainly carrying on the legacy set by his grandfather, Louis Davenport. He is a soft-spoken, humble and extremely hard working man, who is devoted to his family and his livelihood. Although his farming operation requires long, arduous hours, he generously donates time to various civic, youth and church activities. His own personal mission is to feed the poor in Mexico. He is

**Louie and Nita Davenport III in March 2001. (Bamonte photo.)**

not quick to talk about it, but Louie has personally contributed thousands of tons of beans and other food items to missions in Mexico and Southern California. The food donations are either grown or purchased by Louie, and are personally delivered in his own semi-truck. Certainly, "philanthropic" is one adjective to describe Louis Davenport's grandson. Other adjectives, gleaned from some character letters written on his behalf, included "highly ethical," "caring," "generous," and "high-principled," but one would never hear him speak these words about himself.

*Top photos: Lewis Jr. holding Louie III in 1942, and Louie's oldest son, David M. and wife Carole Davenport of Hawaii. Bottom: A family gathering in April 2001. Back row, from left: Micah R. Davenport of California (youngest son), Laura R. Davenport of Seattle (oldest daughter), Louie and Nita Davenport, Lizette James (third daughter), Shaney Clemmons of Bellevue, Washington (youngest daughter), Joe James and John James. Louie, Nita and the James family live in Gooding, Idaho. Front: Ariel Davenport, Bradly James and Emily James. Daughter Joy and grandson Dustin are not shown. (All photos courtesy Louie and Nita Davenport.)*

# Chapter 7

## The Declining Years and Community's Support

The war years had a mixed effect on the Davenport Hotel. When the United States entered World War II and troops were called out, the labor pool was greatly diminished. But occupancy remained at near capacity, as it did for most hotels throughout the county. Within close proximity to the military bases of Geiger, Galena, Ft. George Wright and Farragut, numerous servicemen streamed in and out of the hotel, often sleeping in the lobby and on the mezzanine. The Davenport actually became an auxiliary service center and, according to the late hotel manager Jim McCluskey, took orders from the Army and Navy as if it were a part of the armed forces. The hotel would receive regular calls regarding the number of servicemen needing room or board on a given day. It was a lively place, and the compensation from the government augmented what were already becoming some of the most profitable years in Louis Davenport's entrepreneurial history.

However, there was a downside. By the end of the war in 1945, the hotel was showing signs of wear. Davenport's unusually high standards of maintenance had been compromised by a shortage of labor and materials, and the hotel was lacking some of its former lustre. In accordance with the blackout rules during the war, the lobby atrium had been covered, blocking the flood of natural light. The building's original mechanical systems were in need of upgrading or replacing. During this time in the country's history, most upscale hotels, having suffered the same imposed neglect, embarked on vast rehabilitation and upgrading programs. Had Louis Davenport still been in his prime, his hotel most assuredly would also have undergone a rigorous refurbishing. But he was 77 years old and his health was failing. It was time to retire.

### Entrusting a New Owner With the Grand Old Hotel

After reaching the decision to sell his hotel, Davenport was approached by several potential buyers, from which he selected William Edris of Seattle. During the negotiation stages, Edris publicly stated his ambition to own and operate the two finest hotels in the Northwest: The Olympic in Seattle, which he had acquired just 15 months earlier, and The Davenport. He also owned the Roosevelt Hotel in Seattle and the Robert Treat Hotel in Newark, New Jersey. Not only was Edris an experienced hotel entrepreneur, he was also originally from Spokane, having lived there as a child. This was an important consideration. Davenport was quoted in the April 26,1945 *Spokesman-Review* as saying:

Spokane men originally built the Davenport to promote the interests of the city . . . and we are selling the hotel to Mr. Edris because we feel he, likewise, has the interests of Spokane and the state at heart and will do everything to promote them. We could have sold to other eastern and western hotel interests for a remuneration considerably higher, but felt that they wouldn't do as much for the city or the state as Mr. Edris. He is a man interested only in the best and intends to operate the hotel along the same lines pursued in the past.

**William Edris**

Edris's Spokane connection, coupled with his publicly-expressed sincerity and benevolence toward the Davenport Hotel, gave Louis Davenport a sense of comfort. In April 1945, the sale of the hotel to the Wm. Edris Company, a Washington Corporation, closed at a purchase price of $1.5 million. As his quote stated, this was not the highest offer Davenport received, but he felt it was the best choice for the hotel and the city of Spokane. He turned over his beloved hotel to Edris with confidence and hope. This soon proved to be an ill-placed confidence.

## The Davenport's Turbulent Years Began With Edris

In January 1947, less than two years after his purchase, William Edris sold the Davenport Hotel for $2.5 million dollars, making a $1 million profit in that short time. Whether or not it was his original intent to exploit Louis Davenport's goodwill is not known. Although the hotel was in need of some definite attention after the war, his main contribution was an upscale penthouse for himself on the 14th floor (thus eliminating the public roof garden) and the installation of new laundry facilities. The paternal guidance and care the Davenport Hotel had enjoyed since its inception was gone and, as the hotel passed through the revolving doors of changing ownership (to date, a total of ten), its gradual downward spiral ultimately led to its being closed in 1985.

The Edris sale was recorded on January 3, 1947, to a new corporation called Davenport, Incorporated, which consisted of three investors, two of whom had ties to Spokane: Charles Finucane, William M. Marshall and Robert P. Porter. Charles Finucane, who was a partner in Finucane & Galland Realtors and general manager of the Sweeney Investment Company, was named as the corporate president. Marshall was chairman of the board and Porter was a vice-president. James McCluskey was retained as hotel manager and also named as vice-president. Incidentally, Robert Porter was the son of the R.B. Porter who purchased the Davenports' home on West Eighth in 1912, where Robert lived in his youth.

The first of many alterations immediately began to take place. Sixteen new suites, adjacent to the Edris penthouse addition, were constructed, permanently altering the roof line. By early 1949, plans were well underway for a complete remodeling of the beautiful Italian Gardens into the Crystal Dining Room and Garden Lounge, but not before additional changes in ownership occurred. Porter and Marshall had sold their shares in 1948, which changed hands again in 1949, passing into the hands of Western Hotels, Inc. of Seattle. In 1953, Finucane also sold his interest to Western Hotels, leaving the Davenport now in the possession of a hotel chain with no personal ties to Spokane. It was said by people who knew Louis Davenport that in his final years he seemed sad. No wonder. He saw his hotel rapidly changing hands, the profit Edris made in his quick exit, and the end of the Italian Gardens. Fortunately, he did not live to see the hotel delivered into the impersonal hands of a corporate chain.

Davenport was no stranger to making changes in his establishment and, in fact, never ceased improving and refurbishing. But an insidious attitude of replacing anything old or "old-fashioned" with a new, modern look was seeping into the minds of Americans. Many of the subsequent changes, frequently to give the hotel and restaurant a contemporary look, were not compatible with the hotel's character. Fortunately, before it was scheduled for demolition, a growing awareness of the value in preserving historic buildings began to take hold.

Most of the owners assumed their new roles with enthusiasm and honorable intentions, but few possessed Davenport's innate sense of what the hotel needed or his attention to detail. A prime example was the neglect of the glass in the lobby ceiling, which had been blackened out during World War II. Half a century elapsed before a new owner, the Ng family from Sun International, recognized the loss of aesthetics, removed the covering and, once again, allowed natural light to fill the lobby.

Little by little, the expensive furniture, silver servings and beautiful decorative pieces disappeared from the hotel. What made the hotel so grand during Louis Davenport's era were the thousand little components, the layers of amenities, delights and services that made a guest's stay feel special. With each tiny loss, the hotel slipped a notch. Davenport had offered much more than a place to eat or sleep; he had created a community center – even a shopping center of sorts – with a multitude of conveniences, services and entertainment. The Davenport was a destination spot, a main attraction to draw people downtown, a welcoming place for people from all walks of life.

So what brought this great hotel to the very brink of destruction? Obviously, it did not happen all at once. Some of the changes were subtle, some were glaring. Much of the change was a simple matter of attitude. The hotel had been almost a personal extension of Louis Davenport. He had poured his heart and soul into it, but for most of his successors, it was simply a business. In addition, the hotel was on a collision course with changing lifestyles and attitudes of the public at large.

Louis Davenport was successful at staying abreast of changing times and always several steps ahead of his competitors. For instance, as the pace of life quickened and leisurely lunches gave way to "fast-food," many of the more formal restaurants did not adapt quickly and suffered the consequences. Davenport, however, was quick to recognize a need, increased staffing in the Coffee Shop and Delicacy Shop, and began catering to the rushed noontime crowd; he never sacrificed service or quality, but merely increased the staff to provide quick, quality lunches. But the changes now facing the hotel were far-reaching. The country was entering a new era, and more than ever, the hotel would need management with strength, dedication and vision to weather rough waters. Unfortunately, it just was not there.

## Changing Times

Following World War II, many people began spending their leisure time in more casual ways. With the widespread ownership of the automobile and its growing reliability, America became more mobile than ever. To meet the needs of the traveling public, motels began to spring up along the more heavily used routes. Convenient, affordable and with little formality involved, they were especially attractive for families traveling with children or travelers who just wanted a quick night's sleep and cared little about fancy amenities. Parking was never a problem, nor was dining. A quick meal from any number of drive-in restaurants usually satisfied a family's appetite for a fraction of the cost of a more formal restaurant.

In addition, the advent of television made a significant impact on the local entertainment scene. Satisfying entertainment was being staged in living rooms across the country. Instead of dressing up and going out to attend the attractions "downtown," more people were settling back in their easy chairs. Other developments, such as shopping malls scattered throughout the city – complete with movie theatres and a variety of services – eliminated many of the reasons to frequent downtown. The loss of activity downtown resulted in a loss of business in the hotel.

The Davenport, along with most upscale hotels located in the hearts of America's cities, felt the pinch from these emerging lifestyle changes. On the local level, there was another set of circumstances to contend with. The Davenport Hotel was built at a time when Spokane was one of the richest cities, per capita, in the nation, and money flowed freely from the natural resource-based industries. But after a cooling-down period, with the exception of moderate fluctuations, Spokane's economy has remained fairly stagnant. The cost to maintain such a grand structure as the Davenport is substantial, so the income side of the equation is necessary to keep it afloat. Following the war, as other factors took their toll, rising labor costs affected the degree of service the hotel was able to offer. Higher wages meant increased overhead. To balance the budget, fewer personnel were employed. Historically, Davenport's labor costs had been quite affordable and the high ratio of employees to customers was a major contributor to the excellent service delivered. A vicious cycle of fewer services-fewer guests began to affect the hotel's once-lofty position.

To aggravate the problems facing the Davenport, parking remained a never-ending challenge. In the days when the majority of patrons arrived by train, the location of the Davenport in the heart of downtown Spokane, with the close proximity to the railway depots, was excellent. When the hotel was built, no one was able to foresee the need to accommodate the volume of cars that would soon be delivering guests to the hotel. Consequently, no provisions were made for drive-through traffic near the hotel's registration desk or for convenient loading or unloading of baggage from private vehicles. To make the situation more frustrating, parking meters were installed in the 1940s. And, finally, Sprague and First became one-way streets, resulting in a traffic pattern most inconvenient for delivering passengers to either of the main hotel entrances, as exiting the car meant stepping out into the traffic lane.

The various owners did what they thought would attract business and make the hotel profitable. Repeated efforts were made to solve the parking dilemma, an outdoor swimming pool was installed in 1957, and numerous cosmetic changes were made.

## The "Doo Wop" Era

During the years 1953 to 1967, under the ownership of Western Hotels, the Davenport suffered some of its greatest indignities. To compete with the ubiquitous motel, the hotel received an extensive cosmetic make-over reflecting a popular style of decor, known as "doo wop." It was characterized by shag carpets, paneling, plastics and white paint. The remodeling, largely completed by 1955, began with a new marquee and neon lighting. The arches in the Hall of the Doges were filled in and covered with red flocked wallpaper, much of the marble was painted, and the hotel furnished throughout in '50s style. The former Italian Gardens, remodeled in 1949 as the Crystal Room and Garden Lounge, was again remodeled as the Spanish-style Matador Dining Room. Western Hotels essentially opted to run this first-class hotel as a competitor of the motels; the focus was to provide just the basics – clean rooms, quick meals and a swimming pool. For lesser hotels, these changes may have worked well, but they almost made a mockery of the Davenport, with its classic, timeless beauty. At least they kept the hotel afloat during their ownership.

*It became evident the Davenport Hotel had fallen from its premier position when Elvis Presley came to Spokane on August 30, 1957 and again in 1973 and stayed at the Ridpath Hotel. (Artist's rendering of Elvis Presley following his second concert in Spokane. Courtesy of artist Penny Alexander.)*

The cosmetic changes were one thing, but greater lay trials ahead. Western Hotels sold the Davenport in 1967 to John S. McMillan of San Francisco, who only held it for two years. In 1969 the new corporate manager, J. Harlow Tucker, announced his multimillion dollar renovation plan and began raising capital through stock sales. Part of the renovation included combining some of the smaller guest rooms to create larger ones and more commercial space. But as the remodeling progressed, the financial situation deteriorated. The Pennington Hotel, which was being used for non-transient monthly rentals, was closed and any existing maintenance efforts were virtually abandoned. In 1972 the corporation filed for bankruptcy. Fraudulent activity involving the hotel's stock sales was soon discovered; Tucker was subsequently indicted and convicted for securities fraud. Many people lost substantial personal investments.

## The Hotel Closes

In 1974 the mortgage holders, Lomas and Nettleton Financial Corporation, acquired the hotel through the bankruptcy reorganization. They contracted with Milner Hotels, Inc., headquartered in Detroit, Michigan, to handle the operations until a buyer could be found. The following year a nomination was submitted and approved to place the hotel on the National Register of Historic Places. This succeeded despite resistance from the mayor of Spokane, who claimed "the hotel's financial condition was poor and the listing as a historic site would block demolition if it became necessary in future years." Around that same time, the Matador Room was again remodeled and called Louis D's. It has been said by people who knew Louis Davenport that he probably "turned over in his grave" at the name. By now, any resemblance to Louis Davenport's Italian Gardens had long since disappeared.

*When Babcock and Anderson purchased the hotel, Jan B. Smith from Helena, Montana, became the administrative assistant. After it closed in 1985, she and her two cats, Kitzel and Sylvester, lived in the hotel as caretakers. Dorothy Powers wrote an amusing story in her book "Dorothy: Powers to the People" about Kitzel (left) and his job as Jan's assistant. As the sun streamed into different guest rooms, Kitzel would move from room to room to nap in the sun. Although the hotel had closed, Jan still received reservation requests from around the world. (Photos courtesy Jan Smith.)*

**Jan in her office at the Davenport.**

Finally, in 1979 a new buyer was found. The former governor of Montana, Tim Babcock, and former Davenport Hotel general manager, Warren Anderson, purchased the hotel for $4.25 million dollars. For the first five years of operation, they were required to pay only the interest, with Lomas and Nettleton maintaining title to the property. Even with that arrangement, the hotel still continued to lose money. In 1983, Anderson transferred his interest to Babcock. After struggling for the next two years to keep the hotel afloat while seeking a partner or a buyer, Babcock relinquished control of the property to Lomas and Nettleton. Although it initially appeared they might undertake refurbishing the hotel themselves, in June 1985, Don Cruikshank, managing director at the hotel, announced it would be closed until a buyer could be found. After 71 years of continual operation, this announcement shocked the community and tore at the heart-strings of residents throughout the Inland Northwest.

While the hotel was closed, Lomas and Nettleton continued to tend the building, which included retaining a small housekeeping staff, engineering crew, administrative secretary and building security. This small dedicated staff included, among others, Jan Smith, Evelyn Conant, John Reed and Jerry Peters, the chief engineer. But the annual costs to maintain the closed hotel were in excess of $600,000. Lomas and Nettleton were searching for a buyer, but there was also talk of demolition. In 1987, H.H. "Buddy" Miller, executive vice-president, came up from the corporate headquarters to prepare the hotel for demolition, but was met with quite a surprise. He quickly realized that demolishing the Davenport Hotel would be a serious mistake.

*Evelyn Conant (left) and Katherine Gellhorn, one of the founding members of the Friends of the Davenport, Christmas 1994. Katherine was one of the most loyal and active members. Evelyn began working for the hotel around 1982 as head accountant and was the last of Babcock's staff to leave when the hotel closed in 1985. Shortly after Sun International purchased the hotel in 1990, Jan Smith took a job elsewhere and the Ngs offered Jan's position to Evelyn. She happily moved into the hotel. While living there, she hosted two special events for her granddaughter, Heather Conant. Heather was disappointed at not being able to attend her 1991 high school prom with her boyfriend, John Ledgerwood, so Evelyn arranged a private prom in the hotel lobby (center). Countless weddings took place in the Davenport, including Heather's in 1996. (Photos courtesy Evelyn Conant.)*

# The Friends of the Davenport

In 1986, when Spokane city councilwoman (later mayor), Sheri Barnard, received word of possible demolition of the Davenport Hotel, her immediate thought was to form a committee to protect the city's most outstanding landmark. Among her many cherished memories of the Davenport Hotel was her wedding engagement there in 1958. It was not long before she realized how many other people shared her feelings. A core group consisting of Sheri, Ron Wendle, Katherine Gellhorn and Bud Cox scheduled a meeting for November 5, 1986, calling for the attendance of all citizens interested in the future of the Davenport Hotel. About 60 people attended that first meeting, which resulted in the formation of the "Friends of the Davenport," a non-profit organization whose intent was to promote and save the hotel. More meetings followed and eventually the ranks of their membership rose to over 4,000. Initially,

*Sheri Barnard, 2001.*
*(Bamonte photo)*

*Some Friends of the Davenport board and others following their Mother's Day open house and tour of the closed hotel on May 15, 1989. Front row: David Shockley, Katherine Gellhorn, Ellen Robey (Friends of the Davenport president) and Mertz Wuts. Back row: Bud Cox, Jan Smith, Penni Buckley, Mac McCandless, Marcia Spencer, Roxanne Wuts, Nancy Compau, Steve Franks, Scott Brooks-Miller, Norma Stejer, Marian Evenson. (Photo courtesy Spokane Public Library.)*

*Charles H. "Chuck" Robey and Ellen R. Robey at a Friends of the Davenport function in front of the Davenport Hotel fireplace. Ellen has been president of The Friends since 1988. Her affections for the Davenport are so strong, she named her beloved cat "Louis Gershwin Davenport." (Photo courtesy Ellen and Chuck Robey.)*

Sheri Barnard served as the organization's president, followed by Ron Wendle. In spring of 1988, Ellen Robey was elected president and has held the position ever since. It was apparent the Davenport was Spokane's most beloved building and cherished landmark, and people were taking action to prove it.

Finding an owner, of course, was the primary concern to both The Friends and Lomas and Nettleton. One of the first projects The Friends assumed was preparing a professional packet of information to be used as a market tool by Lomas and Nettleton. As an added enticement, they worked towards establishing a Davenport Historic District, but unfortunately, were unable to convince all the property owners within the proposed boundaries of the benefits. They became directly involved in searching for potential buyers. Leaving no stone unturned, they even contacted wealthy business tycoon Donald Trump and Charles, the Prince of Wales (a reply was received from Buckingham Palace with a "thank you and best wishes").

Finding an owner proved to be a long and trying process, with the wrecking ball looming on the horizon. Periodically, interested buyers presented various ideas. There were not only proposals regarding the rehabilitation of the hotel, but also suggestions of senior citizen housing, a university campus, a new home for the public library, state and commercial offices, and even a gambling casino. Hopes would rise, only to have interested investors slip away, and tensions mounted over concerns about Lomas and Nettleton's ability to continue pouring money into an unproductive investment. The Friends, however, were stalwart advocates and never lost hope.

Countless stories could be told about people's experiences and memories associated with the Davenport. The following story was shared by a woman who wished to remain anonymous, but it is reflective of the Davenport's long-lasting impact on its guests. Of note, this woman lived in an Inland Northwest community quite some distance from Spokane. Her account, as she wrote it, is as follows:

One year, when I was a young child in the early 1950s, our family Christmas present was a trip to Spokane to see the Ice Capades on Christmas day, including a stay at the Davenport Hotel. Since this was rare and special treat, my mother wanted to "do it in style," which led us to the restaurant dressed in our Sunday best. My brother and I were required to be on our very best behavior.

The hotel and dining room were an impressive sight for young eyes. I remember the dazzling white tablecloths and waiters in black uniforms. I tried to sit very ladylike, as I had been told, when a very proper waiter gently took my napkin from the table and carefully laid it across my lap.

My mother suggested an item from the menu, but I requested a hamburger, fries and a chocolate milk shake, this being the <u>only</u> thing I <u>ever</u> ordered from <u>any</u> restaurant. However, because the menu did not include hamburgers, my parents quietly tried to talk me into eating something else. I stubbornly refused to the point of "best behavior" going out the window. I was about to mortify my parents by really making a scene, when the waiter stated: "If the little lady wants a hamburger, then she shall have a hamburger." While I'm sure my parents were very embarrassed by my behavior, I, on the other hand, was quite smug and felt like a princess.

When the meal arrived, I had my hamburger and fries, but with a decided upgrade. The meat looked something like a hamburger patty, but the bun was far fancier than usual, and the fries were larger than those at a drive-in. All was presented as beautifully as my parents' meals. It was the best hamburger I have ever eaten, so perfect, in fact, that I don't even remember if I got a chocolate shake to go with it.

Longtime Friends' board member, Dorothy Rochon Powers of the *Spokesman-Review*, soliciting readers' memories about the Davenport, received an overwhelming response, similar to the one above. She wrote numerous columns, greatly stimulating the public's interest in preserving the Davenport. The articles also made Lomas and Nettleton acutely aware of the how deeply rooted the hotel was in the social life and history of the Inland Northwest, especially in the hearts and memories of its residents. They, too, fell under the Davenport Hotel's spell and, in spite of their own financial losses, remained dedicated to the building until a buyer was secured. This kind of

*Nancy Compau, Spokane Public Library Northwest Room historian; Dorothy Powers, retired Spokesman-Review associate editor and columnist; and Bob Briley, one of Spokane's most recognized television broadcasters, in the Davenport for filming of the video companion to this book, July 2001. (Bamonte photo.)*

genuine, unwavering public support has never been shown to any other cause in the history of Spokane. It was bound to have a positive influence on any potential buyer.

## A Buyer!

Just when all hope seemed lost and the hotel's future most certainly doomed, a buyer appeared. During the Christmas season in 1989, James Hill, originally a native from Coeur d'Alene, was in Spokane for the first time in five years and was

*Wai-Choi Ng at his going-away party hosted by The Friends in 2000. (Photo courtesy Ellen Robey.)*

dismayed to see the old hotel had closed. He had, at one time, been the manager of the Davenport's Matador Dining Room. Hill was in partnership with Wai-Choi Ng of Hong Kong, who had hotel chains and other holdings worldwide, and was himself an experienced hotelier, having started his career with Hyatt Hotels in the mid-1960s. Hill convinced his partner in Sun International Hotels Ltd. to purchase the Davenport and, on March 23, 1990, they closed the purchase of the hotel and furnishings for $5.25 million. Wai-Choi's brother Patrick, as a representative of the Ng family, and Patrick Yap, chief executive officer, were placed in charge of the hotel project and operations.

Finally, it appeared the hotel had owners capable of performing the necessary restoration, who anticipated reopening the hotel the following year. They were serious and enthusiastic about restoring the hotel to its former grandeur and recognized its architectural and historical significance. Plans for the hotel included an estimated investment of $20 million. The Friends of the Davenport and others rejoiced!

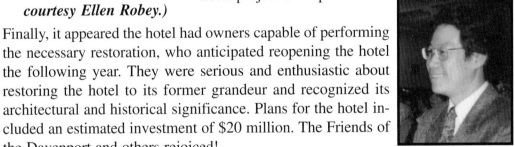

*Jeffrey Ng, 1994.*

Unfortunately, the Davenport's problems were far from over and, almost immediately, the new owners were beset with obstacles. A misunderstood expectation at the time of purchase regarding public funding for a parking facility developed into an irreconcilable rift by the end of the year between Wai-Choi Ng and Jim Hill. Ng felt Hill was to blame for the situation and bought out Hill's share of the partnership. Work temporarily ceased on the hotel project.

Work finally got underway and, in 1993, Patrick Ng had the tinted glass in the lobby atrium, which had been covered over for 50 years, cleaned or replaced and a new skylight built over it. Somewhere along the line, references to the "Tiffany" glass in the skylight began to appear, but it is highly doubtful the glass is Tiffany. When the hotel was preparing to open and the newspaper published its detailed account, a special point was made in naming brand names wherever possible. In reference to the skylight, the only description given was "tinted." In addition, Louis Davenport and Louis Tiffany were friends. If the glass was from Tiffany, which was founded in 1853, undoubtedly, attention would have been drawn to the name at that time.

Revelations of a massive underground oil spill halted the Ngs' progress again in 1994. Apparently, an estimated 75,000 gallons of oil had leaked from the nearby now-defunct steam plant many years earlier and had been concealed from the public. As the battle waged over responsibility for the cleanup, the Friends of the Davenport once again rallied to the support of the beleaguered hotel and, largely through their efforts, the problem was finally resolved. Around this same time, in July 1994, Wai-Choi's brother, Jeffrey Ng, his wife Rowenah and four-year-old son, Eugene, moved into the hotel to oversee the restoration project. Jeffrey's major accomplishment was a complete restoration of the Elizabethan Room. Wallpaper had to be stripped and many wood panels were replicated, as well as some of the silver light fixtures.

Renovation proceeded, but despite the Ngs' best intentions, their progress was wrought by one difficulty after another. In addition to the parking situation and oil spill, numerous constraints and requirements imposed by various regulatory authorities were undermining their efforts. After ten years of sincere efforts, the project was put on hold. In May 2000, Davenport Sun International Hotels Inc. sold the Davenport Hotel to Walt and Karen Worthy. This transaction involved a price of $6.5 million and consisted of an exchange of business property plus a cash balance.

In spite of ongoing financial difficulties and some of the cosmetic indignities suffered in earlier times, the hotel's magnetic attraction never faded. Although the Ngs were unable to reopen the hotel as they had originally hoped, they made progress in the huge renovation project and, at the very least, saved the hotel from the ominous fate that loomed a decade before. In spite of all the trials and challenges, Louis Davenport's influence can still be felt. Employees responsible for maintenance and security during periods when the hotel was closed said they could still almost feel his eyes on them.

*Jeffrey and Rowenah Ng (seated center) and some board members of Friends of the Davenport in the Elizabethan Room on October 22, 1996. Also seated are Bud Cox and Katherine Gellhorn. Ellen Robey is standing between the Ngs. Others, from left, are David Shockley, Mertz Wuts, Marian Evenson, Nancy Compau, Steve Franks, Chuck Robey. (Photo courtesy Nancy Compau.)*

# Chapter 8

## Reemerging Promise

***Walt and Karen Worthy, 2001. (Photo by Nick Follger, Master Photographer)***

Fifty-five years elapsed between the time Louis Davenport sold his hotel to the point where it truly began to reemerge in all its greatness. What began as a simple fascination with Spokane's fading crown jewel has become a focal point of commitment and stewardship by one of Spokane's most celebrated and successful entrepreneurial couples.

In the early 1970s, during their courting years, Walt Worthy and Karen (Milanowski) Powell, would occasionally dine in the Matador Room of the Davenport. Walt always had an interest in the Davenport. However, during those years, their budget prohibited many dates of that nature. For the time being, dining at the Davenport would remain simply a nice place to spend time together. In the far reaches of their imaginations, their future roles in the history of Spokane's most celebrated landmark was never anticipated. From its inception, the Davenport has always seemed to provide a special piece of magic for couples that frequent it. As time passed, the Worthys would soon fall under its spell.

Walt Worthy was born on September 22, 1946, in Great Falls, Montana, while his father was stationed there with the Army Air Corps. He is the son of Walter B. and Virginia Worthy. Following his discharge, the family returned to his father's hometown in rural South Georgia, where he raised cotton, corn and peanuts on the family farm, and shipped decorative evergreens to wholesale florists in the northeast. His father was also a flight instructor during the Korean War and later owned and operated a small 32-unit motel in Cairo, Georgia. Walt was the oldest of four children. He and his sisters grew up on the farm and attended school in Georgetown, Georgia. Walt's graduating class of 17 was one of the largest in the history of Georgetown High School.

In 1964, Walt entered Auburn University in Auburn, Alabama, where he studied engineering and business for three years. In 1968 he enlisted in the Air Force, eventually becoming a survival instructor at Fairchild Air Force Base. While in the service, he started a small roofing company in Spokane, which soon branched into the construction field. Walt built his first speculation house in 1970 and continued to remodel basements and do other small projects until the early 1980s, when the first commercial venture was undertaken. In the years following, several vacant buildings and grocery stores were purchased and renovated into commercial office space. Work commenced on the approximately 600,000-square-foot Rock Point Corporate Center in 1987, which is presently the sixth largest business complex in the state.

Walt and Karen met in the spring of 1970, through a fellow teacher and neighbor of Karen's in Spokane, where she was teaching first grade at Balboa Elementary School. Karen came into the world on May 30, 1944, at Chehalis, Washington. She was the younger of two daughters born to Leo and Margaret Milanowski. For the majority of Karen's early life, the family lived in Centralia, Washington, where she graduated from Centralia High School. Following graduation, she entered Western Washington University in Bellingham, graduating with a degree in elementary education. Karen's parents were both musicians and played in a dance band for various events on weekends, which is how they met. Prior to that, Karen's father toured during the summers between college terms and even played in the Marie Antoinette Room at the Davenport, in the 1930s. At age 92, he recently revisited the hotel.

## The Decision to Buy

Four major elements undoubtedly played a part in the Worthys' decision to buy the once world-renowned Davenport Hotel. The first was the location. It had been a city landmark and symbol of elegance and excellence for over 86 years. Located in the heart of downtown Spokane it was perfectly situated within walking distance of the city's major entertainment, shopping and business district. Twenty-seven years ago, the area around the scenic Spokane River was landscaped in the heart of downtown and the 100 acre Riverfront Park (fifty of these acres include the river) was established within walking distance of the hotel. Two major hospitals are within a five-minutes drive and the Spokane International Airport is less than 15 minutes from the hotel. Views of the river, mountains and city also enhance the pleasure of being a guest of the hotel.

Secondly, the hotel itself was considered a "trophy property." It was originally designed and built to reflect ancient European influence, and was among the few truly grand hotels in America. The combination of its architectural styling, quality building materials and workmanship make it irreplaceable in today's building market. According to Melville Holmes, who is in charge of the Davenport's decorative restoration, the movement toward modernism in the 1950s through the 1970s did away with traditional and rococo designs. As a result, the skilled craftsmen were without work and entire trades disappeared. Artisans to create the kind of ornamentation presently found in the Davenport are not so readily available as they once were.

The third element was its celebrity. The Davenport Hotel was a symbol of Spokane's success and most beloved gathering place for generations of people from throughout the Inland Northwest and the nation. The guest books of the hotel held names of many of the world's most famous and prominent people. Guests who had come to know the splendor of the hotel and excellence of service, returned and conveyed their enthusiasm to others. But the Davenport was losing its original splendor, and its mechanical structures needed to be strengthened, modernized and physically adapted to the current standards. Upon completion, the Davenport Hotel will resume its place in Spokane and become a marketer's dream.

And, finally, probably the most significant factor was Worthys' position to accomplish this project. When the hotel closed in 1985, Tim Babcock gave Walt a tour of the hotel. He was interested in buying it then, but did not quite have all the necessary elements firmly in place to do the job. Virtually every year, he had approached the Ngs with a proposal to buy the old hotel and, finally in 2000, was given the opportunity. By this time, he had in place the key people with a proven track record in restoration projects and experience working as a team. In addition, the Worthys had the capital resources to complete the project.

# The Core Problems

**Davenport's Restaurant and Pennington Hotel**: Worthys' purchase of the Davenport Hotel included the entire block, 155 feet wide by 300 feet long, bounded by Sprague, Lincoln, First and Post. The purchase included the original Davenport's Restaurant, located in the former Wilson Block, and the Pennington Hotel, which had previously held restaurant, banquet and kitchen facilities. These buildings occupied over 33% of the entire ground space and were distinct from the main hotel in both their facade and height.

The Wilson Block and Pennington Hotel (former Bellevue Building) were hastily constructed following the fire of 1889 in accordance with the era's standards and construction methods. They severely lacked the functional capacity and utility of today's standards of construction and safety. By 2001 they had deteriorated almost beyond rescue – 111 years had taken their toll. Structural designs, building codes and features of hotels are constantly evolving to adapt to and comply with the times. Since Louis Davenport sold his hotel in 1945, this has not been done to any significant degree. Simple cosmetics could not cure the functional obsolescence of these buildings. Most importantly, it would not have been cost effective to bring them up to the standards of today's stringent building codes, as they would still be left with an impairment of function.

The Worthys were faced with a tough decision. To insure the hotel's continued existence, the choice was clear. The original Davenport's Restaurant and Pennington Hotel, the most historic structures on the Davenport block, had to be razed and replaced with one compatible with the hotel. The Worthys had a complicated situation of trying to satisfy the preservationist (including the legal ramifications associated with demolishing a building on the Historic Register), an adoring public with more than a casual interest in what was being done to the hotel, and a need to make the hotel profitable to prevent it from falling back into the same unfortunate state. To be competitive with the other major hotels within its class in the area, the hotel would need a drive-through (porte cochere), major ballroom and a grand entrance to the hotel, with valet parking in the basement. Facilities to provide arriving guests easy access to the hotel and the registration desk were imperative.

**The 1914 Davenport Hotel structure**: The second leading problem confronting the hotel owners was the obsolescence in the guest rooms. When Worthys purchased the hotel, there were over 400 guest rooms, the majority of which were quite small and plain. This was a striking contrast to the unique architectural style and magnificence of the public areas. Most of the guest rooms definitely did not reflect the same grandeur. The cure for this would be larger – but fewer – rooms, stately enough to carry the luxurious theme throughout the entire hotel.

**The parking problem**: The third significant problem, yet by no means the least, was the parking. Since the mid-1930s, when it became the goal of most American families to own a car, the Davenport Hotel has experienced a chronic parking problem. It has also lacked easy access for travelers to pull off the busy streets surrounding the hotel to unload passengers and baggage.

## The Renovation Agenda

Almost immediately after their purchase in May 2000, the Worthys began tackling the core problems and have had a steady crew of between 80 to 150 workers on the job at nearly all times. They have embarked on and are committed to the largest overhaul the Davenport Hotel has experienced since its inception. As this publication goes to print, the project has passed the halfway mark, and all the necessary elements are in place for a triumphant conclusion. In effect, with all obstacles considered, the highest and best use for Spokane's beloved hotel is exactly what the Worthys are doing – making it again one of America's finest grand hotels.

The preexisting public rooms have been beautifully restored and are being scheduled for various functions. Some of the original decorative detail was essentially lost through years of being bathed in paint. The ornamentation has been brought back to life. Some of the treatments used in the restoration used better materials than originally, such as gold leaf instead of gold paint. Careful color selection, special techniques and applications by artist Melville Holmes, or under his supervision, have created a stunning effect in the restored Marie Antoinette and Isabella rooms.

The other elements in the renovation are being addressed as follows:

• A new structure, similar in appearance (shown at right), will replace the old Davenport Restaurant portion of the Davenport block. It will include a porte cochere beneath a grand ballroom and, a basement parking garage with a capacity to accommodate 40 to 50 vehicles, will service the hotel's valet parking. A new parking garage will also be built across the street from the south entrance to the hotel on First Avenue, where the OK Stable was located at the turn of the century. This parking garage will be seven stories high and accommodate 450 vehicles.

• The exquisite Hall of the Doges, once Spokane's most famous and beautiful ballroom, was removed intact before the building was demolished. It will be refurbished and placed in the new grand-ballroom addition as a pre-function area. The deteriorating painting on the ceiling shows evidence of harsh cleaning and poor attempts at retouching. It will be restored – or completely redone – by Melville Holmes.

272 ... Reemerging Promise

- The number of preexisting guest rooms will be reduced from 400 to 281. To accomplish this the guest room floors were stripped and gutted down to the exterior walls and supporting structures, with one exception; the Circus Room on the Seventh floor was left intact. All plumbing, wiring and mechanical systems were removed and replaced with state of the art technology. The latest in information technology will be available for the business traveler. (The hardware for this costs half as much as the total construction of the hotel.) The average-sized room will be approximately 450 square feet, variances depending on type and location. Seventy percent of these will have king-sized beds and the remainder will have two queen-sized beds. The new construction is superior in every way and far more luxurious.

- There will be over 25,000 square feet of banquet space. The new ballroom, including the pre-function facility, will be over 11,000 square feet. Portions of Louis Davenport's original apartment, located above his restaurant, were removed and will be reassembled for use as retail space. The grand entrance, grand ballroom, guest rooms and parking garage are expected to be completed sometime in late spring or early summer of 2002.

- There will be one main restaurant, with seating for 130, and a small coffee shop or espresso area. Limited food service will also be available in the bar, which will seat 80-100, and the lobby lounge will probably have the capacity to serve 40-50.

- The penthouse level will feature a 2000-square-foot presidential suite, and a governor's suite, with slightly less space, will feature separate bedrooms, small kitchen and bar areas, additional bathrooms, jacuzzis and fireplaces.

- The goal is to become a four-star hotel. The primary difference between four- and five-star hotels is the ratio of staff to guests, obviously higher at a five-star facility.

The Worthys estimate the costs of the entire project, including the purchase price, to be in excess of $30 million. Following completion, the hotel will offer more functional utility than ever in its lifetime. The Davenport was built to last, but unfortunate circumstances and some intermittent poor choices, almost destroyed it. Its original design freely used symbolic representations – various creatures, both mythological and real, heraldic crests, the Davenport coat of arms. These symbols are a timeless representation of strength, sociability, comfort, protection, time - honored traditions – and life itself. Like the mythological phoenix, the grand old hotel is rising anew. Undoubtedly, Louis Davenport would find great satisfaction in the care and dedication shown by the Worthys and others responsible for the salvation of his legendary hotel. In the spirit of all he represented, he would most assuredly be grateful to Spokane's citizenry for their undying loyalty and affection toward his masterpiece, and the Worthys for their commitment in its preservation and renovation.

*A montage of interior shots of the old Pennington Hotel taken just weeks prior to demolition. Much of the structure was in the advanced dry-rot stages and the floor levels of the two buildings were not in alignment. (Bamonte photos, 2001)*

*The old Pennington Hotel and Davenport's Restaurant in February 2001, just prior to demolition. (Bamonte photos.)*

*Two cranes, a 115 and 125 ton capacity, from Hite Crane & Rigging Inc., removing the 30-ton Hall of the Doges on February 27, 2001, just days before the building was demolished. The Hall of the Doges was the most beautiful banquet room in the Inland Northwest and will be restored in the new ballroom facility.*

*Left: Lura Sheahan, Davenport Hotel project coordinator, and Walt Worthy film-ing the removal of the Hall of the Doges. Right: Clint Weyrauch, project manager for Worthy Enterprises, and Karen Worthy. (Bamonte photos)*

*Two of Worthys' electrical crew, Bill McCraw (left) and Vern Hill, working in the basement level near the location of Davenport's original restaurant.*

*Worthy employees Scott Schmidt (left) applying gold foil to the art deco in the Marie Antoinette Room and Dell Philips dressing up columns in the Isabella Room.*

*Employee Laura Damaceno (left), working on part of the Davenport's electrical system, and Lura Sheahan, the hotel's project coordinator, in the Isabella Room.*

*Melville Holmes with a portrait he painted of his wife Janice. Melville is one of the Inland Northwest's foremost artists and has been an integral part of the Davenport's renovation, responsible for the color treatment and restoration of the detailed decorative ornamentation. After his first exposure to Spokane's little piece of Old Europe in the mid-1990s, Melville decided to do some paintings of the rooms. He was in the midst of that process when Walt Worthy began meeting with decorative art consultants from New York and Salt Lake City. Melville felt he might have something to offer and Walt quickly discovered the depth of Melville's talents. Melville and Janice began the project together, carefully analyzing the rooms for the most appropriate treatment. Their intent was to restore the Old World elegance in the public rooms. They began with the Marie Antoinette Room, which they felt needed a sophisticated, but subtly feminine, touch. Sensitive to the colors in the marble floors and unable to find ready-mixed colors of their choosing, they mixed their own paint. Melville gives his wife equal credit for the exquisite restoration of the Marie Antoinette Room, which was nearing completion in December 2000, when Janice passed away suddenly. This portrait will be hung in the hotel in her memory.*

*From left: Suzanne Bamonte, Gary Zagelow and Clint Weyrauch studying historical details of the Davenport Hotel. Suzanne is the coauthor of this book; Gary was instrumental in researching the history of the physical layout and design of Davenport's buildings; Clint is Worthys' construction project manager and longtime trusted associate.*

*An on-camera interview with former hotel patron Dr. George Wood in the hotel lobby during the filming of the video "Spokane's Legendary Davenport Hotel" by Jim Bolser and Robin Briley of Peak Video Productions. (Bamonte photos)*

# Selected Bibliography

Bamonte, Tony and Suzanne Schaeffer, *History of Pend Oreille County.*
 *Manito Park: A Reflection of Spokane's Past.*
 *Spokane and the Inland Northwest: Historical Images.*
 *Miss Spokane: Elegant Ambassadors and Their City.*
Butte-Silver Bow Public Archives, Butte, Montana.
California Genealogical Society, Oakland, Calif., Archives.
California Historical Society Research Library, Baker, Calif., Archives.
*Chicago Inter-Ocean*, selected articles.
*Dakin Spokane Fire Map*, 1890.
*Davenport Hotel Directory*, 1914.
Davenport Hotel, various publications.
Durham, Nelson W., *Spokane and the Inland Empire.*
Eastern Washington State Historical Society, Research Library Archives.
*Evening Chronicle*, selected articles.
Giles, Dorothy and Franklin, Irma, *Thomas Davenport, Philipstown Pioneer, 1682-
 1759, and His Descendants* and *Supplements I-III*
Hook, Harry H. and McGuire, Francis J., *Spokane Falls Illustrated.*
*Hotel Monthly,* September 1915.
Hubbard, Elbert, *Philistine*, 1906.
Hyslop, Robert B., *Spokane Building Blocks*. Jensen, Derrick and Draffan, George
 with Osborn, John, M.D. *Railroads and Clearcuts.*
Kitsap Regional Library, Port Orchard, WA.
Mathieu, Edward, *The Life of a Chef.*
Matthews, Henry C., *Kirtland Cutter – Architect in the Land of Promise.*
Montana Historical Society Library, Helena, Montana, Archives.
*Morning Review*, Spokane Falls, selected articles.
Nebraska State Historical Society, Lincoln, NE, Archives.
*Northern Pacific Railroad Journal of Congress's 1864 Northern Pacific Railroad
 Land Grant.*
Peters, Lloyd, *Lionhead Lodge – Movieland of the Northwest.*
*Polk's Spokane City Directories*, all volumes.
Powers, Dorothy Rochon, *Dorothy: Powers to the People.*
Putnam County Historical Society, Cold Spring, N.Y. Archives.
San Francisco History Center, San Francisco Public Library, Archives.
*Sanborn Maps*, selected maps.
*Seattle Post-Intelligencer*, selected articles.
Secretary of State, *Articles of Incorporation, State of Washington.*
Spokane County Assessors Office, selected information.
Spokane County Auditor's *Registration of Births.*
*Spokane Daily Chronicle,* selected articles.

# Continued Selected Bibliography

*Spokane Falls City Directory*, selected volumes.
*Spokane Falls Review*, selected articles.
*Spokane Press,* selected articles.
Spokane Public Library, Northwest Room, Archives.
*Spokesman-Review*, selected articles.
Superior Court Civil Division, Red Bluff, Calif., Archives.
*System*, A business journal, May 1919.
Tehama County Genealogical and Historical Society, Red Bluff, Calif., Archives.
Tehama County Records, Red Bluff, Calif., Archives.
*The Western Architect*, July 1913.
United Methodist Church, Pawnee City, Neb., Archives.
*Walla Walla Union*, selected articles.
Washington State Archives, Eastern Region in Cheney, *Records.*
Weston, Mildred, *Vachel Lindsay – Poet in Exile.*
*What Service Means*, A Davenport Hotel publication, 1920.

# The following people provided interviews:

Jamie Baker
Sheri Barnard
Edna Mae and Thoburn Brown
Nancy Gale Compau
Evelyn Conant
Larry and Bernice Davenport
Louie and Nita Davenport
Melville Holmes
Dorothy Powers
John Reed
Ellen Robey
Maxine Rolie
Norma and Dick Stejer
Charlie Willis
George Wood
Walt and Karen Worthy

# Index

288

240
West Point Foundry
240
Western Hotel 191
Western Hotels, Inc.
257, 259-60
Western House 35,
36, 38
Western Life Insurance
Company 249
Western Union 157
Western Washington
University 268
Weston, Mildred 231
Wetzel, Daniel F. 57
Weyrauch, Clint 275,
277
White, Aubrey L. 98,
99, 114, 239, 247
White, Betty 99, 222
White, Ethelyn (see
Binkley) 99
White, Harriet 99
White, Louise 99
White, Mary 99
Whitehouse & Price

252
Whitehouse, Harold
C. 167
Whitmore, Helen
190
Whitten Block 15, 52
Wilbur, Oregon 244
William Edris
Company 256
William Howard Co.
114
Williams, Catherine
(Betts), 192, 194
Williams, Marcy 170
Willis, Charles
Willis, Herald 99
Willis, Melissa 99
Willis, Winfield 99
Wilson Block 16, 19,
21, 53, 55, 58, 60,
62, 67, 108, 141,
270
Wilson, Henry L 19,
52, 62
Wilson Mantor
Photography 157

Windsor Hotel 36,
37, 48
Winston, Warn 205
Winter, Bernice 192
Winters, Elizabeth
114
Winters, William 86
Wolfe, Thomas 222
Wood, George Dr.
277
World War I 164,
204, 229, 234
World War II 149,
183, 197, 213,
214, 255, 257, 258
Worldwide Prayer
Circle 232
Worthy Enterprises
270, 271-72
Worthy, Karen 266,
267, 268, 275
Worthy, Virginia 268
Worthy, Walt 214,
266, 67, 268, 269,
275
Worthy, Walter B.

268
Wraight, Harry 177
Wren, Thomas F.
Wuts, Mertz 262,
266
Wuts, Roxanne 262

**Y**.W.C.A. 223
Yakima, Wash. 235
Yap, Patrick 265
Yellow Cab Company
157
Yenney, Clara 190
Yogananda,
Paramahansa 222,
232

**Z**agelow, Gary 277
Zelinsky, D. 125
Zepp, Arthur 184
Ziegfeld Follies 217,
222
Ziegfeld Jr., Florenz
222
Ziegler, Will H. 114,
190